The Describer's Dictionary

Also by David Grambs

Bernstein's Reverse Dictionary, second edition (editor)

Just Ask Mr. Wordwizard

The Endangered English Dictionary

Did I Say Something Wrong?

The Random House Dictionary for Writers and Readers

Death by Spelling

Dimboxes, Epopts, and Other Quidams

Also by David Grambs and Ellen S. Levine

So You Think You Can Spell?

The Describer's Dictionary

A TREASURY OF TERMS AND LITERARY QUOTATIONS

Expanded Second Edition

DAVID GRAMBS
and ELLEN S. LEVINE

W. W. NORTON & COMPANY | NEW YORK LONDON

Printed in the United States of America

For information about permission to reproduce selections from this book, write to Permissions, W. W. Norton & Company, Inc., 500 Fifth Avenue, New York, NY 10110

For information about special discounts for bulk purchases, please contact W. W. Norton Special Sales at specialsales@wwnorton.com or 800-233-4830

Manufacturing by LSC Harrisonburg
Book design by Barbara Bachman
Production manager: Louise Parasmo

Library of Congress Cataloging-in-Publication Data

Grambs, David.
The Describer's dictionary : a treasury of terms and literary quotations / David Grambs and Ellen S. Levine. — Expanded Second Edition.
pages cm
Previous edition: 1993.
Includes bibliographical references and index.
ISBN 978-0-393-34616-9 (pbk. : alk. paper)
1. English language—Synonyms and antonyms. 2. Description (Rhetoric) I. Levine, Ellen S. II. Title.
PE1591.G67 2014
423'.1—dc23
2014037180

W. W. Norton & Company, Inc.
500 Fifth Avenue, New York, N.Y. 10110
www.wwnorton.com

W. W. Norton & Company Ltd.
15 Carlisle Street, London W1D 3BS

4 5 6 7 8 9 0

For Bill Dorsey and Frank Lyman

CONTENTS

SIZE, POSITION, RELATION, AND PROPORTION

LIGHT AND COLORS

STRUCTURES AND SPACES

EARTH AND SKY

TERRAIN AND LANDSCAPE

WEATHER, FORCES OF NATURE, AND THE SOLAR SYSTEM

ANIMALS

PEOPLE

THE BODY

PREFACE

BY THE TIME YOU'VE BEGUN READING THIS PREFACE TODAY, you've probably already sent at least one email or text message, updated your social media page, posted a comment at an online zine, or perhaps composed a chapter for your forthcoming self-published novel.

Whether your creations are tweets or tomes, *The Describer's Dictionary* means to serve the needs of all communicators, from the published professional, creative-writing student, blogger, and aspiring journalist to the pen-in-hand diarist and dogged snail-mail letter writer.

This revised and expanded *Describer's Dictionary* remains, like the original edition, unique in its format: part dictionary and part anthology. We hope it will serve as an indispensable complement to your standard lexicon and thesaurus. Hundred of entries have been added, but the intent of this book is the same: to make thousands of specific words expediently referable. Nouns (to identify things) and adjectives (to describe them) are the essence of the dictionary portion of the book.

The volume is arranged in five sections—Properties of Things, Structures and Spaces, Earth and Sky, Animals, and People—and within each one the quotations are chosen to illustrate the terms or definitions introduced in that section. (A few quotations do not contain a specific term or definition appearing in the dictionary pages but nevertheless are included because they fall within the subject area and exemplify good descriptive writing.) Lexically, this book's format is for the most part that of a reverse-dictionary, whereby meanings or definitions precede the terms. For example:

having the same shape or boundaries
coextensive
(Properties of Things)

covered or arched and usually columned walkway open on at least one side
gallery, arcade, loggia, cloister
(Structures and Spaces)

small stream
streamlet, brooklet, rivulet, rill, runnel, burn
(Earth and Sky)

having no tail
anurous, acaudal
(Animals)

uneasy
restless, fidgety, fluttery, restive, nervous, unnerved, on edge, jittery, ill at ease, apprehensive, tense, skittish, keyed up, anxious
(People)

A reader might want to know, for instance, the zoological adjective for "like a peacock"; or the momentarily forgotten architectural term that is elusive in the often confusingly clustered and subsumed categories of one's handy *Roget's*; or the right words, for a science-fiction story, to describe features of an apocalyptic landscape; or that word—it's a French borrowing, isn't it?—for a nose that in shape is turned up; or which specific color term one should choose for something that is bluish gray.

Many words in the book should be familiar (if not always remembered). Other adjectives and nouns are less common or are technical and probably quite unfamiliar. Because some of the terms or synonyms are somewhat arcane does not mean that they are preferable or more "correct." Often, successful expert writers use simple language in their verbal depictions (as is shown in so many of this book's illustrative passages).

Thus the familiar "wrinkled" can be just as apt as "rugose"; and the existence of "hippocrepiform" notwithstanding, many writers, including academicians, will be more likely to say "horseshoe-shaped." It is always a question of context, voice, or audience—or the writer's choosing to use the occasional optional (and informative) synonym to avoid repetition.

This edition features more than eight hundred quotations by more than six hundred writers of both fiction and nonfiction. (See the new Index of Quoted Authors.) The quotations have been taken from writers from the nineteenth century to the present, many of them literarily acclaimed nominees or winners of such honors as the National Book Award, MacArthur Foundation Fellowships, and the Pulitzer, O. Henry, Man Booker, and Nobel Prizes. The quotes, from predominantly but not exclusively American and British writers (writing in English), are from diverse genres. Fiction excerpts, from both novels and short stories, are drawn from classic and current general fiction as well as from mystery and espionage fiction, historical novels, and science fiction. Nonfiction quotes are selected from biographies, memoirs, and other books and articles by journalists, humorists, naturalists, scientists, physicians, and travel writers.

We hope that these quotations not only provide engaging illustrations of the use of the terms presented but also will make for interesting, ever browsable reading in their own right—even prompting the reader to look further into a particular book or other works by an author.

The citations should keep one mindful that vivid or memorable writing often involves ineffably subtle touches and obliquities of delineational style—an eye for the striking or surprising detail, a well-crafted sense of phrasing, and the gift of just the right metaphor or simile. As with so many other things, in the art of writing the whole is greater than the sum of its parts. Apposite terminology is but a starting point. It is how the words are put together that counts for so much.

All in all, we hope you find this second edition of *The Describer's Dictionary* to be ever reliable and surprising as a source of terms for painting pictures with the English language. As for its quotations, we trust that they will offer you little tugs of encouragement and inspiration.

ACKNOWLEDGMENTS

WE'RE GRATEFUL TO OUR AGENTS, JIM TRUPIN AND LIZ Trupin-Pulli, for their continuing efforts on our behalf and for being readily accessible across varied time zones.

A lexically complex work such as this would be a handful—possibly a headache—for any editor. For his attentiveness and sound suggestions regarding the manuscript and for patiently shepherding us through the publishing process, we are greatly indebted to our editor, Jeff Shreve.

We'd like to thank our copyeditor, Mary Babcock, for her keen-eyed scrutiny of the manuscript—for alerting us, always in a direct and understated way, about matters needing correction or clarification.

At Norton, we'd also like to thank production manager Louise Parasmo, project editor Don Rifkin, art director Albert Tang, cover designer Steve Attardo, publicist Audrey Walker; and Melody Conroy, the original editor for this new edition with whom we worked briefly.

Toby Richman and Loretta Shapoff were kind enough to help proofread some of the quotations, and Christine Barone provided us with expert keyboarding.

We could never have finished the project without the

aid, comfort, and emergency cures of our computer medicine man, Sebastian Barone.

For their considerate support in other ways, we'd like to acknowledge Claire Angelica, Phil Miller, Richard Pearse and Nancy O'Donohue, Bob and Judy Porter, and Henry Rasoff and to thank Diane Giddis and Steve Weller for their sustaining presence as friends.

Among the many websites we consulted in the course of preparing the manuscript, special mention is deserved here of abebooks.com, longform.org, gutenberg.org, books.google.com, and onelook.com.

Our thanks to WNYC and National Public Radio for introducing us to many emerging writers worth exploring for quotations, and to Simon Loekle for his strangely wonderful radio program, *As I Please* (WBAI), surely the only reason we'd ever willingly choose to be awake—week after week—at six a.m. on Saturday.

The Describer's Dictionary

PROPERTIES OF THINGS

SHAPES

GENERAL SHAPES

having a shape or form
shaped, formed, configured, conformed, fashioned

having no shape, shapeless
unshaped, formless, amorphous, inchoate, unformed, unfashioned, unconfigured, unconformed

having a usually simple plane shape (lines or curves)
geometric, geometrical

having the same shape or boundaries
coextensive

having a similar form
conforming, similiform, equiform

having a different form
diversiform, variform

having many forms
multiform, multifarious, polymorphic, polymorphous, multiplex, omniform, omnifarious

having a shape with equal sides and angles
regular

not having a shape with equal sides and angles
irregular
having an unconventional or uneven shape
irregular, contorted, misshapen, malformed, deformed, twisted, grotesque
having an axially (or in relation to a central line) balanced shape
symmetrical
having an axially unbalanced shape
asymmetrical, dissymmetrical
more prominent or sizable on one side
one-sided, lop-sided
having the sides reversed (as in a mirror)
heterochiral
producing or characterized by distortion of image or shape (as by unequal magnification in a lens or mirror)
anamorphic
having proper or harmonious dimensions relationally
proportional, proportionate, commensurate, eurythmic, eurhythmic
not having proper dimensions relationally
disproportional, disproportionate, incommensurate
longer in one dimension
elongated, oblong, oblongitudinal, lengthened, extended, stretched, prolongated, elliptical, distended, protracted
shorter in one dimension
shortened, truncated, foreshortened
becoming wider
widening, expanding, broadening, dilating, splayed
becoming narrower
narrowing, tapering, tapered

having or coming to a point
pointed, pronged, spiked, acuate, acuminate, mucronate

straight and uncurved in line
rectilinear, rectilineal, linear, lineal

not straight
crooked, bent, askew, awry, oblique

angled or inclined from the perpendicular
raked

flourish-like curve
curlicue

short wiggly line or scrawl
squiggle

represented in outline only
outlined, outlinear, contoured, delineatory, in profile, silhouetted

having a sharp bend or angle
angular, geniculate, orthometric

standing at a right or 90° (L- or gamma-shaped) angle
upright, perpendicular, normal, orthogonal, rectangular, orthometric

having a less than right angle
acute-angled

having three acute angles
triquetrous

having a greater than perpendicular angle
obtuse-angled

having an acute or obtuse (or non-right) angle
oblique-angled, obliquangular

angle greater than 180°
reflex angle

being an angle formed by two planes
dihedral
bent abruptly
geniculate, inflexed, intorted
bent abruptly backward
retroflex, cacuminal
having short and sharp vee-like turns
zigzag, staggered, chevroned, cringle-crangle
having a shape formed by lines rather than by curves (hence having angles)
angular
having a curve or curves (roundness or rondure)
curvilinear, curved, curvate, bowed, curviform, arcing, arciform, flexuous
slightly curved
curvulate
curved upward
upcurved, upturned, arched, arcuate, vaulted, concamerated
curved downward
downcurved, downturned, decurved, decurvate
curved forward
procurved
curved backward
recurved, recurvate
curved inward
incurved, incurvate, involute, hooked, aduncous
curved outward
excurved, excurvate
curving back toward itself
hooked, crooked

curved around farther than a semicircle
gibbous

curved up and around and closed or almost closed
looped

describing a curve that is bold or elongated
sweeping

describing a series of reverse curves
whiplash

curving or arcing (two curved lines) to a point
cusped

curving to a central point with a "dip" (contraflexure) inward on either side of the apex
ogival

making a perfect closed curve (two dimensions)
circular, round, rounded, ringlike, annular, cycloid, cycloidal

flat and circular
discoid

hollowed inward
concave, bowl-like, basin-like, crater-like, dished, sunken, depressed

rounded and bulging outward
convex, protuberant, gibbous, cupped, cupriform, cambered

concave on one side and convex on the other
concavo-convex, convexo-concave

more curved on the concave than on the convex side
concavo-convex

more curved on the convex than on the concave side
convexo-concave

concave on two or both sides
biconcave
convex on two or both sides
biconvex, amphicyrtic
having a common center
concentric
circular in three dimensions or ball-like
round, spherical, spheral, globular, globose, orbicular, orb-like, globate, rotund, spheriform, bombous, conglobate
nearly round
obrotund
like a half-circle
semicircular, hemicyclic
like a half-moon
semilunar, demilune
round but wider in the middle or flattened at the top
oblate
round but longer vertically (as along a polar axis)
prolate
more or less round
spheroidal, ellipsoidal
egg-shaped
ooid, oval, ovoid, ovaliform, oviform, elliptical, elliptic, ellipsoidal
ovoid with the wider end up
obovoid
showing coils or twists
convoluted, convolved, whorled

winding (as if around a pole) in shape

spiral, helical, gyral, heliciform, sirulate, cochleate, corkscrew, tortile, curlicue

spiral or shaped like an inverted cone

turbinate

having numerous turns or bends

bending, winding, twisting, tortuous, sinuous, serpentine, meandering, anfractuous, waving, wavy, undulant, undulating

like a complex or confusing network

maze-like, mazy, labyrinthine, labyrinthian, plexiform

having or in the form of connecting links

chain-like, festooned, catenary, catenate, concatenate, concatenated

enclosing (with either straight or curved lines) a space and constituting a figure

closed

not (either straight or curved lines) enclosing a space or constituting a figure

open

making a closed plane figure of straight lines

polygonal

many-sided

multilateral, polygonal

having equal sides

equilateral

having many angles

multiangular, polyangular

being a two-dimensional figure

plane

being a three-dimensional figure
solid
being a solid figure with many sides
polyhedral, polyhedric
being polyhedral with all vertices in two parallel planes
prismatoidal
four-sided plane figure whose opposite sides are parallel and equal
parallelogram
parallelogram with four equal sides
rhombus, rhomb
many-sided with parallelogram sides and the bases or ends parallel and congruent
prismatic
being a polyhedron with six faces, all of which are parallelograms parallel to the opposite face
parallelepipedal
being a parallelepiped with rhombuses for faces
rhombohedral
having two sides
bilateral
having two faces or fronts
bifacial
three-sided
triangular, deltoid, trilateral, wedge-shaped, cuneate, trigonal, cuneiform, trigonous
triangular with unequal sides
scalene
triangular with two equal sides
isosceles
triangular with equal sides
equilateral

triangular inversely
obcuneate, obdeltoid

being a three-dimensional pointed figure with a base and triangles (usually four or three) for sides
pyramidal

inversely pyramidal
obpyramidal

being a triangular (with three upright sides) pyramid
tetrahedral

having a 90° arc or being a quarter of a circle
quadrantal

having four sides and four angles
quadrilateral, quadrangular, quadrangled, tetragonal

four-sided with all right angles and equal sides
square, foursquare, quadrate

four-sided with all right angles (right-angled parallelogram)
rectangular

having the shape of a narrow rectangle (as a gemstone)
baguette

four-sided with opposite sides parallel and equal
parallelogrammatic

four-sided with two sides parallel
trapezoidal, antiparallelogrammatic

four-sided (parallelogram) with equal but non-right-angled sides (or not a square)
rhombic, rhombical

four-sided (parallelogram) with unequal non-right-angled sides
rhomboid

somewhat like a rhomboid figure
rhomboidal

four-sided with no parallel sides
trapeziform, trapezial
four-sided with two equal acute and two equal obtuse angles (or a long rhomboid figure with the diagonal perpendicular to the horizontal)
diamond, lozenge-shaped
solid with six square faces
cubic
somewhat cubic in shape
cuboid, cuboidal
having an evenly extended or elongated round shape
cylindrical, columnar, columnal, pillar-like, shaft-like
narrowly cylindrical
tubular, tubulate
more or less cylindrical but tapering at one or both ends
terete
being a rounded figure (with a circular base) that tapers upward to a point
conical, conic, funnel-shaped
somewhat conical
conoid, conoidal
conical with the pointed end below
obconic
like two opposite-pointing cones having the same base
biconical
having all angles equal
equiangular
being a four-sided (and -angled) plane figure (polygon)
quadrangular, tetrangular
being a five-sided plane figure
pentagonal, pentangular

being a six-sided plane figure
hexagonal, sexangular, sexagonal

being a seven-sided plane figure
heptagonal

being an eight-sided plane figure
octagonal, octangular

being a nine-sided plane figure
nonagonal

being a ten-sided plane figure
decagonal

being a twelve-sided plane figure
dodecagonal

being a (three-dimensional) polyhedron with three faces
trihedral

being a polyhedron with four faces
tetrahedral

being a polyhedron with five faces
pentahedral

being a polyhedron with six faces
hexahedral

being a polyhedron with seven faces
heptahedral

being a polyhedron with eight faces
octahedral

being a polyhedron with twelve faces
dodecahedral

being a polyhedron with twenty faces
icosahedral

being a polyhedron with twenty-four faces
icositetrahedral

picture-like as a representational form
glyphic, pictographic, hieroglyphic
signifying an idea, concept, or thing but not a particular word or phrase for it
ideogrammatic, ideographic
signifying a word
logogrammatic, logographic

PARTICULAR SHAPES OR LIKENESSES

acorn-shaped
glandiform, glanduliform
almond-shaped
amygdaloid, amygdaliform
alphabet-like
alphabetiform
amoeba-shaped
amoebiform, amoeboid
antenna-shaped
antenniform
apple-shaped
maliform, pomiform
apse-shaped
apsidal
arched or bowed
arcuate, bandy
arch-shaped
arciform
arm-shaped
brachial

arrowhead-shaped
sagittate, sagittiform
arrowhead-shaped (with flaring barbs)
hastate
awl-shaped
subulate, subulated, subuliform
ax- or cleaver-shaped
dolabriform, dolabrate, securiform, axiniform
bag- or pouch-shaped
sacciform, scrotiform, bursiform
ball-shaped
conglobulate
bark-like
corticiform
barley-grain-shaped
hordeiform
barrel-shaped
dolioform
basin-shaped
pelviform
basket-shaped (small basket)
corbiculate
beak-shaped
rostate, rhamphoid, rostriform
bean-shaped
fabiform, fabaceous
beard-shaped
barbate
bell-shaped
campaniform, campaniliform, campanular, campanulate, campanulous, caliciform

berry-shaped
baccate, bacciform

bill-shaped
rostriform, rostate, rhamphoid

bladder- or flask-shaped
ampullaceous, ampulliform, lageniform, utriculate, utriculoid

boat- or canoe-shaped
navicular, naviculiform, naviform, scaphoid, cymbiform, nautiform, hysterioid, hysteriform

bonnet- or miter-shaped
mitrate, mitriform

bowed or arched
arcuate, bandy

bowl-shaped
crateriform, parabolic

brain-like
cerebriform

branched
furcal, furcate

branched slightly
furcellate

brush-shaped
muscariform, scopiform, scopulate, scopuliform, aspergilliform

bubble-like
bulliform

buckler (or round shield)-shaped
scutate, clypeate

bud-like
gemmiform

bulb-shaped
bulbiform, bulbous

buttocks-like
natiform

cactus-shaped
cactiform

canal-like
canaliform

canoe- or boat-shaped
navicular, naviculiform, naviform, scaphoid, cymbiform, nautiform, hysterioid, hysteriform

cat-shaped
feliform

caterpillar-shaped
eruciform

catkin-shaped
amentiform

cavity-like
aveoliform

cell-like
celliform

chain-like
catenary, catenoid, catenular, catenulate

chisel-shaped
scalpriform

chisel-shaped (primitive)
celtiform

cigar-shaped
terete

claw- or nail-shaped
unguiform

claw- or pincer-shaped
cheliform
cleaver- or ax-shaped
dolabriform, dolabrate, securiform, axiniform
cloud-shaped
nubiform
clover-leaf-like
trifoliate, trifoliated, trefoil
club-shaped
clavate, claviform
club-shaped inversely
obclavate
cobweb-like
cortinate
coin-shaped
nummiform, nummular
column-like
columnar, basaltiform, columniform
column-like (small column)
columelliform
comb-shaped or toothed
pectinate
combs-like (series of combs)
cardiform
cone-shaped
conical, coniform, strobile
cord- or rope-like
funiform
cowlike
vaccine (rare)

crab-shaped

cancriform

crater-like

crateriform

crescent-shaped

meniscal, meniscate, meniscoid, menisciform, lunate, falcate, falcicular, falciculate, drepaniform, drepanoid, sickle-shaped, bicorn, bicornuate, bicornuous, half-moon-shaped, crescentiform, crescentic, demilune, semilunar

crescent-shaped (small crescent)

lunulate

crest-shaped

cristiform

cross-shaped

cruciate, cruciform

crown-shaped

coroniform

cube-shaped

cubiform

cucumber-shaped

cucumiform

cumulus-cloud-like

cumuliform

cup-shaped

scyphate, scyphiform, cupulate, cupuliform, cyathiform, calicular, caliculate, calathiform, pocilliform, poculiform

curl-like

cirriform

cushion-shaped or pad-like
pulvilliform, pulvinate

cylinder-shaped
cylindriform

dart-shaped
belemnoid

delta (Δ)- or wedge-shaped
triangular, sphenic, cuneate, cuneiform

disc-shaped
disciform, discoid

dome-shaped
hemispherical

donut-shaped
toroidal

double- or two-faced
janiform

ear-shaped
auriform, auriculate

eel-shaped
anguilliform

egg-shaped
ooid, oval, ovoid, oviform, ovaliform, elliptical, ellipsoidal

egg-to-pear-like in shape
ovopyriform

embryo-like
embryoniform

erect-phallus-shaped
ithyphallic

eye-shaped
oculiform

fan-shaped
flabellate, flabelliform, rhipidate

feather-like
pinnate, pinniform, penniform, plumiform, pennaceous, plumaceous

fern- or frond-shaped
filiciform

fiddle- or violin-shaped
pandurate

fig-shaped
ficiform, ficicoid, caricous

finger-like
dactyloid, digitate, digitiform

fish-shaped
ichthyic, ichthyoid, ichthyoidal, ichthyomorphic

flame-shaped
flammulated

flask- or bladder-shaped
ampullaceous, ampulliform, lageniform, utriculate, utriculoid

flower-like
floriform, floral

flowerpot-shaped
vasculiform

foot-shaped
pediform, pedate

forceps-like
forcepiform

forked
forficate, furcate

fringe-like

fimbriate, fimbricate, lanciniform

fringed (small fringe)

fimbrillate

frond- or fern-shaped

filiciform

fruit-shaped

fructiform

funnel-shaped

infundibular, infundibuliform, choanoid, funnelform

gill-shaped

branchiform

gland-like

adeniform

grain-like

graniform

granule-like

granuliform

grape-cluster-like

botryose, aciniform

grouped together

agminate

hair-like

piliform, capilliform

hammer-shaped

malleiform

hand-shaped

meniform, palmate

handle-shaped

manubrial, ansate

hat-like
galericulate
headlike at one end
capitate
heart-shaped
cordiform, cordate
heart (inverted)- or spade (cards)-shaped
obcordate, obcordiform
helmet-shaped
galeiform, galeate, cassideous
herring-shaped
harengiform
hinged-joint-like
ginglymoid
honeycomb-like
faviform, faveolate, alveolate
hood-shaped
cucullate, cuculiform
hoof-shaped
ungulate
hook-shaped
ankyroid, ancistroid, aduncate, uncinate, unciform, hamiform
horn-shaped
corniform, cornuted
horseshoe-shaped
hippocrepiform
hourglass-shaped
biconical
insect-like
insectiform

ivy-leaf-shaped
hederiform
jelly-like
gelatiniform
jug-shaped (one handle)
urceiform
keel-shaped
carinate, cariniform
keyhole-shaped
clithridiate
kidney-shaped
reniform, nephroid
kidney-bean-shaped
reniform, nephroid
knob-like at one end
capitellate
knot- or node-shaped
nodiform
ladder-like
scalariform
lambda-shaped (Λ)
lambdoid
lance-head-shaped
lanceolate
lance-shaped
lanciform
lance-shaped inversely
oblanceolate
lattice-like
clathrate, clathroid, clathrose

leaf-shaped
phylliform, foliform, foliate, foliated

leather-bottle-shaped
utriform

lens-shaped (flattened oval)
lenticular, lentiform, lentoid

lentil-shaped
lenticular, lenticuliform, lentiform

lily-shaped
liliform

lip-shaped
labial, labellate, labelloid

lobe-shaped
lobate, lobular, lobiform

loop- or sling-shaped
fundiform

lotus-petal-shaped
lotiform

lyre-shaped
lyriform

miter- or bonnet-shaped
mitrate, mitriform

moon-shaped
luniform

mountain-shaped
montiform

mouth-shaped
oriform

mulberry-shaped
moriform

mummy-like
mummiform
mushroom-shaped
fungiform, agariciform
nail- or claw-shaped
unguiform
narrowing at the top
fastigiate
navel-like
umbiliform, umbiliciform
neck-like
colliform
needle-shaped
aciform, acicular, acerose, aciculate, styloid
netlike
retiform, reticular
nipple-shaped
mammiloid, mammiliform
node- or knot-shaped
nodiform
nose-like
nasiform, nasutiform
nostril-like
nariform
nut-shaped
nuciform
oar- or paddle-shaped
remiform
oat-shaped
aveniform

obelisk-shaped
obeliscoid, obeliskoid

omega-shaped (Ω)
omegoid

oyster-shaped
ostreiform

pad-like or cushion-shaped
pulvilliform, pulvinate

paddle- or oar-shaped
remiform

palm-shaped
palmate, palmiform, palmatiform

pea-shaped
pisiform

pear-shaped
pyriform

pear (upside-down)-shaped
obpyriform

pebble-shaped
calciform, calculiform

pencil-shaped
penciliform

petal-shaped
petaliform

phallus-shaped
phalliform, phallic

pie-shaped
sectoral

pie-shaped with a flat end rather than a point
segmental

pincer- or claw-shaped
cheliform
pipe- or tube-shaped
tubular, tubiform, fistulous, fistular, fistuliform
pitcher-shaped
ascidiform
plant-shaped
phytoform
pod-shaped
leguminose, leguminiform
pointed oval (as a gemstone)
marquise
pouch- or bag-shaped
sacciform, scrotiform, bursiform
prickle-shaped
aculeiform
prop-like
fulciform
pruning-knife-shaped
cultrate, cultriform
pulley-shaped
trochleiform
purse-shaped
bursiform
radial in form
actiniform
ram's-head-shaped
arietinous
reed-like
calamiform

rice-grain-like
riziform
ring-shaped (or spirally curled)
circinate, cingular, annular
rodlike
virgulate, bacillary, bacilliform, vergiform, baculiform
roof-shaped
tectiform
rope- or cord-like
funiform
rows-of-bricks-like
muriform
S-shaped
sigmoid, sigmoidal, annodated
saddle-shaped
selliform
sandal-shaped
sandaliform
saucer-shaped
pateriform, acetabuliform
sausage-shaped
allantoid, botuliform
scimitar-shaped
acinaciform
scissors-shaped
forciform
shallow-depression-shaped
glenoid
shark-shaped
squaliform, selachian

shell-shaped
conchiform, conchate

shield-shaped
scutate, scutiform, scutatiform, aspidate, elytriform, peltate, clypeate, clypeiform, peltiform

shovel- or spade (implement)-shaped
palaceous

sickle-shaped
meniscal, meniscate, meniscoid, menisciform, lunate, falcate, drepaniform, drepanoid, bicorn

sieve-like
cribriform, cribrose, cribral, cribrate

sling- or loop-shaped
fundiform

slipper-shaped
calceiform, soleiform

snail-shell-shaped
cochleate, cochleiform, soleiform

snake-shaped
colubriform, anguiform, serpentine

spade (cards)- or inverted-heart-shaped
obcordate, obcordiform

spade (implement)- or shovel-shaped
palaceous

spatula-shaped
spatulate

spear-shaped or arrowhead-shaped (with flaring barbs)
hastate

sphere-shaped
spherical, spheriform

spike-shaped
spiciform, spicate
spindle-shaped
fusiform
spine- or thorn-shaped
aculeiform, spiniform
spoon-shaped
cochleariform, spatulate
spread-fingers-like
digitate
stake-shaped
sudiform
stalk-like
stipiform
star-shaped
astroid, actinoid, stellate, stellar, stelliform
star-shaped (small star)
stellular
stemlike
cauliform
stirrup-shaped
stapediform
stone-like (small stone)
lapilliform
strap-shaped
ligulate, lorate
string-of-beads-like
moniliform, monilioid
sword-shaped
gladiate, ensate, ensiform, xiphoid, xiphiiform

tail-like
caudiform
teardrop-shaped
guttiform, lachrimiform, stilliform
tendril-like
pampiniform
tent-shaped
tentiform
thorn- or spine-shaped
aculeiform, spiniform
threadlike
filiform, filose, filariform
tongue-shaped
linguiform
tooth-like
odontoid, dentiform
toothed or comb-shaped
pectinate
top-shaped or top shell-shaped
trochiform
torpedo-shaped
terete
tower-shaped
turriform, pyrgoidal, turrical, turricular
tree-shaped
arboriform, dendritic, dendriform, dendroid, dendritiform
trumpet-shaped
buccinal
tube- or pipe-shaped
tubular, tubiform, fistulous, fistular, fistuliform

turnip-shaped
napiform
turret-shaped
turriculate, turriculated
two- or double-faced
janiform
U-shaped
hyoid, oxbow-like, hippocrepiform, parabolic
upsilon (ϒ)- or Y-shaped
hypsiloid, ypsiliform, hypsiliform
valve-shaped
valviform
violin- or fiddle-shaped
pandurate
vortex-like
vorticiform
wedge- or delta (Δ)-shaped
triangular, sphenic, cuneate, cuneiform, deltoid
wedge-shaped inversely
obcuneate, obdeltoid
wheel-shaped
rotiform, rotate
winglike
aliform
X-shaped
decussate, chiasmal
Y- or upsilon (ϒ)-shaped
hypsiloid, ypsiliform, hypsiliform

COMMON EMBLEMS AND SYMBOLS

figure of the earth
geoid

horizontal figure eight symbolizing infinity or eternity
lemniscate

circle with arrow pointed outward toward the upper right
male symbol, Mars symbol

circle with a suspended cross
female symbol, Venus symbol

seven- or nine-branched (Jewish) candelabrum
menorah

Hebrew symbol of life
chai

Judaic hexagram (intersecting triangles)
Star of David, Magen David, Mogen David, Shield of David

intersecting triangles, one of which is light and one dark
Solomon's seal

Buddhist or Hindu symbol of the universe, typically a design with a circle enclosing a square or a circle divided into four sections
yin-yang symbol, mandala

loop-topped cross (symbol of life)
ankh, crux ansata, key of life, key of the Nile, looped Tau cross

circle divided vertically by a line with two arms (like a downward vee) from the center to the circle
peace symbol

three loops interlaced into a roughly triangular form
triquetra

Japanese (Shinto) shrine-gate symbol
torii

hooked cross
swastika, gammadion, fylfot, crux gammata

figure with three curved branches or legs from the same center (or a three-armed swastika)
triskelion, triskele, triskelis

five interlocking circles (three above two)
Olympic symbol

flame-shaped symbol
flammulation

almond-shaped object or ornament
mandorla

five-pointed star
pentacle, pentagram, pentalpha

diamond-shaped scale or plate
mascle

triangular or wedge-shaped symbol
delta

moon (first or last quarter) or sickle shape
crescent

three-pronged spear associated with the god of the sea
trident

L-shape
gamma

V or upside-down-V emblem
chevron

two coiled snakes on a winged staff, associated with the Greek god Hermes (medical symbol)
caduceus, kerykeion

human skull (as a symbol of mortality)
death's-head, memento mori

skull and crossbones (pirate or poison symbol)
Jolly Roger

iris symbol (royal emblem of France)
fleur-de-lis

roselike ornament
rosette, cockade (when worn as an ornament)

upward-pointing three-lobed or three-petaled (trifoliate) floral shape
trefoil, shamrock

four-lobed or four-petaled floral shape
quatrefoil

five-lobed or five-petaled floral shape
cinquefoil

common ornament showing spread leaves or petals
palmette

common ornament showing a radiating floral cluster
anthemion, honeysuckle ornament

common ornament showing sprouting pointed leaves
lotus

common ornament showing shapely "billowing" leaves
acanthus

upright eagle with wings outstretched
spread eagle, heraldic eagle

ceremonial-staff emblem of authority
scepter

sphere with a cross atop it (monarchial symbol)
orb

bundle of rods with a projecting ax blade, borne before magistrates of ancient Rome as an indicator of authority
fasces

sun surrounded by (a representation of) its rays
sunburst

wheel whose spokes project beyond the rim
catherine wheel, spider wheel

map's circular symbol with N, S, E, and W indicated
compass rose

ornamental oval or somewhat curved frame
cartouche

Egyptian beetle-like symbol or ornament
scarab

stylized asp worn on ancient headdresses
uraeus

symbolic or memorial cluster of weapons or armor
trophy

curved band (often bearing an inscription)
ribbon

thin curling or spiral form like a leafless stem
tendril

finely interlacing curves or floral or animal figures
arabesque

typographic symbols
dingbats

selected keyboard characters used to depict a smiley face or signal the writer's emotion, attitude, or tone
emoticon

QUOTATIONS

I walked my rented bicycle through the gate to the Boudhanath stupa, turned left, then rode clockwise around the massive white dome. A plastic bag of tangerines dangled from my handlebars, jerking as the bike bounced along the cobblestone road. The wide, circular path surrounding the shrine was an important *kora*: a devotional path, followed clockwise around a holy mountain or Buddhist monument. The ancient white dome of Boudha itself—symbolic of a lotus, an egg, and/or Buddha's overturned begging bowl—rests upon a three-tiered plinth. The entire site, viewed from above, is revealed as a giant earthwork: an elaborate geometric mandala.

—JEFF GREENWALD, *Snake Lake*

The shapes of the letters are remarkably strong, written with expertise and confidence in symmetrical lines. Vertical strokes, both straight and rounded, are penned thickly with bold triangular pennant heads. Horizontal strokes are thin and are frequently used to join letters, sometimes with a slight triangular terminal.

—PETER BROWN, *The Book of Kells*

Mysticism always gripped the Welsh creative imagination, as we can see from the few Celtic artifacts still extant in the country. There is nothing straightforward to the manner of these objects, nothing right-angled or self-explanatory. They are neither realist in style nor entirely abstractionist—pictures which have evolved into patterns, triangles blurred into rhomboids, ritual combinations of curls and circles which may have some magic meaning, but have been stylized into an art form. When living creatures appear, they are caricature humans, schematic animals, and time and again there emerges the strange triskele, the wavy pattern of connected spirals which seems to have had some arcane fascination for the Celtic mind. —Jan Morris, *The Matter of Wales*

"I used to play basketball," he explained.

"You must've been pretty good."

"I wasn't bad, but all the shoes and balls are Cancer Perks." He walked toward the TV, where a huge pile of DVDs and video games were arranged into a vague pyramid shape. He bent at the waist and snatched up *V for Vendetta*. "I was, like, the prototypical white Hoosier kid," he said. "I was all about resurrecting the lost art of the midrange jumper, but then one day I was shooting free throws—just standing at the foul line at the North Central gym shooting from a rack of balls. All at once, I couldn't figure out why I was methodically tossing a spherical object through a toroidal object. It seemed like the stupidest thing I could possibly be doing."

—John Green, *The Fault in Our Stars*

Aulus recommended a mass-attack in diamond formation. The head of the diamond would consist of a single regiment in two waves, each wave eight men deep. Then would follow two regiments marching abreast, in the same formation as the leading one; then three regiments marching abreast. This would be the broadest part of the diamond and here the elephants would be disposed as a covering for each flank. Then would come two regiments, again, and then one. The cavalry and the rest of the infantry would be kept in reserve. Aulus explained that this diamond afforded a protection against charges from the flank; no attack could be made on the flank of the leading regiment without engaging the javelin-fire of the overlapping second line, nor on the second line without engaging the fire of the overlapping third.

—Robert Graves, *Claudius the God*

Misha listened, but with a certain ethereal inattention. As I talked, he was twisting and folding a napkin into . . . something. He had lately become a master of origami, the Japanese art of paper folding. He had filled an entire room with his paper menagerie: octagons, tetrahedrons, storks, bugs.

—David Remnick, *Lenin's Tomb: The Last Days of the Soviet Empire*

The pommel in gilt brass was composed of acanthus leaves and swept forward in the French style, the guard fitting into the foremost part which was split resembling the beak of a bird.

—Robert Wilkinson-Latham, *Swords in Color*

The body of the machine was small, almost cylindrical, and pointed. Forward and aft on the pointed ends were two small petroleum engines for the screw, and the navigators sat deep in a canoe-like recess, the foremost one steering, and being protected by a low screen with two plate-glass windows, from the blinding rush of air. On either side a monstrous flat framework with a curved front border could be adjusted so as either to lie horizontally or to be tilted upward or down.

—H. G. WELLS, "The Argonauts of the Air,"
The Complete Short Stories of H. G. Wells

Weber tried a different approach when he included the subway in his 1915 painting *Rush Hour: New York*. Showing the height of the daily commute, it is a swirl of solid and transparent planes of color composed of irregularly shaped diamonds, hexagons, and semicircles that rotate around the canvas. The lower half of the composition is devoted to the underground spaces of urban transport with brown arches alluding to the underground tunnels of the subway.

—TRACY FITZPATRICK, *Art and the Subway: New York Underground*

The stalagmites of Armand are a rather unusual variety—they appear to be made of rounded, irregular, hollow cones, which are concave upwards.

—TONY WALTHAM, *Caves*

When she'd stepped through to the other side, she turned and found that he was watching her from behind a glass wall. She went right up to it and pressed her face to it, near to his, so near that her eyelashes fluttered on the cold screen between them. He breathed on the glass and a nimbus of condensation billowed between them, and suddenly a fingertip was etching lines, curves, shapes into the mist. Letters. —MAGGIE O'FARRELL, *Instructions for a Heatwave*

The Russian defences consisted of a semi-elliptical-shaped fort containing 62 casemates on each of two floors from which heavy guns mounted in the centre could sweep the bay almost at water level. Behind the ellipse, and part of the fort, stood a large horseshoe-shaped work on two floors with casemates armed with heavy guns to flank the landward approaches. In the hills behind lay three round towers, also casemated, their guns commanding the countryside. All the masonry was granite, constructed in polygonal form similar to the method used by the Austrians at Verona. —QUENTIN HUGHES, *Military Architecture*

When Hal comes in, Howard is standing at the counter, emptying a medicinal-looking powder into a fishbowl containing a single vermilion fish. The fish is shaped like the end of a shovel and has both eyes on one side of its head; the powder turns the water electric green. The vermilion shovel fish hovers meditatively in the electric green orb, like a bizarre Christmas ornament.

—STACEY D'ERASMO, *A Seahorse Year*

Volcanic islands generally are circular or elliptical cones or domes, and it is easy to visualize the influence of their shape upon erosion by imagining simple circular cones that lie in seas without waves and on which rain falls uniformly. The consequent rivers that develop on a cone are radial because the slopes of the cone are radial. The side slopes of the river valleys tend to be relatively constant but the longitudinal slopes are steeper in the headwaters than at the shoreline. Thus the valleys of the radial streams are funnel shaped; they are narrow and shallow at the shoreline and spread into great, deep amphitheaters in the interior. —H. W. MENARD, *Islands*

The complex tangential and integer-ratio geometries found in most crop circles, even those of 1,000 feet in diameter, are awesomely accurate. The diatonic ratio (the white notes on the piano) has also been detected from triangle, square and hexagon ratios in certain formations, as have fractals and the Fibonacci sequence.

—LUCY PRINGLE, *Crop Circles*

The great breakthrough, however, was in the development of the medieval Christian labyrinth design. This had eleven rings instead of seven, a characteristic cruciform design, and most significantly, the paths ranged freely through the quadrants, rather than methodically proceeding quarter by quarter in the Roman way. A manuscript in the Vatican dated AD860–2 contains a prototype of this innovatory medieval Christian design, and the tenth-century Montpellier manuscript portrays the design more formally. It was executed in two main forms, circular and octagonal. —ADRIAN FISHER AND GEORG GERSTER, *Labyrinth*

A *Vexierbild* (puzzle-picture) by Schon, a Nuremberg engraver and pupil of Dürer, has been described by Rottinger: of large dimensions (0.44 metre × 0.75 metre) it is formed of four trapezoidal rows in which striped hatchings are continued by landscapes peopled with living figures. Towns and hills, men and animals are reabsorbed and engulfed in a tangle of lines, at first sight inexplicable. But by placing the eyes at the side and very close to the engraving one can see four superimposed heads inside rectilinear frames. Perspective causes the apparent images to disappear and at the same time the hidden outlines to appear.

—JURGIS BALTRUŠAITIS, *Anamorphic Art*

The ball took place in the fair's Natatorium, a large building on the Midway devoted to swimming and bathing and equipped with a ballroom and banquet rooms. Bunting of yellow and red hung from the ceiling. The galleries that overlooked the ballroom were outfitted with opera boxes for fair officials and socially prominent families. Burnham had a box, as did Davis and Higinbotham and of course the Palmers. The galleries also had seats and standing room for other paying guests. From railings in front of the boxes hung triangles of silk embroidered with gold arabesques, all glowing with the light of adjacent incandescent bulbs. Its effect was one of indescribable opulence.

—ERIK LARSON, *The Devil in the White City*

If you draw a small irregular shape on the oblong edge of the pack, every tiny part of that picture will change when you shear the oblong to form a rhomboid. Only the area remains the same; and only the sides, which are straight and parallel, remain straight and parallel. But oceans and continents are not parallelograms!

—DAVID GREENHOOD, *Mapping*

The Catherine-wheel window, and rude tracery below it, is the only portion clumsily adopted from the Lombards.

—JOHN RUSKIN, "Assisi," *The Lamp of Beauty*

Harald Alabaster's study, or den, was next to Bredely's small chapel. It was hexagonal in shape, with wood-panelled walls and two deep windows, carved in stone in the Perpendicular style: the ceiling too was carved stone, pale grey-gold in colour, a honey-comb of smaller hexagons.

—A. S. BYATT, "Morpho Eugenia," *Angels and Insects: Two Novellas*

If the long sides, given by joining the Station positions, were to be related to the Moon in the same way, the Station positions would need to form not a rectangle, but a parallelogram with corners that were not right angles. Shifting Stonehenge only 50 miles to the north or south would change the required angles by as much as 2°.

—FRED HOYLE, *On Stonehenge*

Besides the uncial writing on the convex side of the sherd, at the top, painted in dull red on what had once been the lip of the amphora, was the cartouche already mentioned as appearing on the *scarabaeus*, which we had found in the casket.

—H. RIDER HAGGARD, *She*

Fixed with cannons that could fire twenty miles, honeycombed with deep tunnels and lateral shafts, Corregidor was stuck like a steel bit in the mouth of Manila Bay. The island was shaped like a tadpole, its squirmy tail pointing off toward Manila, its bulbous head aimed at Bataan. The Rock, it was called. The Impregnable Fortress. The Asian Gibraltar.

—HAMPTON SIDES, *Ghost Soldiers: The Epic Account of World War II's Greatest Rescue Mission*

Often the edges bounding a face make up a fairly simple plane figure—a triangle, or a square, or the like. And often the faces bounding the whole crystal make up a corresponding simple solid figure—a cube, a tetrahedron, or an octahedron. . . .

—ALAN HOLDEN AND PHYLIS MORRISON, *Crystals and Crystal Growing*

Workers fabricated the javelin-like spire in pieces, lifted it into the tower, and riveted it together. A 30-ton crane stood ready. Van Alen waited for a perfectly calm morning. When it came, as the architect watched nervously from the street, the crane lifted the 28-ton needle into place. It took just 30 minutes. With that, Walter Chrysler's skyscraper topped out at 1,048 feet, taller than the 986-foot Eiffel Tower, then the world's tallest structure, and more important, taller than anything yet proposed by John Raskob.

—MITCHELL PACELLE, *Empire: A Tale of Obsession, Betrayal, and the Battle for an American Icon*

These consist of cylindrical cells set together to form a palisade-like layer. . . . Each cell is polygonal in horizontal section; cuboidal cells are square in vertical section, whereas columnar cells are taller than their diameter. Commonly, microvilli are found on the free surface of such cells, providing a large, absorptive area . . . , as in the epithelium of the small intestine (columnar cells with a striated border), the gall bladder (columnar cells with a brush border) and the proximal and distal convoluted tubules of the kidney (large cells with brush borders).

—Henry Gray, *Gray's Anatomy*,
36th edition (Peter L. Williams
and Roger Warwick, eds.)

Piet was by profession a builder, in love with snug right-angled things, and he had grown to love this house, its rectangular low rooms, its baseboards and chair rails molded and beaded by hand, the slender mullions of the windows whose older panes were flecked with oblong bubbles and tinged with lavender, the swept worn brick of the fireplace hearths like entryways into a sooty upward core of time, the attic he had lined with silver insulation paper so it seemed now a vaulted jewel box or an Aladdin's cave, the solid freshly poured basement that had been a cellar floored with dirt when they had moved in five years ago. He loved how this house welcomed into itself in every season lemony flecked rhomboids of sun whose slow sliding revolved it with the day, like the cabin of a ship on a curving course.

—John Updike, *Couples*

Eucalyptus trees with their smoky, oily smell grew everywhere, very tall, the boles going far up before sending out a branch. They were untidy trees, with wood soft and weak. They kept losing branches, so that there were great gaps along the trunks. They kept dropping their narrow tan, spear-shaped leaves, which littered the ground under them, and layers of bark fell from them in long strips along with little wooden buttons, brown with crosses carved out of them on one side, powdery blue on the other.

—LYDIA DAVIS, *The End of the Story*

Immediately on passing through Porta del Popolo the visitor enters a square, Piazza del Popolo. Today it is an oval but at that time it was a long, narrow trapezoid converging toward the gateway and with long garden walls on either side. Facing the city, one saw the three thoroughfares thrusting deep into the town. The two triangular building sites form an effective front with two symmetrical domed churches strongly emphasizing the solid mass of the houses advancing toward the open space of the piazza.

—STEEN EILER RASMUSSEN, *Towns and Buildings*

This monumental female saviour of his movement was to have carried a torch in one hand, lighting her kindly face, while the other would have supported a globe containing an entire theatre. Her robes would fall away to a great parade-ground where people could disport themselves in gentle diversions amid the scent of orange blossom. The basic idea is not new at all. As the mythographer Marina Warner notes, a Stone Age temple uncovered at

Skara Brae on Orkney adopts the "cinquefoil form of a schematic female body, the entrance lies through the birth passage."

—HUGH ALDERSEY-WILLIAMS, *Anatomies: A Cultural History of the Human Body*

On the computer-enhanced images they could see a patchwork of sinuous valleys like those found on Mars. There were also areas of grooved terrain, similar to that found by *Voyager* on the surface of one of Jupiter's satellites, Ganymede. Elsewhere, the surface of Miranda resembled the cratered highlands of our own Moon, and there were also giant scarps higher than the Grand Canyon. In the centre of the satellite was a large rocky area shaped rather like a chevron, and two multi-ringed features rather like archery targets bracketed it.

—ARTHUR SMITH, *Planetary Exploration: Thirty Years of Unmanned Space Probes*

It was an almost perfect cone of snow, simple in outline as if a child had drawn it, and impossible to classify as to size, height, or nearness. It was so radiant, so serenely poised, that he wondered for a moment if it were real at all. Then, while he gazed, a tiny puff clouded the edge of the pyramid, giving life to the vision before the faint rumble of the avalanche confirmed it.

—JAMES HILTON, *Lost Horizon*

Flora was ironing barefooted. Her habit of going without shoes in the house I found somewhat obscene because her feet were childishly shapeless and uncared-for. I thought of Nonie's visits to her chiropodist to have her long, narrow feet soaked and sanded and the corns on the knobbly joints shaved away and her almond-shaped toenails blunt-cut and buffed to a high pink sheen, though nobody was going to see them but us.

—GAIL GODWIN, *Flora*

On another sculptured relief, showing the king, in a chariot, hunting lions, his tunic is embroidered with a disk encircled by a ring-border decorated with a palmette design, which contains a pictorial representation of a sacred tree confronted on either side by a priest, and surmounted by a winged solar disk, here a flower-like rosette.

—ARCHIBALD H. CHRISTIE, *Pattern Design: An Introduction to the Study of Formal Ornament*

There were always subtle differences, but for the most part, a lamb chop tended to maintain its basic shape. That is to say it looked choplike. It had a handle made of bone and a teardrop of meat hugged by a thin rind of fat. Apparently, though, that was too predictable. Order the modern lamb chop, and it's likely to look no different than your companion's order of shackled pompano.

—DAVID SEDARIS, *Me Talk Pretty One Day*

First of all, when you consider the shape of a chickadee's body, you will notice that it's round. Whereas a blue jay is elongated, and a nuthatch tapered and slightly flattened, a chickadee is like a little ball. This roundness helps the small bird balance itself in the topsy-turvy positions it assumes while it's searching for insect eggs on the twigs and outer branches of trees.

—Gale Lawrence, *A Field Guide to the Familiar: Learning to Observe the Natural World*

Marburg is one of a family of viruses known as the filoviruses. Marburg was the first filovirus to be discovered. The word *filovirus* is Latin and means "thread virus." The filoviruses look alike, as if they are sisters, and they resemble no other virus on earth. While most viruses are ball-shaped particles that look like peppercorns, the thread viruses have been compared to strands of tangled rope, to hair, to worms, to snakes. When they appear in a great flooding mess, as they so often do when they have destroyed a victim, they look like a tub of spaghetti that has been dumped on the floor. Marburg particles sometimes roll up into loops. The loops resemble Cheerios. Marburg is the only ring-shaped virus known.

—Richard Preston, *The Hot Zone: A Terrifying True Story*

Earth flows move slower than debris flows and mudflows. They usually have a spoon-shaped sliding surface with a crescent-shaped cliff at the upper end and a tongue-shaped bulge at the lower end. . . .

—Peter W. Birkeland and Edwin E. Larson, *Putnam's Geology*

If we look through a window at a mass of buildings, or any external objects, and observe that part of the glass to which each object, line, or point, appears opposite, we find that their apparent situation is very different from their real. We find that horizontal lines sometimes appear oblique, or even perpendicular, that circles, in certain situations, look like ellipses, and squares like trapezoids or parallelograms. —JACOB BIGELOW, *The Useful Arts: Considered in Connexion with the Applications of Science*

Two of the most famous, long landmarks of Manhattan are the Flatiron Building, erected in 1902, and the Times Building (recently remodeled as the Allied Chemical Building), in 1904. Both have odd, trapezoidal floor plans, dictated by the pie-shaped real-estate slices Broadway strews along its diagonal path as it crosses Manhattan avenues, Fifth at Twenty-third, site of the Flatiron, and Seventh at Forty-second, site of the Times. The resulting slenderness of the two buildings, plus the absence of scientific data on wind stresses, caused the New York engineers to take special precautions. Triangular "gusset plates" were inserted as braces, four to each joint of horizontal beam and vertical column.

—JOSEPH GIES, *Wonders of the Modern World: Thirteen Great Achievements of Modern Engineering*

Later, experimenting with small and full-size gliders, he found that setting the wings at a slight dihedral (or shallow V-shaped) angle to each other gave lateral stability, and that a tail plane set behind the main wings was necessary for longitudinal stability.

—*The American Heritage History of Flight* (Alvin M. Josephy, ed.)

c. Ovoid or circular shape. This type of craft is described as being shaped like an ice cream cone, being rounded at the large end and tapering to a near-point at the other end. They are approximately 30–40 feet long and the thick end diameter is approximately 20 percent of the length. There is an extremely bright light at the pointed end, and this craft usually travels point down. They can appear to be any shape from round to cylindrical, depending upon the angle of observation. Often sightings of this type of craft are elliptical craft seen at an inclined angle or edge-on.

—Stanton Friedman, *Top Secret/Majic: Operation Majestic-12 and the United States Government's UFO Cover-up*

We had crossed the high and relatively level sands which form the base of the Fork, and were entering the labyrinth of detached banks which obstruct the funnel-shaped cavity between the upper and middle prongs. This I knew from the chart. —Erskine Childers, *The Riddle of the Sands*

A geometric plan of Beaux-Arts derivation organized the main exhibit area into a *rond-point* system of radiating streets and fanlike segments. Symmetrical axes led to the

Fair's central theme building, the Trylon and Perisphere. The longitudinal central axis of Constitutional Mall extended from the Trylon and Perisphere eastward to the oval Lagoon of Nations and beyond, to the Court of Peace, which was flanked by foreign-sponsored pavilions and terminated by the symmetrical U.S. Government Building. Extending at 45° angles from either side of the Trylon and Perisphere were the Avenue of Patriots and the Avenue of Pioneers, both of which culminated in circular plazas—the former at Bowling Green, before the IRT and BMT entrances, and the latter at Lincoln Square.

—Eugene A. Santomasso, "The Design of Reason," *Dawn of a New Day: The New York World's Fair, 1939–1940* (Helen A. Harrison, ed.)

For the structural supports Wright devised dendriform (tree-shaped) columns with elongated tapered shafts carrying broad flat disks. Forming the roof of the secretarial staff room is a forest of these columns, three stories high. . . .

—Leland M. Roth, *A Concise History of American Architecture*

The Old River Control Auxiliary Structure is a rank of seven towers, each buff with a white crown. They are vertical on the upstream side, and they slope toward the Atchafalaya. Therefore, they resemble flying buttresses facing the Mississippi. The towers are separated by six arciform gates, convex to the Mississippi, and hinged in trunnion blocks secured with steel to carom the force of the river into the core of the structure. Lifted by cables, these tainter gates, as they are called, are about as light and graceful as anything could be that has a composite weight of twenty-six hundred tons. Each of them is sixty-two feet wide.

—JOHN MCPHEE, *The Control of Nature*

At the other end of the series we have the cells of the hive-bee, placed in a double layer: each cell, as is well known, is an hexagonal prism, with the basal edges of its six sides beveled so as to join on to a pyramid, formed of three rhombs.

—CHARLES DARWIN, *On the Origin of Species*

In the evenings Mrs. Chaudhuri sometimes sang to them. Directly she was seated cross-legged on the rush mat, gently supporting the onion-shaped tamboura, she became a different woman; self-assured, holding her bony body gracefully erect, not unlike the way Lady Chatterjee held hers when sitting on a sofa at the DC's.

—PAUL SCOTT, *The Jewel in the Crown*

To bring light into the center of the room, a portion of the roof was raised about 4 meters higher than the roof over the side sections; the columns supporting the two sections differed, with bundle papyriform columns used at the side and full-blooming open papyriform columns in a larger size standing along the central aisle.

—DORA P. CROUCH, *History of Architecture: From Stonehenge to Skyscrapers*

"As you can see, the missile tubes are located forward of the sail instead of aft, as in our subs. The forward diving planes fold into slots in the hull here; ours go on the sail. She has twin screws; ours have one propeller. And finally, her hull is oblate. Instead of being cylindrical like ours, it is flattened out markedly top and bottom."

—TOM CLANCY, *The Hunt for Red October*

They were much shorter than any animal he had yet seen on Malacandra, and he gathered that they were bipeds, though the lower limbs were so thick and sausage-like that he hesitated to call them legs. The bodies were a little narrower at the top than at the bottom so as to be very slightly pear-shaped, and the heads were neither round like those of *hrossa* nor long like those of *sorns*, but almost square.

—C. S. LEWIS, *Out of the Silent Planet*

As long ago as 340 B.C. the Greek philosopher Aristotle, in his book *On the Heavens*, was able to put forward two good arguments for believing that the earth was a round sphere rather than a flat plate. First, he realized that eclipses of the moon were caused by the earth coming between the sun and the moon. The earth's shadow on the moon was always round, which would be true only if the earth was spherical. If the earth had been a flat disk, the shadow would have been elongated and elliptical, unless the eclipse always occurred at a time when the sun was directly under the center of the disk.

—STEPHEN HAWKING, *A Brief History of Time: From the Big Bang to Black Holes*

Deep between two hills was an old quarry, which we were fond of pretending we had discovered. In places the stone stood in vertical shafts, six-sided or eight-sided, the height of stools or pillars. At the center of each of them was a sunburst, a few concentric circles, faint lines the color of rust. These we took to be the ruins of an ancient civilization. If we went up to the top of the quarry, we could ease ourselves a quarter of the way down its face on our toes along a diagonal cranny, till we came to a shallow cave, just deep enough for the two of us to sit in.

—Marilynne Robinson, *Housekeeping*

Fish scientists describe white sharks as traumatogenic to humans, meaning capable of causing an injury. The largest grow to nearly twenty feet and weigh five thousand pounds, about the same as a Lincoln Navigator. They are among the most modern looking of animals—eight fins on a tapered cylinder, a Bauhaus fish—yet their form is prehistoric. One woman told me that when she saw a white shark for the first time she felt as if she were seeing a dinosaur rising from the depths.

—Alec Wilkinson, "Cape Fear: Tracking the Sharks of New England," *The New Yorker*, September 9, 2013

He reached the top of the hill; he turned a corner and the town was hidden. Down he looked into a deep valley with a dried up river bed at the bottom. This side and that was covered with small dilapidated houses that had broken stone verandahs where the fruit lay drying, tomato lanes in the garden, and from the gates to the doors a trellis of vines. The late sunlight, deep, golden, lay in the cup of the valley; there was a smell of charcoal in the air. In the gardens the men were cutting grapes. He watched a man standing in the greenish shade, raising up, holding a black cluster in one hand, taking the knife from his belt, cutting, laying the bunch in a flat boat-shaped basket. —Katherine Mansfield, "The Man without a Temperament," *Stories*

With the lights out, the desert was gray tufted with black spots of desert growth. Here and there loomed tall columns, and one rocky mass shaped like a pipe organ.

—Louis L'Amour, *The Haunted Mesa*

Their discoverers may ambitiously have planned a concentric circle for which the eighty-two Q and R holes were intended, arranged in thirty-eight pairs with an additional six at the north-eastern entrance. But when the last bluestone was unearthed and the countryside scoured no more were to be found. In frustration, the scheme was modified into a less impressive single circle of about fifty-seven stones enclosing an elegant horseshoe of nineteen pillars. Even in the golden age of prehistory there could be blunders. Stonehenge was no exception.

—Aubrey Burl, *Great Stone Circles: Fables, Fictions, Facts*

Topology studies the properties that remain unchanged when shapes are deformed by twisting or stretching or squeezing. Whether a shape is square or round, large or small, is irrelevant in topology, because stretching can change those properties. Topologists ask whether a shape is connected, whether it has holes, whether it is knotted.

They imagine surfaces not just in the one-, two-, and three-dimensional universes of Euclid, but in spaces of many dimensions, impossible to visualize. Topology is geometry on rubber sheets.

—JAMES GLEICK, *Chaos: Making a New Science*

Under his eyes new cities grew. Mesa Verde, Aztec, Wupatki, Keet Seel. Each built and at the height of its prosperity abandoned until the people were gathered for their last great migration into the desert itself. Into four groups they divided themselves and in four directions they left, making a cross over the land until more hundreds of years passed and they wheeled right, forming a swastika. As this swastika wheeled, they broke into smaller groups, all returning but all moving in circles until the land was a giant's pattern of moving swastikas and serpentines. A pueblo would live for an instant. Another group would find it and a spiral map of their predecessors' path and then turn in the opposite direction, one eddy twisting from another, yet always directed to the finally permanent gathering at the center of the world. —MARTIN CRUZ SMITH, *Nightwing*

The phone rings on the little chest squeezed between the refrigerator and the swinging door to the dining room, its drawers containing things rarely or never used (owner's manuals for such broken appliances as the deep-fat fryer whose cord likewise lies hidden deep under a pile of ruffled aprons, a lemon zester, a muddler, a croque-monsieur mold, a set of pastel plastic heart-, spade-, diamond-, and club-shaped cookie cutters, a bartender's guide called

Here's How bound by rawhide thongs to a pair of wooden covers, etc. etc.). —KATHRYN DAVIS, *Hell*

He had been dreaming, and he saw his dream in its exact form. It was, first an emerald. Cut into an octagon with two long sides, it was shaped rather like the plaque at the bottom of a painting. Events within this emerald were circular and never-ending.

—MARK HELPRIN, "The Schreuderspitze," *Ellis Island and Other Stories*

In the jargon of his trade, this region was covered by "the semi-permanent Pacific High." He looked at it malignantly. Then he smiled, for he noticed that the High had today accidentally assumed the shape of a gigantic dog's head. Rising from the Pacific waters it looked out stupidly across the continent. The blunt nose just touched Denver; the top of the head was in British Columbia. A small circle over southern Idaho supplied an eye; three concentric ovals pointing southwest from the California coast furnished a passable ear. —GEORGE R. STEWART, *Storm*

After dinner, I put clean towels on the bed in the guest room. My mother is sitting on the bed. The room has Harold's minimalist look to it: the twin bed with plain white sheets and white blanket, polished wood floors, a bleached oakwood chair, and nothing on the slanted gray walls.

The only decoration is an odd-looking piece right next to the bed: an end table made out of a slab of unevenly cut marble and thin crisscrosses of black lacquer wood for the legs. My mother puts her handbag on the table and the cylindrical black vase on top starts to wobble. The freesias in the vase quiver.

—AMY TAN, *The Joy Luck Club*

My instructor, Donald Defler, a gnomish balding man, paced at the front of the lecture hall and flipped on an overhead projector. He pointed to two diagrams that appeared on the wall behind him. They were schematics of the cell reproduction cycle, but to me they just looked like a neon-colored mess of arrows, squares, and circles with words I didn't understand, like "MPF Triggering a Chain Reaction of Protein Activations."

—REBECCA SKLOOT, *The Immortal Life of Henrietta Lacks*

All the gold, and stucco ornamentation, the cartouches of pan-pipes and tambourines, the masks of Comedy, and the upholstery in garnet plush were democratic stabs at palatial luxury; these were the palaces of the people.

—ROBERTSON DAVIES, *World of Wonders*

On the prow of that stone ship in the centre of the strait, and seemingly a part of it, a shaped and geometrical outcrop of the naked rock, stood the pueblo of Malpais. Block above block, each story smaller than the one below, the tall houses rose like stepped and amputated pyramids into the blue sky. At their feet lay a straggle of low buildings, a criss-cross of walls; and on three sides the precipices fell sheer into the plain. A few columns of smoke mounted perpendicularly into the windless air and were lost.

—Aldous Huxley, *Brave New World*

But there were other objects of delight and interest claiming his instant attention; there were quaint twisted candlesticks in the shape of snakes, and a teapot fashioned like a china duck, out of whose open beak the tea was supposed to come. And there was a carved sandal-wood box packed tight with aromatic cotton-wool, and between the layers of cotton-wool were little brass figures, hump-necked bulls, and peacocks and goblins, delightful to see and to handle. Less promising in appearance was a large square book with plain black covers. . . .

—Saki, "The Lumber-Room," *The Complete Saki*

Very clever were some of their productions—pasteboard guitars, antique lamps made of old-fashioned butter boats covered with silver paper, gorgeous robes of old cotton, glittering with tin spangles from a pickle factory, and armor covered with the same useful diamond-shaped bits left in sheets when the lids of tin preserve pots were cut out.

—Louisa May Alcott, *Little Women*

"Which Renatus kindly hatched for that occasion," Burlingame interrupted. "And what's more he allows his globules both a rectilinear and a rotatory motion. If only the first occurs when the globules smite our retinae, we see white light; if both, we see color. And as if this were not magical enough—*mirabile dictu!*—when the rotatory motion surpasseth the rectilinear, we see blue; when the reverse, we see red; and when the twain are equal, we see yellow. What fantastical drivel!"

—JOHN BARTH, *The Sot-Weed Factor*

I cut from a tree a score of long, blunt thorns, tough and black as whalebone, and drove them through a strip of wood in which I had burnt a row of holes to receive them, and made myself a comb, and combed out my long, tangled hair to improve my appearance.

"It is not the tangled condition of your hair," persisted the voice, "but your eyes, so wild and strange in expression, that show the approach of madness. Make your locks as smooth as you like, and add a garland of those scarlet, star-shaped blossoms hanging from the bush behind you—crown yourself as you crowned old Cla-cla—but the crazed look will remain just the same."

—W. H. HUDSON, *Green Mansions*

Building the hive, the workers have the look of embryonic cells organizing a developing tissue; from a distance they are like the viruses inside a cell, running off row after row of symmetrical polygons as though laying down crystals.

—LEWIS THOMAS, *The Lives of a Cell: Notes of a Biology Watcher*

These 2D beings can explore the geometry of their two-dimensional universe by making measurements on straight lines, triangles, and circles. Their straight lines are the "geodesics" discussed in Chapter 2 . . . : the straightest lines that exist in their two-dimensional universe. In the bottom of their universe's "bowl," which we see in Figure 3.2 as a segment of a sphere, their straight lines are segments of great circles like the equator of the Earth or its lines of constant longitude.

—KIP S. THORNE, *Black Holes and Time Warps: Einstein's Outrageous Legacy*

Quite different from these nests of paper and clay are those of thickly felted vegetable hairs made by large wasps of the genus *Apoica.* Round or hexagonal in shape, five or six inches in diameter, these nests have the form of an umbrella without a handle or a stalkless mushroom.

—ALEXANDER F. SKUTCH, *A Naturalist in Costa Rica: How Movement Shapes Identity*

It was in this place of astonishing miniatures that I came upon the lairs of the lions in the sunny sand—ant lions, that is. Small funnel-shaped pits dimpled the sand—inverted cones an inch or two in diameter across the top, tapering to the bottom perhaps an inch deep in the sand.

—VIRGINIA S. EIFERT, *Journeys in Green Places: Shores and Woods of Wisconsin's Door Peninsula*

Later he stared at his finished work and longed to know if anyone other than Mr. Cromarty would be able to make sense of the miniature circles, dashes, and curlicues that floated freely above the lines with their sudden cruel hooks. —IAN McEWAN, *The Child in Time*

Particles may seem like a Platonic abstraction at first. They are fundamental and indivisible. They have no shape, size, color, or any other macroscopic properties. And any particle of a type will be completely identical and indistinguishable from one of the same type. Quite literally, if you've seen one electron, you've seen them all.

—DAVE GOLDBERG, *The Universe in the Rearview Mirror: How Hidden Symmetries Shape Reality*

Probably the best known of the moths are the sphinx or hawk moths, some of which are so large they resemble hummingbirds. The bodies of these moths are relatively stout and torpedo-shaped.

—DAVID F. COSTELLO, *The Prairie World: Plants and Animals of the Grassland Sea*

But the ends of the "horseshoe" ran into the river which formed the northern boundary—and fourth side—of the plantation. And at the end nearer the house and outbuildings in the middle of the plantation, Leiningen had constructed a dam. By means of the dam, water from the river could be diverted into the ditch.

So, now, by opening the dam, he was able to fling an imposing wall of water, a huge quadrilateral with the river as its base, completely around the plantation, like the moat encircling a medieval city.

—Carl Stephenson, "Leiningen versus the Ants," *Great Stories of Suspense and Adventure*

Colored red ochre, blue and tan, they paraded along the walls in that peculiar frontal way of Egyptians, with vultures on their palms, sheaves of wheat, water lilies and lutes. They were accompanied by lion, scarabs, owl, oxen and dismembered feet. —E. L. Doctorow, *Ragtime*

But being accepted one day doesn't mean one will be welcome the next—the Jews of Buenos Aires couldn't resist planning for dark times. So atop that modest wall they'd affixed another two meters of wrought-iron fence, each bar with a fleur-de-lis on its end. All those points and barbs four meters up gave that wall an unwelcoming, unclimbable, pants-ripping feel.

—Nathan Englander, *The Ministry of Special Cases*

Kayerts stood still. He looked upwards; the fog rolled low over his head. He looked round like a man who has lost his way; and he saw a dark smudge, a cross-shaped stain, upon the shifting purity of the mist.

—Joseph Conrad, *An Outpost of Progress*

The room's one window, too high for a woman not standing on a stool to peer out of, had lozenge panes of leaded glass, thick glass bubbled and warped like bottle bottoms. —John Updike, *The Witches of Eastwick*

But at first sight from the Derwent River—from which most museumgoers approach by ferry from downtown Hobart, the capital—MONA looms above like a post-apocalyptic fortress, waffled-concrete walls intersecting with great trapezoidal battlements clad in rusting steel.

—Richard Flanagan, "Tasmanian Devil," *The New Yorker,* January 21, 2013

The rich benignant cigar smoke eddied coolly down his throat; he puffed it out again in rings which breasted the air bravely for a moment; blue, circular—I shall try and get a word alone with Elizabeth to-night, he thought—then began to wobble into hour-glass shapes and taper away; odd shapes they take, he thought.

—Virginia Woolf, *Mrs. Dalloway*

The world's first ballistic missile was the Nazi's V-2 rocket, designed by German scientists under the leadership of Wernher von Braun. As the first object to be launched above the Earth's atmosphere, the bullet-shaped, large-finned V-2 (the "V" stands for *Vergeltungswaffen*, or "Vengeance Weapon") inspired an entire generation of spaceship illustrations.

—Neil deGrasse Tyson, *Space Chronicles: Facing the Ultimate Frontier*

This miniature world demonstrated how everything was planned, people lived in these modern streamlined curvilinear buildings, each of them accommodating the population of a small town. . . . —E. L. Doctorow, *World's Fair*

Directly across the way stood a top-heavy dockhouse, a weatherbeaten cube of pure nineteenth century raised up on out-curving supports for the purpose of enabling elderly ladies to sit out on good afternoons to watch the sailboats leaning at their work—a setting rendered completely other-day and unreal by this thick, moist air.

—JOHN HERSEY, *Under the Eye of the Storm*

PATTERNS AND EDGES

PATTERNS

having a pattern or design

patterned, designed, figured

having a planned and orderly design

schematic

deployed or arranged in a prescribed or definitive pattern, as geese, marching bands, military aircraft, or skydivers

in formation

having varied colors or a varied pattern

variegated, motley, harlequin, diverse, multifarious

having a consistent or recurrent conceptual element

having a motif

represented in a simplified or symbol-like form

formal

represented in a realistic or somewhat detailed form

naturalistic

designed with a pattern of rectilinear and/or curvilinear motifs

geometric, geometrical

having a pattern of uniformly spaced vertical and horizontal lines (as to locate points on a map)
grid-like, graticulated

irregular geometric pattern repeating similar shapes on smaller scales
fractal

having many dots
dotted, punctate

having any dots that from a distance seem to merge
pointillist

having gold dots made with a pointed tool
pointillé

having spots
spotted, speckled, dappled, menald, macular, maculose, pardine, flecked

having colored spots, blotches, or speckles
varicolored, mottled

having dots or spots in a textile pattern
polka-dot, polka-dotted

having spots like the petals of a rose (as those of a leopard)
rosette

having eyelike spots
ocellate

having soft shadow-like small touches or spots
stippled

having softened or blurred outlines or colors, as in a painting
scumbled

having holes
holey, pierced, porous, perforated, spongeous, cribriform

having small holes as a design in embroidery
eyelet
having bowl-like depressions
cratered
having small depressions
pitted, cuppy, cavernulous, foveate
having small fissures or chinks
rimulose
having scoop-like indentations
chiseled, gouged
having a rounded recess
scooped, hollowed, concave
constructed to be windingly intricate or complicated
maze-like, labyrinthine, labyrinthian, tortuous
having a structure of rows and openings
honeycombed, faveolate, faviform, alveolate, compartmentalized, chambered
having any of many interwoven, plaited patterns
basket weave
having an angular-labyrinth or straight-pathways design
fretted
cavity-divided or compartmentalized
locular, loculate
having a horizontal marking or strip
banded, barred, belted
having a horizontally encircling band or stripe
crossbanded
having lines or stripes
lined, striped, lineate, scored
having thin lines or stripes
pinstriped

having black and white stripes
zebra
a pattern of alternating short and slanted lines
herringbone
having spaces or interruptions rather than being continuous or consistent as a pattern
broken
having narrow markings or irregular stripes
streaked
having variegated marble-like streaks or a swirling pattern
marbled, marmoreal
having fine lines
lineolate
having longitudinal (lengthwise) stripes
vittate
in sequence or in rows
serial
having vertical ranks
rectiserial
arranged in two rows or series
biserial
having grooves
grooved, fluted, channeled, cannellated, rutted
having rectangular grooves
dadoed
having long furrows or grooves
sulcated, canaliculated, canaliculate
having rows of folds or ridges and grooves
corrugated, plicate
having minute grooves
striated

having raised lengthwise strips
ridged
having hairlike ridges
lirate
having many ripples or short bends
crinkled
having spiral grooves
rifled
having long or row-like thin projections
ribbed, costate
having cord- or tube-like trimming
piped
having cracks
cracked, crackled, craquelé, crazed
wound together
interlaced, intertwined, interwoven, entwined, plaited, braided, plexiform
having ornamental curls or plaiting
goffered
having crossed lines
crisscross, crisscrossed, crosscut, reticulate, reticulated, cancellate
having a design of crossed strips
latticed
marked or shaded with two or more sets of intersecting parallel lines
crosshatched
having a netlike pattern
reticular, reticulated
an all-over network of fine lines or dots (as on a postage stamp)
burelé

map line representing connecting places having the same elevation
contour line
map shading line to suggest relief or depth
hachure
having sharp back-and-forth turns
zigzag, staggered, chevroned, chevronwise, cringle-crangle
having a pattern of contrasting or variegated squares
checkered, checkerboard, chessboard, counterchanged, tessellated
having a weblike construction or pattern
mesh-like
assembled from varied pieces of cloth or other materials
patchwork
set or inserted into a surface as part of a design
inlaid
having or resembling a design of inlaid pieces
mosaic
having a recessed checkered pattern
waffle, waffled
having a pattern of unbalanced or irregular squares
plaid
having a plaid pattern designating a Scottish clan
tartan
having a pattern of varicolored diamond shapes
argyle
having irregular, swirled patterns of a particular shade or shades to blend in with a natural terrestrial environment
camouflage, camo
having pieces or elements overlapping
imbricate, imbricated, obvolute

having a pattern of tangent or overlapping circles or semicircles
scaled, perulate
having thin and flat or gill-like plates
lamellate, lamellated
having coils or spirals
whorled
having several whorls
multispiral
having a pattern of wormlike curves
vermiculate, vermiculated
having irregular crooked or sinuous lines
rivulose
having wavy lines
undé, damascened, flexuous
having waves or undulations
rippled
having a shimmering rippled or watery pattern (from two superimposed patterns)
moiré
showing circular continuation or movement
rotary, rotational
having flower-shaped or flower-like ornaments
floriated, floral, floreted
arranged in a pattern of rosettes
rosular
having an ornamentally curled design
scrolled
curled or coiled inward
involute
having starlike rays
asteriated

radially symmetrical
actinoid
having encircling parallel rings
ringed
showing delicately ornamental openwork
filigreed
interlaced and branching ornamental work, as in a Gothic window
tracery
puckered, blistered
bullate, bulliform
knobbed
bosselated
bulging
bombé
having a hammered appearance
malleated

EDGES

having an uneven and sharp edge
jagged
having a rough and untrimmed edge (as a piece of paper)
deckle-edged
having a special edge to prevent raveling, or an edge meant to be discarded
selvage, selvedge
having cuts along the edge
indented, nicked, nocked
having vee-shaped indentations
notched

having teeth or notches

toothed, saw-toothed, notched, crenellated, serrated, serrulate, dentate, denticulate, dentelated, dentellated, shark's-tooth, shark's-teeth, serried

having an irregular wavy or toothed outline

crenulate

having deep and sharp indentations

vandyked

having curled indentations

foiled

having curled projections along the edge

scalloped, crenate, invected, invecked

having rounded projections

lobed, lobate, lobular

having sharp backward projections

barbed

having concave indentations along the edge

engrailed

having a beveled or flattened edge (cut on an angle)

chamfered

having teeth along the edge

saw-toothed, dentate

having small teeth along the edge

serrate, denticulate, dentellated

having a notch near the edge

rabbeted

having cuts on the surface

scratched, scarred, scored

having an edge of threads or strips

fringed, fimbriate

QUOTATIONS

It was a short flight, a leaping of time and space, from the chaotic but warm swirl of India to the extreme hardness and violence of a medieval state in the throes of a war, India green and fertile at takeoff, Afghanistan pure unadulterated brown and snow-swept, serrated mountain ridges, all in two hours.

—CARL HOFFMAN, *The Lunatic Express: Discovering the World . . . via Its Most Dangerous Buses, Boats, Trains, and Planes*

He outspread his arms, laid his feet primly side by side, and gave himself a slow once-over, looking prepared to be shocked at what he found. Ill-fitting pin-striped suit, hatless, tie loosely knotted, one shirttail hanging out, something teenage in his unruly ginger curls.

—MICHAEL CHABON, *The Yiddish Policemen's Union*

With such exuberant invention, the identity of the animals represented can become very obscure. Usually there are precise clues. Two prominent teeth and a rectangular cross-hatched tail among the maze of symbols indicate a beaver; a wide toothless mouth and no tail, a frog; a dorsal fin and a blow-hole, a killer whale.

—DAVID ATTENBOROUGH, *The Tribal Eye*

In contrast, the common dolphin (*Delphinus delphis*) often leaps from the water and plays in the bow waves of boats. Its taller dorsal fin has a curved trailing edge. Also called the saddleback, Delphinus has a black back, white belly and distinctive crisscross pattern along the sides.

—PHILIP KOPPER, *The Wild Edge: Life and Lore of the Great Atlantic Beaches*

We discover that we've left the guide-book in Och-na-cock-a-leekie and wander the streets disconsolately, looking for something of architectural or historical interest, settling eventually on the Wee Highland Gift Shop where we buy many totally useless objects adorned with thistles and heather, although personally, I am delighted with my Illustrated Pocket Guide to Scottish Tartans, even if half the tartans are reproduced in hazy black-and-white.

—KATE ATKINSON, *Behind the Scenes at the Museum*

Set on a basement of "rusticated" stonework of varying tones, its principal story is built of tan brick banded with strips of gaily-floriated tiles, which parallel the lines of the basement. Then, based on the module of the square flower tile, there rises an intricately corbelled cornice, a series of chimneys and a cylindrical tower, all of which are harmoniously interrelated by patterns such as chevrons and prisms. —GEORGE R. COLLINS, *Antonio Gaudi*

How are we going to clean those windows? Foster's proposal featured curtain walls of glass and stainless steel hung in a diagonal grid that meet at each corner of the structure in a dramatic chamfer, a zigzag beveled edge formed of four concave diamond shapes, each sixteen feet deep and eight stories high, known as "bird's mouths" by the architect.

—ADAM HIGGINBOTHAM, "Life at the Top," *The New Yorker*, February 4, 2013

Bichrome wares accompany the prevalent monochrome pottery described above, but with the addition of white-painted motifs. The primarily geometric designs include bands, circles, dots, scrolls, frets, zigzags, triangles, diamonds, chevrons, and sunbursts, either singly or in combination, although some may represent stylized animals. Common shapes are water jars, with designs painted on the vessel shoulders and handles, and tripod-supported bowls with flaring walls, often painted white on both interior and exterior surfaces.

—SYLVANUS G. MORLEY AND GEORGE W. BRAINERD, *The Ancient Maya*

On our penultimate jump of the day, out of a D18 Beechcraft at 10,500 feet, we made a ten-man snowflake. We managed to get ourselves into a complete formation before we passed 7,000 feet, and thus were able to enjoy a full eighteen seconds of flying the formation down a clear chasm between two towering cumulus clouds before breaking apart at 3,500 feet and tracking away from each other to open our chutes. —EBEN ALEXANDER, *Proof of Heaven: A Neurosurgeon's Journey into the Afterlife*

The North Rim is so deeply excavated by side canyons that in certain sections its pattern resembles a giant-toothed comb. The side canyons of the South Rim merely serrate it in gentle scallops. —ROBERT WALLACE, *The Grand Canyon*

In no time Tool was hopelessly hooked, his dosage escalating to levels that would have euthanized a more highly evolved organism. The only serious obstacle to his drug habit was his excess of body hair, so dense and oily as to defy conventional adhesives. Daily cropping was required, often in checkerboard patterns to accommodate multiple stolen patches.

That was how Red Hammernut found him, buck naked in a rusty washtub behind the house trailer, scraping brutally at his shoulder blades with a disposable razor. —CARL HIAASEN, *Skinny Dip*

Within the channels are many features, such as teardrop-shaped islands, longitudinal grooves, terraced margins, and inner channel cataracts, that are also found in regions on Earth affected by large floods.
—*Viking Orbiter Views of Mars* (Cary R. Spitzer, ed.)

Men swore. They pushed at the wheels with long oak poles and slashed at the oxen till their backs were cross-hatched with bleeding welts and their noses ran pink foam.

—JOHN GARDNER, *Grendel*

The plate has scalloped edges that curve upward slightly. The curving indentations on the rim are perfect, having been stamped by a machine, a contraption that is surely a masterpiece of modern engineering, made possible only by very precise computations and the manipulations of Euclidean geometry.

—CARLOS EIRE, *Learning to Die in Miami: Confessions of a Refugee Boy*

The sparks were not a pattern on a dark ground, they were themselves the background, that of a flaming evening sky. The black lines, and stripes upon it, were the lower branches of a fir thicket; these branches were dead and bare because the growth was so dense that no light reached down here.

—ISAK DINESEN, "The Caryatids, An Unfinished Tale"

He was a young snake, not even two feet long. Like the other poisonous snakes found in the Ozarks, the cottonmouths, copperheads belong to the genus Agkistrodon, which means fish-hook toothed. The copperheads in my part of the Ozarks are the southern variety, *Agkistrodon contortrix contortrix*, which makes them sound very twisty indeed. They are a pinkish coppery color with darker hourglass-patterned markings. They have wide jaws, which give their heads a triangular shape.

—SUE HUBBELL, *A Country Year: Living the Questions*

The large 420-pound bongo's bright chestnut-red is also disrupted by mottled ears, a white chevron on the forehead, white cheek spots, a white crescent on the chest and, like the eland of the savanna, by ten or thirteen narrow transverse white stripes across back and sides.

—RICHARD PERRY, *Life in Forest and Jungle*

Immediately other cars started swerving into each other, trying to knock them off the better tracks. The tracks themselves were a spaghetti pattern, winding about, crossing and recrossing each other. It was almost impossible to be sure of avoiding collisions.

Indeed, other cars were gleefully racing to the intersections, trying to catch each other broadside. One succeeded, and the victim car was not only pushed off the trail, it rolled over and finished on its roof. It was out of the race. —PIERS ANTHONY, *Esrever Doom (Xanth)*

They scuttled for days and days till they came to a great forest, 'sclusively full of trees and bushes and stripy, speckly, patchy-blatchy, shadows, and there they hid: and after another long time, what with standing half in the shade and half out of it, and what with the slippery-slidy shadows of the trees falling on them, the Giraffe grew blotchy, and the Zebra grew stripy, and the Eland and the Koodoo grew darker, with little wavy grey lines on their backs like bark on a tree trunk. . . .

—RUDYARD KIPLING, "How the Leopard Got His Spots," *How the Leopard Got His Spots and Other Just So Stories*

Thoughts rise up in me, take odd turns, vanish like bits of smoke. At the same time I'm wide open to striking impressions—that ladder leaning against the side of a house, with its shadow hard and clean against the white shingles, which project a little, so that the shingle-bottoms break the straight shadow-lines into slight zigzags; that brilliant red umbrella lying at an angle in the recycling container on a front porch next to the door; that jogger with shaved head, black nylon shorts, and an orange sweatshirt that reads, in three lines of black capital letters: EAT WELL / KEEP FIT / DIE ANYWAY. A single blade of grass sticks up from a crack in a driveway. I come to a sprawling old house at the corner, not far from the sidewalk. Its dark red paint could use a little touching up. Under the high front porch, on both sides of the steps, are those crisscross lattice panels, painted white. Through the diamond-shaped openings come pricker branches and the tips of ferns.

—STEVEN MILLHAUSER, "Phantoms," *The PEN O. Henry Prize Stories 2012*

The tattoos were freshened by the air. Oriental dragons climbed Karp's arm, green claws splayed from his feet, ink-blue women wrapped around the columns of his thighs, and with each steamy breath the vulture picked at his heart. More vivid were the whitening scars, dead stripes on his chest, where the accusation had been burned away. Across his narrow brow spread a livid band. —MARTIN CRUZ SMITH, *Polar Star*

Scientists can also spy the escalating threats that trilobites confronted by studying the evolution of their eyes. Trilobite eyes were unlike those of virtually any other known animal, the lenses built not of protein but of calcite crystals, lending the animals a "stony stare," as Dr. Fortey put it.

In most trilobites, each compound orb held hundreds of tiny calcite lenses, arranged in a tightknit honeycomb pattern, like the eye of a fly. But fairly late in trilobite evolution one group developed a different sort of eye, composed of a smaller number of larger, separated calcite lenses.

—NATALIE ANGIER, "When Trilobites Ruled the World," *New York Times*, March 3, 2014, Times Science

. . . she could only look out at the brown marshes and the million black factories and the puddly streets of towns and a rusty steamboat in a canal and barns and Bull Durham signs and roundfaced Spearmint gnomes all barred and crisscrossed with bright flaws of rain. The jeweled stripes on the window ran straight down when the train stopped and got more and more oblique as it speeded up. —JOHN DOS PASSOS, *The Morning of the Century*

They lay on a ledge high upon the sunny east slope and looked out to the north through the notch cut as sharply as a wedge out of a pie. Far below them the golden plain spread level, golden-tawny grass and golden-green wheat checker-boarded in a pattern as wide as the world.

—WALLACE STEGNER, "Two Rivers," *Collected Stories of Wallace Stegner*

The blossom-covered surface of the river is smooth, stretched taut from bank to bank like a polka-dotted fabric. The prow of the boat rips a passage through with a sizzling hiss. —KEN KESEY, *Sometimes a Great Notion*

The bedstead, chairs, and lounges, were of bamboo, wrought in peculiarly graceful and fanciful patterns. Over the head of the bed was an alabaster bracket, on which a beautiful sculptured angel stood, with drooping wings, holding out a crown of myrtle-leaves. From this depended, over the bed, light curtains of rose-colored gauze, striped with silver, supplying that protection from mosquitoes which is an indispensable addition to all sleeping accommodation in that climate.

—HARRIET BEECHER STOWE, *Uncle Tom's Cabin*

Her checkered black-and-white fingernails looked beautiful and modern against the dull, scuffed cover of her book. She mouthed the words as they came to her and rolled each page softly between her fingertips before turning it. —DENNIS BOCK, *Going Home Again*

I do not remember a great deal about early childhood, a season that has never consciously obsessed me. The shining gilt serrations of the Albert Memorial's spire; the great groups of white statuary—Europe, Asia, Africa, America—the wide flights of marble steps leading to the frieze of figures representing the arts and sciences throughout history, the rich greenery of Kensington Gardens beyond, together formed the central landmark of my first continuously remembered existence.

—Anthony Powell, *To Keep the Ball Rolling: The Memoirs of Anthony Powell*

. . . Hunt never commented on her appearance again, though a year later he gave her a present—a long, thin, limp, old silk scarf, with slanted ends and a black border and a small geometric pattern of green, beige and white checks and diamonds, a scarf from the thirties, which smelt faintly of age and old-fashioned face powder and cats and sawdust.

—Margaret Drabble, *The Middle Ground*

What Clark balked at was tearing up the carpet, which was the same in every room and the thing that she had most counted on replacing. It was divided into small brown squares, each with a pattern of darker brown and rust and tan squiggles and shapes. For a long time she had thought these were the same squiggles and shapes, arranged in the same way, in each square. Then when she had had more time, a lot of time, to examine them, she decided that there were four patterns joined together to make identical larger squares.

—Alice Munro, "Runaway," *Runaway*

He blames the broccoli for today's predicament. The broccoli on his plate put him in a state of great agitation in the dining hall. It was pungent and fractal with the texture of a small bush. He likes his food smooth. Lumpiness or random texture plunge him into anxiety.

—JANNA LEVIN, *A Madman Dreams of Turing Machines*

I couldn't comfortably hold the rubber handrail, and sensibly wasn't allowed to steady myself with the high step ahead of me. As we drew close to the next floor, I could see a green glow coming from under the crenellated slit where the escalator steps disappeared; and as soon as I stepped off, onto oddly immobile linoleum and then a tundra of carpeting, the soft sounds reached me from some department I knew nothing about, like the "Miss" department. . . . —NICHOLSON BAKER, *The Mezzanine*

Aadam's eyes are a clear blue, the astonishing blue of mountain sky, which has a habit of dripping into the pupils of Kashmiri men; they have not forgotten how to look. They see—there! like the skeleton of a ghost, just beneath the surface of Lake Dal!—the delicate tracery, the intricate crisscross of colorless lines, the cold waiting veins of the future. —SALMAN RUSHDIE, *Midnight's Children*

SURFACES, TEXTURES, AND COMPOSITION

SURFACES AND TEXTURES

flat or without varying elevation

plane, level, planate, tabular, tabulate

made flat, flattened

applanate, planiform, complanate

on a plane or unbroken surface

flat, level, planar, tabular, flattened, even, applanate, homaloidal

constituting the final coating on a surface

finished

the process of painting a finish that has the look of a solid material such as marble, stone, or wood

faux finishing

sheen produced, by age or use, on a surface

patina

diminished in luster owing to the effect of air, dust, or dirt

tarnished

green patina, as on copper, bronze, or brass, produced by long exposure to air or seawater

verdigris

bent or twisted out of its plane

warped, buckled

smooth and free of roughness

even, uniform, glabrous, levigate

smooth and shiny

lustrous, glossy, polished, burnished, buffed, glazed, gleaming, glistening, glinting, glassy, suave, silken, silky

coated to be smooth and shiny

varnished, shellacked, lacquered, enameled

like glass

glassy, glazed, glazy, vitreous, vitriform, hyaline

not shiny

lusterless, dull, matte

having an uneven surface

irregular, bumpy, humpy, hummocky, lumpy

rough

coarse, prickly, scabrous, abrasive, scratchy, choppy, ragged, jagged, sandpapery

rough with prominent irregularities

scraggly, scraggy

soft and lustrous

silken, silky, satiny

finished with a nap produced by brushing

brushed

soft and silky with a deep pile

plush

felt-like

pannose

velvety

velutinous

hairy

hirsute, bristly

fuzzy

shaggy, nubby

having wrinkles

wrinkled, corrugated, rugose, crinkly, crinkled, crispate, creased

having a pushed-up surface

raised, embossed, relief, in relief

having rounded protuberances

knobbed

having small rounded protuberances

pimpled

having hard ornamental protuberances

studded

having raised (relief) patterns made by hammering the other side

repoussé

knobby

studded, lumpy, nubby, nubbly, knubbly, nubbed, noded, noduled

having a cut-into surface

carved, incised, inscribed, etched, engraved, tooled

having small plane surfaces, as a cut gem

faceted, facetted

having (produced) minute cracks in the surface or glaze

crazed

worn or aged by the elements
weathered, weather-beaten, eroded
deliberately marred or faded so as to appear aged or worn
distressed
having small pits or indentations
pitted, pocked, pockmarked, dimpled, depressed, indented
having hammered indentations
chased
sharp
acute, cutting, keen-edged, keen, knife-edged, knife-like, razor-edged, razor-like, cultrate
having sharp projections
thorny, prickly, barbed, spiny, echinated
not sharp
dull, blunt, obtund, obtuse
having a sliced opening or openings
slit, cut, slashed, incised, gashed, scissored, hacked
having scratches
scratched, scored, abraded, scuffed, scraped, scarred
dyed or stained
tinged, imbrued, imbued, infused
splashed or sprinkled upon, as with a different substance or color
splattered, spattered
having a distinct, often protective top plate or layer
laminated
sticky
viscous, viscid, adhesive, gummy, pasty, mucilaginous, glutinous, tacky
covered with another material or substance
overlaid

coated

covered, bedaubed, lacquered, filmy, overlayed, glossed, dipped

coated with a surface of metal

plated, electroplated, clad

coated with a glossy surface

enameled

painted thickly

pastose, impasted, impasto

covered with a crust

encrusted, caked

marked irregularly or dirtied

smudged, smeared, streaked

COMPOSITION

solid

substantial, dense, concrete, material, palpable, intact

hard

firm, unyielding, inflexible, rock-hard, stonelike, flinty, adamantine, indurate, steely

hardened

toughened, indurated

marble-like

marmoreal, marbled

granite-like

granitic

cement-like

cementitious

diamond-like

adamantine, diamantine

having a grain-like composition

grainy, granular, gritty, coarse-grained, rough-grained, granulated, branny

having a sand-like composition

sandy, sabulous, tophaceous, arenaceous, arenarious

stiff

rigid, starchy, inelastic, inflexible, inextensible, unyielding

tight

taut

tough

fibrous, leathery, coriaceous, sinewy, ropy, stringy, gristly, chewy

soft

yielding, pliant, pulpy, doughy, mushy

limp

flaccid, slack, loose, baggy, droopy, floppy, loppy

lacking solidity

flimsy, unsubstantial, gossamer

breakable or brittle

fragile, crisp, frangible, frail, crackable, crushable

easily pulverized or crumbled

friable, crumbly, pulverizable, shivery

easily cuttable or splittable

scissile

rubbery, elastic

blubbery, resilient, springy

yielding

clay-like, doughy, pudding-like, pulpy, porridge-like, pultaceous

flexible
bendable, pliable, pliant, elastic, resilient, ductile, plastic

moldable
supple, malleable, fictile

stretchable
tensile, ductile, extensible, extensile

mealy
floury, farinaceous

flaky
scaly, squamate, shivery

without moisture
dry, arid, desiccated, parched, sere

offering poor or no traction
slippery, slippy, slick, lubricated, lubricious, glossy

oily, greasy, fatlike
slick, oleaginous, unguinous, sebaceous, pinguid

soapy
saponaceous, lathered

moist, damp
dank, bedewed, dewy, roral, rorid, imbrued, embrued

wet, watery
fluid, serous, liquid

very wet
sodden, soaked, saturated, permeated, soggy, suffused

coolly moist and sticky
clammy

absorbent
porous, leachy

wet and yielding

spongy, semiliquid, pulpy, mushy, slushy, squashy, squishy, oozy, slimy, gooey

thick

clotted, grumous

soft like nap or down

fluffy, downy, fleecy, cottony, feathery, lanuginous, lanuginose

woolly

flocculent, lanate, lanose

feathery

plumy

pillow-like

cushiony, puffy

dense

compact, compacted, close-textured, thick, consolidated, condensed

clotted

congealed, coagulated, bunched, compacted

separable

fissile, scissile, partable, dissociable

very thin

sheer, lawny

light and somewhat transparent

filmy, gauzy, gossamer, cobwebby

powdery, dusty

floury, chalky, triturated, comminuted, pulverous, pulverulent

foamy

frothy, spumescent

jelly-like
gelatinous, colloidal, jelled
cork-like
suberose
rocky
petrous, calcified
stony
pebbled, pebbly, gravelly

QUOTATIONS

In the pool of light shed onto her lap, an exquisitely manicured hand guides a slender gold-plated propelling pencil across the lines of print, occasionally pausing to underline a sentence or make a marginal note. The long, spear-shaped finger-nails on the hand are lacquered with terracotta varnish. The hand itself, long and white and slender, looks almost weighed down with three antique rings in which are set ruby, sapphire, and emerald stones.

—David Lodge, *Small World*

Pseudo-Arabic minarets, dentils, and spindled galleries silhouette the outlines of furniture designed on the circle and its parts—the arc and chord. The wooden frame was covered in chamois leather within *repoussé* metal mounts or veneered in pewter and brass with insect-like motifs and Middle Eastern calligraphy.

—Alastair Duncan, *Art Nouveau Furniture*

On the men drifted. Several days passed with no food and no rain. The raft was a gelatinous mess, its patches barely holding on, some spots bubbling outward, on the verge of popping. It wouldn't bear the men's weight much longer.

In the sky, Phil noticed something different. There were more birds. Then they began to hear planes. Sometimes they'd see a tiny speck in the sky, sometimes two or more together, making a distant buzz. They were always much too far away to be signaled, and both men knew that as far west as they had probably drifted, these planes were surely Japanese.

—LAURA HILLENBRAND, *Unbroken: A World War II Story of Survival, Resilience, and Redemption*

Sometimes the ice is black and glossy, blasted smooth by the endless wind, with only a few swaths of snow lying on it. Sometimes it is hummocky, with drifts of snow sheltered behind the hummocks. Sometimes it is ridged and buckled from the enormous strains of the wind, the currents and the line of advancing bergs.

—RICHARD BROWN, *Voyage of the Iceberg: The Story of the Iceberg That Sank the* Titanic

Momma Hattie served blackened everything, fried foods that had to be coaxed out of the skillet with a metal spatula and serious scraping. Then she poured the greasy residue into a Crisco can, where it congealed into schmaltz: a slippery mass whose consistency would hold your thumbprint until it came time to melt it down again.

—DAVID BERG, *Run, Brother Run*

It was a wild, cold, seasonable night of March, with a pale moon, lying on her back as though the wind had tilted her, and a flying wrack of the most diaphanous and lawny texture. —ROBERT LOUIS STEVENSON, *Dr. Jekyll and Mr. Hyde*

And my mother, of course. I linger over her. But reluctantly, memory going cloudier, Mom in her best little smart suit, short tweed skirt, great gams, Mom in her perfect makeup, her hair in a perfect coil glistening with lacquer, secret pins. —BILL ROORBACH, *Life among Giants*

My horse was not above medium size, but he was alert, slender-limbed, muscled with watch springs, and just a greyhound to go. He was a beauty, glossy as silk, and naked as he was when he was born, except for bridle and ranger saddle. —MARK TWAIN, *A Connecticut Yankee in King Arthur's Court*

In the first week of April, before Lavender died, Lieutenant Jimmy Cross received a good-luck charm from Martha. It was a simple pebble, an ounce at most. Smooth to the touch, it was a milky white color with flecks of orange and violet, oval-shaped, like a miniature egg. In the accompanying letter, Martha wrote that she had found the pebble on the Jersey shoreline, precisely where the land touched water at high tide, where things came together but also separated.

—TIM O'BRIEN, *The Things They Carried*

The drama classroom was in a portable, one-room prefabricated building on cinder blocks in the middle of the schoolyard. It was a shoes-off environment, no desks, just wall-to-wall nylon broadloom in a mottled goldenrod. The carpet was pilled, matted with staples and crumbs, and waxy with years of adolescent foot sweat. About fifteen hopefuls sat on the floor in a circle around the drama teacher, who sat with her legs folded under her, Zen tea master-like. She surveyed us and then her eyes lit upon me. She gave me a small smile, the corners of her mouth turning up slightly, while at the same time from her nose I could hear a small puff, the softest whisper of breath. The sound a pillow makes when you sink your head into it. —DAVID RAKOFF, *Half Empty*

He lets the book fall closed. It makes an exhausted sound, like a padded door shutting, by itself, at a distance: a puff of air. The sound suggests the softness of the thin oniony pages, how they would feel under the fingers. Soft and dry, like *papier poudre*, pink and powdery, from the time before, you'd get it in booklets for taking the shine off your nose, in those stores that sold candles and soap in the shapes of things: seashells, mushrooms. Like cigarette paper. Like petals. —MARGARET ATWOOD, *The Handmaid's Tale*

Janice owned one pair of boots which she wore in all seasons, repairing them with Sellotape when they threatened to fall apart. Over the boots she wore a filmy gypsy skirt of no colour that Treslove could distinguish and over that a grey-and-blue cardigan the sleeves of which she wore long, as though to protect her fingertips from the cold. In all weathers, Janice's extremities were cold, like those of an orphan child, as Treslove imagined, in a Victorian novel. —HOWARD JACOBSON, *The Finkler Question*

She had a vision of her mad wet face against the sky, as she rocked on the slippery stone. She tried to catch at her habit to help her, but the stuff was slimy with wet and dirt. Then Sister Ruth seemed to fall into the sky with a scream, as she went over the railings.

—RUMER GODDEN, *Black Narcissus*

In the estimation of here and there a man of weak judgment, it was greatly in the parson's power to have helped the figure of this horse of his,—for he was master of a very handsome demi-peaked saddle, quilted on the seat with green plush garnished with a double row of silver-headed studs, and a noble pair of shining brass stirrups, with a housing altogether suitable, of grey superfine cloth, with an edging of black lace, terminating in a deep, black, silk fringe, *poudre d'or*,—all which he had purchased in the pride and prime of his life, together with a grand embossed bridle, ornamented at all points as it should be. —LAURENCE STERNE, *Tristram Shandy*

A grainy, porous overlay might account for the waffling or graham-cracker appearance of much of the surface in the photos. —RICHARD S. LEWIS, *Appointment on the Moon*

Mostly it was the timid who perished: they died easily, and their corpses were thrown into the rivers and irrigation ditches or just left in the sun to rot. Let them know that you are dangerous. The crows ate the grasshoppers and let the wasps alone.

Martin, convinced of his logic but not free of dread, started down the road toward Tepazatlán.

The asphalt was still tacky from the day's heat. There were only a few clouds tonight, rows of wispy crescents drifting down from the north. The cambered black road, curving down through low hills, reminded him of the river. There were fields and pastures and patches of scrub forest on both sides of the road.

—Ron Faust, *In the Forest of the Night*

In front were the dark green glassy waters of an unvisited backwater; and beyond them a bright lawn set with many walnut trees and a few great chestnuts, well lit with their candles, and to the left of that a low white house with a green dome rising in its middle and a veranda whose roof of hammered iron had gone verdigris colour with age and the Thames weather. This was the Monkey Island Inn.

—Rebecca West, *The Return of the Soldier*

The buttress merged with roof and floor in flowing and perfectly proportioned curves. And on its face was superimposed a small, delicately sculptured column, so oddly weathered that it seemed almost a decorative afterthought. The surface of this column was rounded and smooth, as if it had been sandpapered by a patient carpenter, and its fine-drawn strata stood out sharp and clear, like the grain on unstained, highly polished wood. —ERNEST BRAUN, *Grand Canyon of the Living Colorado*

This whole apartment is gleaming and slidey. You could be inside a bubble, here—a dark pearl hanging in the middle of the sky. Monday, Tuesday, Thursday, Friday: four mornings a week Lupe comes to clean and launder and put things in order. The floors have been bleached almost translucent, and stained, and a crew of other painters has done something to the walls to make them dark and glassy, so that Jamie's leaves look like they're twining right in the air. —DEBORAH EISENBERG, "Rosie Gets a Soul," *The Collected Stories of Deborah Eisenberg*

But after a foot or two of this ladder-like progression they are faced either with the battering fall of white water at their left or with a smooth black stretch of rock wall in front, hit every few seconds by heavy splashes of spray. For a few feet at the bottom of this wall grows a close slimy fur of waterweed, and among its infinitesimal tendrils the elvers twine themselves and begin, very slowly, to squirm their way upwards, forming a vertical, close-packed queue perhaps two feet wide.

—GAVIN MAXWELL, *Ring of Bright Water*

If I were a speck of slime mold, both one and many, a single-celled swarm, a gelatinous glob of peanut butter—like ooze on the forest floor, I would hustle after prey at a flat-out 1 mile per hour, streaming my slime one way, then another, to gather up bacteria, protozoa, grass, and rotting leaves.

—DIANE ACKERMAN, *Dawn Light: Dancing with Cranes and Other Ways to Start the Day*

The injury was much worse than when they had heard her screaming and had run through the habitat and pulled her up through the A Cyl hatch. Now, running diagonally down her leg was a series of saucer-shaped welts, the center of each puffed and purple. "It's swollen a lot in the last hour," Tina said.

Norman examined the injuries. Fine toothmarks ringed swollen areas. "Do you remember what it felt like?" he said.

"It felt awful," Tina said. "It felt *sticky*, you know, like sticky glue or something. And then each one of these round places burned. Very strong."

—MICHAEL CRICHTON, *Sphere*

Monday dawns a full gale, the seas building to twenty feet and the wind shearing ominously through the rigging. The sea takes on a grey, marbled look, like bad meat.

—SEBASTIAN JUNGER, *The Perfect Storm*

The cross-legged one (wearing a woman's dress, but it may be a boy) puts out his hands over the eggs and gently shuffles them a little closer together, letting a couple of the outer ones roll back into his palms. The eggs are a creamy buff, thick-shelled, their glaze pored and lightly

speckled, their shape more pointed than a hen's, and the palms of the small black hands are translucent-looking apricot-pink.
—NADINE GORDIMER,
The Conservationist

Fifty dirty, stark-naked men elbowing each other in a room twenty feet square, with only two bathtubs and two slimy roller towels between them all. I shall never forget the reek of dirty feet. Less than half the tramps actually bathed (I heard them saying that hot water is "weakening" to the system), but they all washed their faces and feet, and the horrid greasy little clouts known as toe-rags which they bind round their toes.
—GEORGE ORWELL, *Down and Out in Paris and London*

I gave the cabbie a ridiculous tip, and as the taxi departed I noticed that awful old car backed down in the neighbours' parking space again. This time, seeing the front of the old ruin I realized it was an Armstrong Siddeley, a grand English dinosaur from 1950. The paints of the period were all toxic toluene nightmares, polluting the air even as they began their life. In 2010 its skin was cracked and chalky, more like dead fish than a dinosaur, a skate, dead shark skin amongst the sand and seaweed.
—PETER CAREY, *The Chemistry of Tears*

They would never be like Mrs. Grandlieu's old timber house, with its worn decorative woodwork, its internal arches of fretwork arabesques that caught the dust, its mahogany-stained floor springy but polished smooth, the hard graining of the floorboards standing out from the softer wood. —V. S. NAIPAUL, *Guerrillas*

The flour falls solidly, in a mound that loosely echoes the shape of the measuring cup. A bigger cloud rises, almost touches his face, then vanishes. He stares down at what he's made: a white hill, slightly granular, speckled with pinpoint shadows, standing up from the glossy, creamier white of the bowl's interior. —MICHAEL CUNNINGHAM, *The Hours*

Cobblestones, which for aeons have rubbed against each other, are ideally smooth. They are firm and pleasant to the touch, smooth and definitive in form, absolutely precise in textural effect. Granite flagstones which have been worn smooth by the feet of generations of walkers have the same character. —STEEN EILER RASMUSSEN, *Experiencing Architecture*

I could not go abroad in snow—it would settle on me and expose me. Rain, too, would make me a watery outline, a glistening surface of a man—a bubble. And fog—I should be like a fainter bubble in a fog, a surface, a greasy glimmer of humanity. —H. G. WELLS, *The Invisible Man*

SIZE, POSITION, RELATION, AND PROPORTION

GENERAL TERMS

large, big

huge, vast, great, massive, extensive, bulky, sizable, considerable, ample, substantial, hefty, jumbo, bounteous, oversize, oversized

very large

giant, gigantic, mountainous, colossal, mammoth, behemoth, brobdingnagian, gargantuan, stupendous, amplitudinous, monstrous, gross, extensive, far-ranging, far-reaching, enormous, titanic, humongous, immense, megatherian, astronomical, Bunyonesque, elephantine, pachydermatous, pythonic, cyclopean, supersized, supersize, whopping

large in capacity

capacious, voluminous, roomy, spacious, comprehensive, commodious

whole

complete, entire, intact, sum, all, full

partial

incomplete, portion, percentage, fraction, slice

increased

raised, augmented, expanded, added to, supplemented, ratcheted up, ramped up, went up, appended, tacked on, heightened

decreased

lowered, lessened, fell, reduced, diminished, declined, went down, rolled back, phased down, curtailed, shortened, subtracted from

small, little, or short

inconsiderable, pint size, diminutive, puny, wee, petite, slight, undersize, squat, bantam, truncated

very small

tiny, teeny, teeny-weeny, minuscule, infinitesimal, minute, miniature, midget, microscopic, trace

wide

broad, thick, latitudinous, spread, outspread

very wide

expansive, panoramic, widespread

narrow

thin, slender, slim, constricted, spindly

sparse

scanty, meager, exiguous, slight

at rest

stationary, not moving, motionless, fixed, stopped, static, inert, at a standstill, still, stuck

in motion

moving, going, running, operating, in action, active, kinetic, advancing, progressing, proceeding, dynamic, locomoting, locomotive, in a state of unrest, motile

high, tall

elevated, lofty, altitudinous

very high

towering, soaring

long

lengthy, extensive, elongated

very long

far-reaching, endless

very deep

profound, abyssal, bottomless, depthless, unplumbed, yawning, cavernous

related

connected, interconnected, associated, affiliated, interrelated, correlated, correlative, correlational, interlinked

interconnected

intermingled, entwined, interlocking, entangled, intertwined, conjoined, bonded

placed or occurring at intervals within or among

interspersed, intermingled, interposed, interjacent, interlarded

in direct relation to

corresponding, correlative, mutual, reciprocal, vis-à-vis

in order

ordered, orderly, systematic, grouped, arranged, arrayed, aligned, organized, sequential, serial, alphabetical, numerical, hierarchic, hierarchical, regimented

not in order, out of order

disarranged, unordered, disarrayed, unaligned, jumbled, muddled, out of kilter

in a line or something like a line

lined up, aligned, ranged, arranged, arrayed, in a row

in proportion

proportionate, proportional, prorated

not in proportion

disproportionate, disproportional, ill-proportioned

in balance

balanced, equipoised, equiponderant, equiponderous, counterbalanced, counterweighted, counterpoised, even, evened out

not in balance

unbalanced, disequilibriate, off-balance, off-kilter

larger or heavier on or leaning to one side

lop-sided, tilted, one-sided

heavier or larger on top

top-heavy

having a perfectly divisible order left and right (bilaterally) or top and bottom

symmetrical

not symmetrical

asymmetrical

having radial symmetry

actinoid, actinomorphic, actinomorphous

north

northern, northerly, boreal, hyperborean

south

southern, southerly, austral, meridional

east
eastern, easterly, oriental
west
western, westerly, occidental
opposite
contraposed, antipodal, counterposed, contrary, opposing
pertaining to opposite sides
heterolateral
at the top
apical, topmost
at the bottom
basal, bottommost
on or to the right
dextral
on or to the left
sinistral
to or at the side
lateral, flanking
on the same side
ipsilateral, ipselateral, homolateral
on the opposite side
contralateral
upright or up-down in direction
vertical, standing, perpendicular, plumb, erect, true
at a 90° angle
right-angled, orthogonal
side to side in direction
horizontal, level, plane
extending across or at a right angle to linearly
cross, crosswise, transverse, athwart, diagonal

at a slanted angle or in a sloping direction or position (from the perpendicular)

angled, aslant, slanting, slanted, oblique, raked, canted, inclined, tilted, leaning, bent, crooked, askew, on a bias, turned, deflected, veering, on a slope

diagonally positioned

catercornered, catercorner, catty-cornered, kitty-cornered

on the outside

external, exterior, without, outer, outermost, superficial

on the inside

internal, interior, within, inner, innermost

center

core, nucleus, middle, centrum, heart, nexus, nub, hub

edge

periphery, border, margin, marge, fringe, boundary, frontier, perimeter, circumference

extending out from a center

radial, radiating, spoked

middle (linearly)

central, midway, medium, mean, medial, mesial, midmost, middlemost

constituting a central line or axis

axial

coming together linearly

meeting, converging, convergent, intersecting

going in two different directions

forked, forking, separating, diverging, divergent, bifurcating, bifurcate, bifurcal, dichotomous, diffluent

running in directional alignment without touching
parallel, nonconvergent, nondivergent, paradromic, collateral, collimated, running side by side

not with or near or set aside
apart, separate, individual, discrete, disjunct, detached, independent, asunder, portioned off

apart
detached, disconnected, unfastened, sundered, disjoined, parted, independent

in pieces or parts
divided, partitioned, compartmentalized, segmented, sectored, fragmented

in two parts
bipartite, dual, double, twofold

in three parts
tripartite, triple, threefold, triform

in four parts
quadripartite, quadriform, fourfold

divided into two usually equal parts
bisected

divided into three usually equal parts
trisected

divided into four usually equal parts
quadrisected

scattered
dispersed, distributed, disseminated, strewn, diffused

continuous
continual, uninterrupted, serial, unbroken, steady, flowing, of a piece

not continuous
discontinuous, interrupted, broken, disjunct

at a point farther than

beyond, in excess of, over, over and above, above and beyond

having the same position or place

coinciding, coincident, coextensive

coinciding when superimposed

congruent

lying along the same straight line

collinear

even or continuous with a given surface

flush

having coinciding axes (or being concentric)

coaxial

of the same size

equal, equivalent, equisized

near

nearby, close, close by, proximal, proximate, nigh, immediate, in the area of, propinquous, propinquant, neighboring, vicinal

next to

adjacent, contiguous, apposite, paradromic (parallel), bordering, side by side, juxtaposed, cheek by jowl, conterminous, coterminous, abreast, beside, by, alongside, apposed

up against or connected to

abutting, adjoining, against

lying close against

adhering, clinging

distant

far, far away, far off, at a distance, long-range, a good way, remote

equally near to or far from
equidistant
at the edge
peripheral, border, marginal
at or near the beginning
initial
at or near the end
terminal, final
near the point of attachment
proximal
at the far end from the point of attachment
distal
over
above, atop, upward, higher, superior
lying above
superjacent, superincumbent, overlying
placed above
superposed
extending over and covering part of
overlapping
on the surface of
atop, superincumbent, superimposed
overhanging or sticking out
overhung, projecting, beetling, jutting, lowering, pensile, protruding, protrudent, outjutting, outstanding, extrusive, protrusive
under
below, beneath, downward from, lower, inferior
lying below
subjacent, underlying, surmounted

underhanging
underhung

hanging from
dependent, pendent, suspended, pendulant, dangling, suspensory, nutant

supporting
bracing, buttressing, underpinning, carrying, bearing, propping up, sustaining, bolstering, shoring up, girding, suspensory

ascending
rising, climbing, acclivous, acclivitous

descending
dipping, dropping, falling, declivous, declivitous

set back
recessed, in a cleft

surrounding
encompassing, enclosing, encircling, circumscribing, enveloping, enfolding, enwreathing, engirding, circumambient, circumjacent, circumferential

surrounded
encompassed, encircled, circumscribed, enveloped, enwreathed, enfolded, engirded

enclosing
containing, confining, closeting, cloistering, immuring, entombing, harboring

enclosed
contained, confined, closeted, cloistered, immured, entombed

between or in between
in the middle, betwixt, interjacent, intervenient

between two lines
interlinear, interlineal
among
amid, amidst, in the midst of, mid, midst
in the middle or center
central, middlemost, centralized
near the center
paracentral
placed in between or among
inserted, interposed, insinuated, interpolated, interjected, intercalated, sandwiched, spatchcocked
situated at intervals
spaced out, interspaced, interspersed, intermittent, intervaled, intervallic
in a space or opening
interstitial, interspatial
facing directly or frontally
head-on
with the side facing
broadside
regarded from the end or longest dimension or with the longitudinal end forward
lengthwise
regarded from one side or with one side forward
sideways, crosswise, widthwise
in front of
anterior, to the fore
at or to the front
frontal, anterior, ventral, obverse, in the foreground, fore, vanward

behind

posterior, to the rear, in the background, aft of

at or to the back

rear, posterior, reverse, dorsal

at or to the side

lateral, on the flank, sideward

facing

face-to-face, vis-à-vis, fronting

facing or moving ahead or to the front

forward

facing or moving back or to the rear

backward

upside down

topsy-turvy, bottom up, turned over, inverted, upturned

inside out

outside in, everted

backwards

reversed, inverted

back to front

reversed, retroverted

turned so as to show a different surface

obverted

in contact

touching, tangent, tangential, abutting, contactual

joined

affixed, in conjunction, conjoined, bound, tied, adjoined, adjoining, connected, combined, combinative, fastened, yoked, bridged, linked, united, interlocked, dovetailed, bonded

brought together

gathered, amassed, heaped, collected, accumulated, bunched, piled, stacked, conglomerate, agglomerate, glomerate, assembled, combined, cumulate, massed, conjoined, of a piece, clustered, grouped, united, conjunct, serried, integrated, melded, conflated, compacted

lying directly in the path of or in front of

athwart

crossing one another

intersecting, crisscross, decussate

second from the last

antepenultimate

next to last

penultimate

as seen from high above

bird's-eye (view)

as seen (graphically) were the exterior or wall removed

cutaway

as seen (graphically) were the parts shown individuated or apart

exploded

Unspecific Quantities or Amounts

pile
gang
drop
sliver
soupçon
snatch

lump
passel
whit
shard
herd
bevy
tinge
cornucopia
welter
strip
potpourri
scintilla
wisp
bunch
quantity
chunk
tuft
snippet
profusion
hunk
body
clutch
squirt
particle
clump
multitude
droves
legion
bite
flood
team

glob
morsel
slice
wad
dab
group
mountain
stack
gazillion
deal
horde
modicum
crumb
trifle
quantum
slew
handful
pocketful
boxful
roomful
jarful
mob
shipload
covey
tad
raft
mishmash
conglomeration
spritz
heap
fraction

truckload
slab
zillion
fragment
bulk
pittance
smear
bit
pinch
scrap
mess
contingent
dash
spate
few
plague
crop
flock
number
galaxy
mass
dribs and drabs
growth
litter
bundle
smidgen
pack
sampling
dollop
symphony
infinity

agglomeration
hair
smattering
congeries
tribe
load
smithereens
gaggle
abundance
series
knot
collection
slip
trickle
piece
speck
myriad
file
crock
riot
troop
plenitude
host
nibble
snack
iota
spark
panoply
lot
gobs
shred

batch
boatload
touch
scads
hint
army
trace
swarm
mound
sheaf
amalgam
litany
sprinkling
tidbit
clot
ort
daub
assortment
parcel
complement
stash
oodles
splash
carload
segment
part
cluster
wealth
remainder
drizzle
spray

portion
serving
patch
fleet
plethora

QUOTATIONS

At the fair each summer when I was a kid, we visited the Fun House, with its creepy grinning plaster face, two stories high. You walked in through its mouth, between its giant teeth, along its hot-pink tongue. Just from that face, you should've known. It was supposed to be a lark, but it was terrifying. The floors buckled or they lurched from side to side, and the walls were crooked, and the rooms were painted to confuse perspective. Lights flashed, horns blared, in the narrow, vibrating hallways lined with fattening mirrors and elongating mirrors and inside-out upside-down mirrors.

—Claire Messud, *The Woman Upstairs*

(The Planck energy is a quadrillion times larger than the energy produced by our largest atom smasher, the Large Hadron Collider outside Geneva. It is the energy at which Einstein's theory of gravity finally breaks down. At this energy, it is theorized that the fabric of space-time will finally tear, creating tiny portals that might lead to other universes, or other points in space-time.) Harnessing such vast energy would require colossal machines on an unimaginable scale, but if successful they might make possible shortcuts through the fabric of space and time, either by compressing space or by passing through wormholes.

—Michio Kaku, *Physics of the Future: How Science Will Shape Human Destiny and Our Daily Lives by the Year 2100*

The portal, flanked on either side by shops, contained two seats outside for clients. The atrium, in process of being redecorated at the time of the eruption, contained a marble impluvium. Beyond, the peristyle and its adjacent chambers resembled a suburban villa, with the major difference that, being in the crowded city, it was self-contained and inward-looking. At the rear of the house, a spacious portico, with its sunken water channel, overlooked a spacious garden, containing pear, chestnut, pomegranate and fig trees. . . .

—G. B. Tobey, *A History of Landscape Architecture*

Their dark branches grow to an extraordinary extent laterally; are endlessly angled, twisted, raked, interlocked, and reach quite as much downward as upwards.

—John Fowles, *The Tree*

Carolyn was blond and wore minks. She had gigantic jade and diamond rings on nearly every finger. And a gold charm bracelet that made a soft tinkle sound when she waved her hands in the air. At night, she slipped into a nightgown with fur trim along the neck and at the hem.

And even her slippers had high heels. I thought she was beautiful, like a movie star.

—Augusten Burroughs, *Possible Side Effects*

Beneath the strongest of the lantern beams they saw that the ladder or iron staircase Scott had found leading from the next to last platform to the plating of the double bottom of the vessel had been twisted around sideways offering a not too difficult climbing angle, except that the last five steps had been sheared off, leaving a gap about level with their heads. A man could take hold of the bottom and swing himself up. Above, at the top, the light showed the gleaming silver cylinder of the propeller shaft, the entrance to the tunnel and the reversed walkway of solid piping that followed it to the stern of the ship.

—Paul Gallico, *The Poseidon Adventure*

But the Flatlander could discover that he lived on the surface of a sphere, rather than on a flat plane, by noting that every time he went on a trip in what he thought was a straight line, he would return to where he started. If he brought out his surveying instruments, he would discover that the sum of angles in a triangle was greater than 180 degrees. In other words, his world did not obey the laws of Euclidean geometry. The Flatlander could even construct a triangle with three right angles by connecting the North Pole to a point on the equator with a north-south line, then going a quarter of the way around the equator, and finally turning north to return to the North Pole.

—J. Richard Gott, *Time Travel in Einstein's Universe: The Physical Possibilities of Travel through Time*

These abandoned channels are best preserved on the slip-off side of a bend—usually as a nest of crescentic loops. Artificial levees form a regular pattern and roughly parallel the course of the river. Drainage or irrigation canals are generally at right angles to the river, although lateral canals may parallel it.

—WILLIAM C. PUTNAM, *Map Interpretation with Military Applications*

Having fastened on coincidence as crucial, Euclid may well have remembered that in his definitions, he affirms that a line, although it has length, has no width. What investigation might justify the conclusion that two lines without width coincide? If no investigation, how could we say that two lines coincide even in length if we cannot say whether they coincide at all?

—DAVID BERLINSKI, *The King of Infinite Space: Euclid and His Elements*

Keen to secure some photographs, I scaled the bank and climbed between the tensioned strands of the fence in sight on my right as I fought my way along the edge of the plantation for what I estimated to be about two hundred yards on a course roughly parallel to the road.

—JOHN LISTER-KAYE, *The White Island*

I feel like a female character in some kind of Pearl S. Buck novel . . . battling for a spot in the old master's house. But I'm like Wife Number Two or Three or Ten. I come with lots of baggage, lots of demands, no skills . . . and a passel of blond children! —SANDRA TSING LOH, *Mother on Fire*

In one case the entire residence unit consists of juxtaposed rectangular rooms enclosing a roughly trapezoid court. —David L. Clarke, *Spatial Archeology*

On the opposite shore stood the recently completed concert-hall, with Laing's medical school and the new television studios on either side. The massive scale of the glass and concrete architecture, and its striking situation on a bend of the river, sharply separated the development project from the rundown areas around it, decaying nineteenth-century terraced houses and empty factories already zoned for reclamation.

—J. G. Ballard, *High-Rise*

The act of pious charity performed, Cedric again motioned them to follow him, gliding over the stone floor with a noiseless tread; and, after ascending a few steps, opened with great caution the door of a small oratory, which adjoined to the chapel. It was about eight feet square, hollowed, like the chapel itself, out of the thickness of the wall; and the loophole which enlightened it being to the west, and widening considerably as it sloped inward, a beam of the setting sun found its way into its dark recess. . . . —Sir Walter Scott, *Ivanhoe*

My way of excitedly repaying my dad for these weekday mornings that I would keep in my heart for the rest of my life was to wake the poor man with seizurelike drumming at around seven in the morning on weekends; one toy metal drum, just marching and pounding. First, the length of the hallway in front of my parents' bedroom a couple of times, then the perimeter of the backyard; a pounding and marching that was at once obsessive-compulsive, extremely punctual, and eerily, calmly emphatic, like a new recruit to the Naval drum corps honoring the dead or a tiny drumming version of Christopher Walken.

—DAN KENNEDY, *Rock On: An Office Power Ballad*

Away to his right was a dark, formless blur lying on the water, a blur that might have been Cape Demirci: straight ahead, across the darkly velvet sheen of the Maidos Straits, he could see the twinkle of far-away lights—it was a measure of the enemy's confidence that they permitted these lights at all, or, more likely, these fisher cottages were useful as a bearing marker for the guns at night: and to the left, surprisingly near, barely thirty feet away in a horizontal plane, but far below the level where he was standing, he could see the jutting end of the outside wall of the fortress where it abutted on the cliff, the roofs of the houses on the west side of the square beyond that, and, beyond that again, the town itself curving sharply downwards and outwards, to the south first, then to the west, close-girdling and matching the curve of the crescent harbour. Above—but there was nothing to be seen above, that fantastic overhang above blotted out more than half the sky; and below, the darkness was equally impenetrable, the surface of the harbour inky and black as night.

—ALISTAIR MACLEAN, *The Guns of Navarone*

Many people felt that if Broadway could not be crossed at street level it should be bridged, and there were many fantastic schemes for doing so. In 1848, John Randel published a proposal for six miles of elevated track, constructed in cast iron and glass, which would run for three miles over Broadway's sidewalks. Passengers would be raised from the ground to an elevated train through elevators complete with sofas and then board a horse-drawn car making all stops. This tender car would gain the speed of a continuously moving horse-drawn car on a parallel track to which passengers would transfer while in motion. To exit, they would transfer back to the all-stops tender car. —STACY KIRKPATRICK, *Art and the Subway: New York Underground*

An interesting point is that in this particular "ideal" theme, the fundamental diagram of the face is the same as the one of the whole body; the link between the two is that the height of the face is equal to the vertical distance between the middle of the body (intersection of the legs in "ideal" specimens) and the navel (the *minor* of the two segments in the Φ proportion determined by the navel) is equal to the distance between the tip of the medium finger (the arm hanging vertically) and the floor or horizontal level supporting the whole.

—MATILA GHYKA, *The Geometry of Art and Life*

The movement made to swing the left arm holding the muleta, which is crossed in front of the body, out and past the right side to get rid of the bull is called crossing.

Any time the man does not make this cross he will have the bull under him. Unless he swings him far enough out the horn is certain to catch him.

—Ernest Hemingway, *Death in the Afternoon*

Had Kennedy been flying during the day or with a clear moon, he would have been fine. If you are the pilot, looking straight ahead from the cockpit, the angle of your wings will be obvious from the straight line of the horizon in front of you. But when it's dark outside, the horizon disappears. There is no external measure of the plane's bank. On the ground, we know whether we are level even when it's dark, because of the motion-sensing mechanisms in the inner ear. In a spiral dive, though, the effect of the plane's G-force on the inner ear means that the pilot feels perfectly level even if his plane is not.

—Malcolm Gladwell, *What the Dog Saw: And Other Adventures*

The process begins with a simple geometric form, a triangle, positioned in three dimensional space. The midpoint of each edge of the triangle has been connected to the other midpoints dividing the original triangle into four triangles. The midpoints are deflected randomly upward or downward to give volume to the form.

—Richard Mark Friedhoff, *Visualization: The Second Computer Revolution*

The stakes are high. Peering into the unknown for the first time, anything could happen. There are scads of competing theoretical models hoping to anticipate what the LHC will find. You don't know what you're going to see until you look. At the center of the speculation lies the Higgs boson, an unassuming particle that represents both the last piece of the Standard Model, and the first glimpse into the world beyond.

—SEAN CARROLL, *The Particle at the End of the Universe: How the Hunt for the Higgs Boson Leads Us to the Edge of a New World*

Above him Escher's head grew smaller and smaller against the bright circle of sky at the mouth of the Moulin. At this depth the shaft divided into two parts like the legs of a pair of trousers. Agassiz chose the wider of the two ways but soon found it repartitioned into a number of impassable holes. Upon signaling to Escher, he was hoisted back up to the bifurcation and then allowed to descend the other passage. He was now more than 100 feet below the surface of the glacier.

—RONALD H. BAILEY, *Glacier*

Away from people—they must get away from people, he said (jumping up), right away over there, where there were chairs beneath a tree and the long slope of the park dipped like a length of green stuff with a ceiling cloth of blue and pink smoke high above, and there was a rampart of far irregular houses hazed in smoke, the traffic hummed in a circle and on the right, dun-coloured animals stretched long necks over the Zoo palings, barking, howling.

—VIRGINIA WOOLF, *Mrs. Dalloway*

. . . detailed features are shown not by conventional signs nor by their outline ground-plans, but by pictures of their actual appearance as viewed from above at an oblique, near vertical, angle. At first sight this seems to be simply the technique of the bird's-eye view, and we might say that Varle's plan of Philadelphia is a mixture of bird's-eye view and map. —P. D. A. Harvey, *The History of Topographical Maps*

The final element of the surround was a gate. A sturdy young tree, stripped of its branches, was positioned upright at one side of an opening in the fence. A hole was dug for the base, and a mound of stones was piled up around it for support. It was reinforced by tying it with thongs to the heavy mammoth tusks. The gate itself was constructed of leg bones, branches, and mammoth ribs lashed firmly to cross-pieces of saplings chopped to size.
—Jean M. Auel, *The Mammoth Hunters*

Jack looked at him sharply, then down at the chart and at Stephen's drawing: it showed a little bay with a village and a square tower at the bottom of it: a low mole ran twenty or thirty yards out into the sea, turned left-handed for another fifty and ended in a rocky knob, thus enclosing a harbour sheltered from all but the south-west wind.
—Patrick O'Brian, *Master and Commander*

A fleet of barges were coming lazily on, some sideways, some head first, some stern first; all in a wrong-headed, dogged, obstinate way, bumping up against the larger craft, running under the bows of steamboats, getting into every kind of nook and corner where they had no business, and being crunched on all sides like so many walnut shells. . . . —CHARLES DICKENS, *The Old Curiosity Shop*

Screwed at its axis against the side, a swinging lamp slightly oscillates in Jonah's room; and the ship, heeling over towards the wharf with the weight of the last bales received, the lamp, flame and all, though in slight motion, still maintains a permanent obliquity with reference to the room; though, in truth, infallibly straight itself, it but made obvious the false lying levels among which it hung. The lamp alarms and frightens Jonah; as lying in his berth his tormented eyes roll round the place, and this thus far successful fugitive finds no refuge for his restless glance. But that contradiction in the lamp more and more appals him. The floor, the ceiling, and the side, are all awry. —HERMAN MELVILLE, *Moby-Dick*

She closed the magazine and set it on the grass beside her chair. The smell of roses was heavy, almost hypnotic. Claire heard bees. Across the Parkers' yard next door, she could see a gaggle of boys walking down the street, the tops of their summer buzzed haircuts shining in the late afternoon sun. —ANN HOOD, *The Obituary Writer*

On the other side, to their left, Geoffrey's house came in sight, almost a bird's-eye view, the bungalow crouching, very tiny, before the trees, the long garden below descending steeply, parallel with which on different levels obliquely climbing the hill, all the other gardens of the contiguous residences, each with its cobalt oblong of swimming pool, also descended steeply toward the barranca, the land sweeping away at the top of the Calle Nicaragua back up to the pre-eminence of Cortez Palace.

—Malcolm Lowry, *Under the Volcano*

I descended upon the glacier. The surface is very uneven, rising like the waves of a troubled sea, descending low, and interspersed by rifts that sink deep. The field of ice is almost a league in width, but I spent nearly two hours in crossing it. The opposite mountain is a bare perpendicular rock. —Mary Shelley, *Frankenstein*

The tower, described in the prospectus as "probably very old", made of old stones culled from some ruin or ruins, was, as various architectural features suggested, no doubt set up in the late nineteenth century. It had been at some point, perhaps in its original construction, attached by a rough stone and brick arched passage to a closely adjacent, indefinitely ancient, stone-built cottage or cabin. The wooden floors and cast-iron spiral staircase in the tower were sound, and both buildings had been sufficiently "modernised". —Iris Murdoch, *The Book and the Brotherhood*

There are twenty-six tables in a railed off section to the right and rear of the room. Fourteen more tables are portioned off in the section to the left. Between these areas, with its own sense of importance, is the platform holding the final table. It's circled with TV camera stations and a row of chairs reserved for family and close friends. Tall bleachers sit on adjacent sides.

—ANNIE DUKE, *How I Raised, Folded, Bluffed, Flirted, Cursed, and Won Millions at the World Series of Poker*

At these meals his wife, Asun, appeared from the kitchen with a cornucopia—salads drenched in olive oil, deviled eggs, tasty chorizo, a potato soup, a good piece of meat or fish, a bottle or two (or three) of homemade wine, brandy, some flan—while Ambrosio sat expectantly, rubbing his prodigious belly, joined by whichever of the now almost-adult Molinos children happened to rotate through that day.

—MICHAEL PATERNITI, *The Telling Room: A Tale of Love, Betrayal, Revenge, and the World's Greatest Piece of Cheese*

Beneath them, from the base of the abrupt descent, the city spread wide away in a close contiguity of red earthen roofs, above which rose eminent the domes of a hundred churches, beside here and there a tower, and the upper windows of some taller or higher-situated palace, looking down on a multitude of palatial abodes. At a distance, ascending out of the central mass of edifices, they could see the top of the Antonine column, and near it the circular roof of the Pantheon, looking heavenward with its ever-open eye.

—NATHANIEL HAWTHORNE, *The Marble Faun*

Just opposite him hung a "Last Judgment": curly-headed cherubs with rotund behinds flying up into a thunderstorm, blowing trumpets. To Richard's left hung a pen drawing by a German master; Rubashov could only see a part of it—the rest was hidden by the plush back of the sofa and by Richard's head: the Madonna's thin hands, curved upwards, hollowed to the shape of a bowl, and a bit of empty sky covered with horizontal pen-lines.

—ARTHUR KOESTLER, *Darkness at Noon*

The book was a standard-issue 1950s schoolbook—battered, unloved, grimly hefty—but near the front it had an illustration that just captivated me: a cutaway diagram showing the Earth's interior as it would look if you cut into the planet with a large knife and carefully withdrew a wedge representing about a quarter of its bulk.

—BILL BRYSON, *A Short History of Nearly Everything*

The harbour lies below me, with, on the far side, one long granite wall stretching out into the sea, with a curve outwards at the end of it, in the middle of which is a lighthouse. A heavy sea-wall runs along outside of it. On the near side, the sea-wall makes an elbow crooked inversely, and its end too has a lighthouse. Between the two piers there is a narrow opening into the harbour, which then suddenly widens. —BRAM STOKER, *Dracula*

The Mews was one of the most important parts of the castle, next to the stables and the kennels. It was opposite to the solar, and faced south. The outside windows had to be small, for reasons of fortification, but the windows which looked inward to the courtyard were big and sunny. The windows had close vertical slats nailed down them, but no horizontal ones.

—T. H. WHITE, *The Once and Future King*

There was a steep wall of sand, behind which the firing could be heard. They made the people form up into short lines and led them through the gap which had been hurriedly dug in the sandstone wall. The wall hid everything from view, but of course the people knew where they were. The right bank of the Dnieper is cut by deep ravines, and this particular ravine was enormous, majestic, deep and wide like a mountain gorge. If you stood on one side of it and shouted you would scarcely be heard on the other. The sides were steep, even overhanging in places; at the bottom ran a little stream of clear water. Round about were cemeteries, woods and garden plots. The local people knew the ravine as Babi Yar.

—D. M. THOMAS, *The White Hotel*

The tip of the nose of the Stansbury Mountains had been sliced off by the interstate to reveal a sheer and massive section of handsome blue rock, thinly bedded, evenly bedded, forty metres high. Its parallel planes were tilting, dipping, gently to the east, with the exception of some confused and crumpled material that suggested a snowball splatted against glass, or a broken-down doorway in an otherwise undamaged wall.

—JOHN MCPHEE, *Basin and Range*

I moved quickly, sliding open the window, slithering on my stomach through the frame to the bathroom sink below, flipping myself over and landing on the bathroom floor. I replaced the screen, closed the window, and opened the cabinet above the sink. There was volumizing mousse, mousse with extra hold, mousse with extra body, and mousse with both extra body and extra hold. A "dollop"? How much was a dollop?

—SHALOM AUSLANDER, *Foreskin's Lament*

After that they went on again; and now the road struck westwards and left the river, and the great shoulder of the south-pointing mountain-spur drew ever nearer. At length they reached the hill path. It scrambled steeply up, and they plodded slowly one behind the other, till at last in the late afternoon they came to the top of the ridge and saw the wintry sun going downwards to the west.

—J. R. R. TOLKIEN, *The Hobbit*

A few hundred yards to my right was the lip of the gorge, obscured by a rise in the land, and rolling away to the left and ahead was the harsher landscape of the Causse, hard parched soil, sagebrush, telegraph poles. Just past the ruined farm, La Prunarède, I turned down a sandy track on the right, and five minutes later I was at the dolmen.

—IAN MCEWAN, *Black Dogs*

LIGHT AND COLORS

LIGHT

without light

dark, dusky, unlighted, unilluminated, unlit, obscure, tenebrous, stygian, caliginous, fuliginous, sunless

having or showing forth little light

dim, dingy, murky, darkish

shadowy

shady, gloomy, umbral, umbrageous, tenebrous

emanating light

shining, beaming, bright, illuminated, illumined, luminous, irradiated, radiant, lucent, lustrous, luminiferous, luminant, luminative, luminificent, illuminant

lighted

alit, lit, lit up, alight, aglow, irradiated, illuminated, lightened, ablaze

very bright

brilliant, glaring, blazing, blinding, refulgent, effulgent, fulgurant, resplendent

sparkling

glittering, scintillating, scintillescent, coruscating, twinkling, clinquant

sparkling or shining in a subdued way

shimmering, shimmery

giving off reflected light

glinting, gleaming

shining or glossy with reflected light

glistening

flashing

flickering, fulgurant, fulgurating

flashing occasionally or fitfully

winking

flashing regularly

blinking, stroboscopic

flashing weakly or going out

fluttering, guttering, sputtering, dimming

showing deflected light rays or distortion of image

refracted, refractive

burning unsteadily or suddenly

flaring, blazing

giving off flame-like light

flickering, wavering, lambent

flame-colored

flammeous

glowing

aglow, lucent, lambent, shimmering

electromagnetic radiation having wavelengths longer than those of visible light (or beyond the red end of the spectrum)

infrared light

electromagnetic radiation having wavelengths shorter than those of visible light (or beyond the violet end of the spectrum)

ultraviolet light

glowing or luminescent with absorbed radiation in a continuing way

phosphorescent

glowing or luminescent with electromagnetic radiation

fluorescent

visible or glowing at night

noctilucent

glowing whitely with light or intense heat

incandescent, candescent

giving off a reddish or golden glow

rutilant

having a milky or cloudy iridescence (like an opal)

opalescent, opaline

having a pearly iridescence (like a pearl)

nacreous, pearlescent

transparent

sheer, clear, lucid, pellucid, limpid

not transparent

untransparent, nontransparent, opaque, adiaphanous, impervious, cloudy, beclouded

admitting the passage of (or letting show through) light

translucent, diaphanous, pellucid, sheer

transparent in water or when wet

hydrophanous

COLORS

without color

colorless, hueless, achromatic, achromic, untinged

any of three groups of colors from which all other colors can be obtained by mixing

primary colors (including the so-called additive, physiological, or light primaries red, green, and blue; the subtractive or colorant primaries yellow, magenta, and cyan; and psychological primaries red, yellow, green, and blue as well as the achromatic black and white)

colored

colorful, hued, toned, painted, chromatic, pigmented, tinctured (dyed or stained)

slightly or weakly colored

tinged, tinted, tinctured

having one color or hue

monochrome, monochromatic, monochromous, monochromic, monotone

of a color or colors that are relatively muted and do not attract attention

neutral

having many colors

many-colored, multicolored, parti-colored, variegated, motley, varicolored, versicolor, versicolored, polychromatic, polychrome, polychromic, kaleidoscopic, prismatic

rainbow-like

iridescent, iridian

changeable in or showing a shift or play of color

iridescent

highly or brilliantly colored

prismatic

having altered or poor coloration

discolored

white as chalk

chalk white, cretaceous, chalky

leached-out white

blanched, etiolated

not pure white or slightly grayish

off-white (e.g., oyster, cream, eggshell)

thinly or translucently white

bone white

bluish white

alabaster, pearl

yellowish white

eggshell, cream, ivory, bone

grayish white

oyster, platinum, tattletale gray

silvery white

argent

bright or vivid red

crimson, scarlet, vermilion, vermeil, cardinal, carmine, geranium, cinnabar, apple red, tomato, lobster red, beet red, fire-engine red, fiery

moderate red

cherry, cerise, blood red

brick red

lateritious

rust red

rufous, ferruginous

orangish red
poppy, persimmon

dark red
wine, wine red, maroon, ruby, cranberry, garnet, currant, puce

brownish red
burgundy

grayish or bluish red
strawberry

purplish red
raspberry, magenta, grape, raisin, claret, amaranthine, Tyrian purple

red or rosy
blush

pink
rose, rosy, carnation

deep pink
melon

vivid or glowing pink
hot pink, shocking pink

yellowish pink
seashell, coral, flesh-colored, flesh-toned, peach, salmon

whitish-to-yellowish pink
shell

moderate orange
apricot, pumpkin

medium dark orange
burnt orange

moderate reddish orange
flamingo

reddish orange

tangerine, carrot, grenadine, Chinese red

dark reddish orange

burnt sienna

brownish orange

terra-cotta, Titian, tawny

yellowish or turning yellow

flavescent

bright or vivid yellow

goldenrod, daffodil

light yellow

canary

pale yellow

straw yellow, flaxen, primrose, ocher

moderate yellow

brass

dark yellow

old gold

orange yellow

champagne, saffron

greenish yellow

citron, lemon, mustard, lime

grayish yellow

buckskin, oatmeal, parchment, honey yellow, chamois

brownish yellow

amber, buff, gold

pinkish yellow

apricot, peach

greenish or turning green

virescent

slightly green or greenish
viridescent

bright or vivid green
emerald, smaragdine

clear light green
apple green

pale green
celadon

dark green
forest green, evergreen, bottle green, marine green, peacock green, British racing green

bluish green
aquamarine, turquoise, jade green

pale yellow green
glaucous

golden green
chrysochlorous

yellowish green
Kelly green, leek green, hunter green, Nile green, absinthe green, pistachio, verdigris, pea green, grass green, sea green, verdant green, leaf green, malachite, moss green, lime green, cobalt green, zinc green

dull yellow green
ocher green

grayish olive
olive drab

greenish olive
olive green, avocado

brilliant yellow green
chartreuse, Paris green

grayish green

sage green, reseda, loden

bright or vivid blue

ultramarine

pale blue

baby blue, sky blue, aquamarine, powder blue, Persian blue, Wedgwood blue, cerulean, azure, lapis lazuli

deep blue

royal blue

greenish blue

turquoise, peacock blue, cobalt, Prussian blue, aqua, teal blue, china blue, Nile blue, cyan

purplish blue

sapphire, moonstone blue, gentian, hyacinth, violet, marine

reddish blue

violet

grayish blue

Dresden blue, shadow blue, delft blue, robin's egg, steel blue, Copenhagen blue, electric blue (or electric green), slate blue

dark grayish blue

navy

violet blue

periwinkle

light purple

orchid

pale purple

lavender

moderate purple

lilac, amethyst

dark purple
aubergine, eggplant, mulberry, sloe
reddish lavender
heliotrope
reddish purple
fuchsia, raspberry, plum
bluish purple
mauve
brownish purple
puce
brown or brownish colors in general
earth tones, umber
having a brownish tinge
infuscate
bright or vivid brown
café au lait
moderate brown
auburn, coffee, cocoa, saddle tan, saddle brown
dark brown
chocolate, nut brown
light or yellowish brown
tan, khaki, beige, fawn, caramel, sienna (raw sienna), fox, bister, bistre, camel, ecru, sand, tawny
golden brown
butterscotch
yellowish brown
ginger
reddish brown
mahogany, umber, chestnut, bay, cinnamon, henna, russet, copper, walnut, oxblood, roan, rosewood

dark reddish brown

burnt umber

grayish brown

nutmeg, sepia, dun, sandalwood

metallic or greenish brown

bronze

mottled brown and yellow

tortoiseshell

grayish

grizzled, grizzly, hoary

pale gray

ash gray

moderate gray

platinum

dark gray

field gray, charcoal, Oxford gray

bluish gray

battleship gray, steel gray, slate, Wedgwood blue, pearl, pewter, gunmetal

purplish gray

dove

brownish gray

smoke, mouse gray, taupe, fuscous, dun

yellowish gray

sand

black

ebony, ebon, sable, jet, onyx, ink black, coal black, anthracite

glossy black

raven, japan

purplish black

sooty black, elderberry, slate black, mulberry, murrey

black and white finely mixed

salt and pepper, pepper and salt

Common Color Modifiers

washed-out
cool
pastel
slate
bleeding
vibrant
deep
bright
vivid
rich
faded
clashing
muted
warm
electric
unsaturated
discordant
garish
fluorescent
dusky
dazzling
pure
brilliant

faint
medium
dark
moderate
burnt
dusty
light
soft
hot
neon
glowing
metallic
streaky
drab
lustrous
antique
mellow
dun
smoky
riot (of)
dull
bleached-out
gaudy
saturated
pale
strong
Day-Glo
phosphorescent

QUOTATIONS

She came in chilled from the sea-mist that I felt on my cheek, in turn; she stroked the scrapey shadow that by five comes upon me, grizzled old bear that I am. The smell of the water-soaked air clung to her. A vibration in the dusk about her, a deep-sea coruscation, bright, unseen. She had left her mind looking out, I think. Her eyes were still full of it; slowly, slowly she seemed to see me again, from a depth. —AMY SACKVILLE, *Orkney*

And there I saw myself as a man might expect, except that my skin was very white, as the old fiend's had been white, and my eyes had been transformed from their usual blue to a mingling of violet and cobalt that was softly iridescent. My hair had a high luminous sheen, and when I ran my fingers back through it I felt a new and strange vitality there. —ANNE RICE, *The Vampire Lestat*

Store windows were filled with silver-painted nude fauns, great glowing puppets, skeletons and witches of every type. Hollowed-out pumpkins lined the gate of Patchin

Place: I felt you could lay my head down among them. The streets looked lonely. I looked lonely as I made my way each morning to work, and each evening home to a slighter, darker twilight, my street trading all its colors for blue, while from the west came the bright, streaming lavender sunset on the Hudson.

—ANDREW SEAN GREER, *The Impossible Lives of Greta Wells*

The advance guard of the expected procession now appeared in the great gateway, a troop of halberdiers. They were dressed in striped hose of black and tawny, velvet caps graced at the sides with silver roses, and doublets of murrey-and-blue cloth embroidered on the front and back with the three feathers, the prince's blazon, woven in gold. Their halberd staves were covered with crimson velvet, fastened with gilt nails, and ornamented with gold tassels.

—MARK TWAIN, *The Prince and the Pauper*

The slender crayons and the round pans of paint in the watercolor tin scatter unlikely chips of pigment on the cream-colored sandstone. The ridge bears the palette of a numb moon. The winter sun's low arc casts ebony shadows of me and the juniper tree, whose shaggy silver bark holds up a rough-needled canopy of brassy green. I place a scarlet crayon on a patch of aquamarine lichen on the slickrock.

—ELLEN MELOY, *The Anthropology of Turquoise: Meditations on Landscape, Art, and Spirit*

These men who looked steadily into their platinum igniter flames as they lit their eternally burning black pipes. They and their charcoal hair and soot-colored brows and bluish-ash-smeared cheeks where they had shaven close; but their heritage showed.

—RAY BRADBURY, *Fahrenheit 451*

He turned slowly, lifting his head, a solitary ray of sunlight pooling under his hat brim. Even though the glare must have been intense, he didn't blink. He was a white man with the profile of an Indian and eyes that seemed made of glass and contained no color other than the sun's refracted brilliance. His complexion made her think of the rind on a cured ham.

—JAMES LEE BURKE, *Light of the World*

The earth grows wan and weird, defertilized, dehumanized, neither brown nor gray nor beige nor taupe nor ecru, the no color of death reflecting light, sponging up light with its hard, parched shag and shooting it back at us. . . .

—HENRY MILLER, *The Colossus of Maroussi*

It was a little like working on a puzzle: grouping the cartons into various modular configurations, lining them up in rows, stacking them one on top of another, arranging and rearranging them until they finally began to resemble household objects. One set of sixteen served as the support for my mattress, another set of twelve became a table, others of seven became chairs, another of two became a bedstand, and so on. The overall effect was rather monochromatic, what with that somber light brown everywhere you looked, but I could not help feeling proud of my resourcefulness.

—PAUL AUSTER, *Moon Palace*

We turned onto a narrow side street, and at once there was an explosion of Mediterranean color: green doorways, turquoise shutters, splashes of soft red and lavender. We parked and walked into the Kasbah, where a few hundred people live, and there the streets were ten-foot-wide footpaths that wound through the ancient mud buildings and into dimly lit tunnels that led to massive wood doors. —BILL DONAHUE, "Under the Sheltering Sky," *The Best American Travel Writing 2004* (Pico Iyer, ed.)

At Stenness, only three of an original twelve or thirteen stones survive; but the ruins remain impressive, as much because of the peculiar characteristics of the flagstone as because of the massive size of the slabs. All are more than fifteen feet tall, quite broad, but remarkably slender, one waif-like sheet being less than a foot in thickness. The Brodgar stones are of the same flagstone; changing colour according to the light, they sometimes seem a pinkish buff, but the hues are spangled with white and lemon lichen blotches, and sometimes a furry, blue-green lichen growth. —RICHARD MUIR, *The Stones of Britain*

As a rule parrots may be termed green birds, the majority of the species having this colour as the basis of their plumage relieved by caps, gorgets, bands and wing-spots of other and brighter hues. Yet this general green tint sometimes changes into light or deep blue, as in some macaws; into pure yellow or rich orange, as in some of the American macaw-parrots (*Conurus*); into purple, grey, or dove-colour, as in some American, African, and Indian species; into the purest crimson, as in some of the lories; into rosy-white and pure white, as in the cockatoos; and into a deep purple, ashy or black, as in several Papuan, Australian, and Mascarene species.

—ALFRED RUSSEL WALLACE, *Tropical Nature and Other Essays*

Eventually I identified the rocks. The petrified roses were barite, probably from Oklahoma. The scratchy brown mineral was bauxite—aluminum ore. The black glass was obsidian; the booklet of transparent sheets was mica; the goldeny iridescent handful of soft crystals was chalcopyrite, an ore of copper. . . .

—ANNIE DILLARD, *An American Childhood*

The water splashed over the margin of the pond, the nearer kites were writhing and plunging. The nearer they were, the more contorted and wild. One came down in the pond. Another, after prolonged paroxysms, behind the cast of the Physical Energy of G. F. Watts, O.M., R.A. Only two rode steadily, a tandem, coupled abreast like the happy tug and barge, flown by the child from a double winch. She could just discern them, side by side high above the trees, specks against the east darkening already. The wrack broke behind them as she watched, for a moment they stood out motionless and black, in a glade of limpid viridescent sky. —SAMUEL BECKETT, *Murphy*

This disrupter of seasons was a new girl in school named Maureen Peal. A high-yellow dream child with long brown hair braided into two lynch ropes that hung down her back. She was rich, at least by our standards, as rich as the richest of the white girls, swaddled in comfort and care. The quality of her clothes threatened to derange Frieda and me. Patent-leather shoes with buckles, a cheaper version of which we got only at Easter and which had disintegrated by the end of May. Fluffy sweaters the color of lemon drops tucked into skirts with pleats so orderly they astounded us. Brightly colored knee socks with white borders, a brown velvet coat trimmed in white rabbit fur, and a matching muff. There was a hint of spring in her sloe green eyes, something summery in her complexion, and a rich autumn ripeness in her walk.

—TONI MORRISON, *The Bluest Eye*

The scattered polychrome of the exterior, strewn with blobs and drops as if handfuls of coloured confetti have been thrown at it, evokes the atmosphere of a Venetian carnival with gondolas and crinolines.

—LARA VINCA MASINI, *Gaudi*

But when his eye was accustomed to the shade within, it withdrew gladly from the glaring sea and glaring tide-rocks to the walls of the chasm itself; to curved and polished sheets of stone, rich brown, with snow-white veins, on which danced for ever a dappled network of pale yellow light; to crusted beds of pink coralline; to caverns in the dark crannies of which hung branching sponges and tufts of purple sea-moss; to strips of clear white sand, bestrewn with shells; to pools, each a gay flower-garden of all hues, where branching seaweed reflected blue light from every point, like a thousand damasked sword blades. . . . —CHARLES KINGSLEY, *Two Years Ago*

The smaller man was looking around, with the air of a child just come to a birthday party—at the clumsy old island schooners tied up at the water's edge, with red sails furled; at the native women in bright dresses and the black ragged crewmen, bargaining loudly over bananas, coconuts, strange huge brown roots, bags of charcoal, and strings of rainbow-colored fish; at the great square red fort, and at the unique cannons atop its slanted seaward wall, pointing impotently to sea; at the fenced statue of Amerigo Vespucci, almost hidden in purple, orange, and pink bougainvillea; at the houses of Queen's Row, their ancient plaster facades painted in vivid colors sun-bleached to pastels; at the old gray stone church, and the white-washed Georgian brick pile of the Sir Francis Drake Inn. —HERMAN WOUK, *Don't Stop the Carnival*

In college, fiddling in the laboratory for his robotics class on a Saturday night, Jonah breathed in the scent of machine parts and electrical wiring and, especially, underwashed MIT undergraduates, who definitely had their own scent; and it seemed to him that an unspiritual life engineered solely by humans, busy in their fluorescent academic hive, would be perfectly acceptable.

—MEG WOLITZER, *The Interestings*

Ahead of them lay the Nile, bathed in mist like a white sea; behind them lay the dark desert, like a petrified purple ocean. At last, a streak of orange light appeared to the east; and gradually the white sea in front of them became an immense expanse of fertile green, while the purple ocean behind turned shimmering white.

—JULIAN BARNES, *Flaubert's Parrot*

The picture was her final treasure waiting to be packed for the journey. In whatever room she had called her own since childhood, there it had also lived and looked at her, not quite familiar, not quite smiling, but in its prim colonial hues delicate as some pressed flower. Its pale oval, of color blue and rose and flaxen, in a battered, pretty gold frame, unconquerably pervaded any surroundings with a something like last year's lavender.

—OWEN WISTER, *The Virginian*

The sight was dazzling. The entire Greensward, the magnificent vision that was Manhattan's great public space, was laid out in its entirety—in the original silver version—upon a landscaped green suede base, with bright blue paint shimmering as we lighted it, in all the places in the Park that were filled with water.

—LINDA FAIRSTEIN, *Death Angel*

From the basic blackness of the flesh of the tribe there broke or erupted a wave of red color, and the people all arose on the white stone of the grandstands and waved red objects, waved or flaunted. Crimson was the holyday color of the Wariri. The amazons saluted with purple banners, the king's colors. His purple umbrella was raised, and its taut head swayed.

—SAUL BELLOW, *Henderson the Rain King*

She woke before dawn coughing. She could make out the shape of the glass of water on the table but it was too far to reach and after a while she managed to stop coughing without drinking.

She lay still as the room grew light. The blue ceiling turned grey then light grey. It was thoroughly quiet. It seemed to be the beginning of something more than just day. For a few long moments she lay and felt—what was it? The dawn light put her in mind of creation. It must have been this way on the actual first day of the world. A thin yellow light spread out and all the sorrows which sat in her seemed suddenly to lift up and fly off and were replaced with the most inappropriate hope.

—SUSAN MINOT, *Evening*

Thundery day along Greenback. All the willows standing still with their leaves pricked. Dusty green. Pale lilac shadows. Tarred road reflecting the sky. Blue to make you jump. A great cloud over on the Surrey shore. Yellow as soap and solid as a cushion. Shaped like a tower about a mile high and half a mile thick, with a little Scotch pepper pot in front. Dresden blue behind full of sunlight floating like gold dust. River roughed up with little waves like the flat side of a cheese grater. Dark copper under the cloud, dark lead under the blue. I could use that cloud in the Fall, I thought. It's a solid square. To give weight in the top left-hand corner, opposite the Tower. Salmon on pink. It's an idea worth trying. —JOYCE CARY, *The Horse's Mouth*

But the only aura of the granite quarry that clung to Owen was the granular dust, the gray powder that sprang off his clothes whenever we lifted him up. He was the color of a gravestone; light was both absorbed and reflected by his skin, as with a pearl, so that he appeared translucent at times—especially at his temples, where his blue veins showed through his skin (as though, in addition to his extraordinary size, there were other evidence that he was born too soon).

—JOHN IRVING, *A Prayer for Owen Meany*

The mountains were covered with a rug of trees, green, yellow, scarlet and orange, but their bare tops were scarfed and beribboned with snow. From carved rocky outcrops, waterfalls drifted like skeins of white lawn, and in the fields we could see the amber glint of rivers and the occasional mirror-like flash of a mountain lake. . . . —GERALD DURRELL AND LEE DURRELL, *Durrell in Russia*

Above the field the swollen palpitating tangle of light frayed and thinned out into hot darkness, but the thirty thousand pairs of eyes hanging on the inner slopes of the arena did not look up into the dark but stared down into the pit of light, where men in red silky-glittering shorts and gold helmets hurled themselves against men in blue silky-glittering shorts and gold helmets and spilled and tumbled on the bright arsenical-green turf like spilled dolls, and a whistle sliced chillingly through the thick air like that scimitar through a sofa cushion.

—ROBERT PENN WARREN, *All the King's Men*

I haven't (the seeing eye), unfortunately, so that the world is full of places to which I want to return—towns with the blinding white sun upon them; stone pines against the blue of the sky; corners of gables, all carved and painted with stags and scarlet flowers and crowstepped gables with the little saint at the top; and grey and pink palazzi and walled towns a mile or so back from the sea, on the Mediterranean, between Leghorn and Naples.

—FORD MADOX FORD, *The Good Soldier*

Newts are the most common of salamanders. Their skin is a lighted green, like water in a sunlit pond, and rows of very bright red dots line their backs. They have gills as larvae; as they grow they turn a luminescent red, lose their gills, and walk out of the water to spend a few years padding around in damp places on the forest floor. Their feet look like fingered baby hands, and they walk in the same leg patterns as all four-footed creatures—dogs, mules, and, for that matter, lesser pandas.

—ANNIE DILLARD, *Pilgrim at Tinker Creek*

Then he saw his old house, no longer green, though to my family and me it would always be "the green house."

The new owners had painted it a lavendery mauve and installed a pool and, just off to the side, near the basement window, a gazebo made of redwood, which overflowed with hanging ivy and children's toys.

—Alice Sebold, *The Lovely Bones*

Light, line, and color as sensual pleasures, came later and were as crude as the rest. The New England light is glare, and the atmosphere harshens color. The boy was a full man before he ever knew what was meant by atmosphere; his idea of pleasure in light was the blaze of a New England sun. His idea of color was a peony, with the dew of early morning on its petals. The intense blue of the sea, as he saw it a mile or two away, from the Quincy hills; the cumuli in a June afternoon sky; the strong reds and greens and purples of colored prints and children's picture-books, as the American colors then ran; these were ideals. The opposites or antipathies were the cold grays of November evenings, and the thick, muddy thaws of Boston winter.

—Henry Adams, *The Education of Henry Adams*

I jiggled my brush in the water jar. The liquid turned the color of my first urine in the morning. I stroked my purple cake, and a bruise-colored cat and then a brown stick cat darted out.

I was so much to myself as I worked that I did not hear her warning shout or the slapping of her Island thongs on the linoleum as she swooped down upon me. Her crimson nails clawed my sheet off its board and crumpled it into a ball. "You, you defy me!" she cried out. Her face had turned the muddy red of my water jar. She lifted me by the forearm, hurried me across the room through a door into a dark parlor, and plunked me down on a stiff cane-back chair.

Her green eyes glared at me like a cat's. They were speckled with brown as if something alive had gotten caught and fossilized in the irises.

—JULIA ALVAREZ, *How the García Girls Lost Their Accent*

The smallest of the tree flocks consisted of about fifteen gobblers. They were huge, wary birds. They were the most beautiful wild things that he had seen. Most were dark, purple-breasted, with a long beard, and a small cunning red head, dark in the back, flecked with brown, and they had a spread of reddish-white tail that dazzled Clint.

—ZANE GREY, *Fighting Caravans*

But in the alleyways behind the marketplace, fruit and meat rotted in crates. Rats crawled; pigeons crowded and pecked each other savagely trailing feathers and lice. This was reality, and though living with Ernest was giving me more tolerance for the real than ever before, it made me feel sick even so. It was like looking into the gutters at the Place de la Contrescarpe, where colored dyes ran freely from the flower vendors' carts: brief false lushness, and ugliness underneath.

—PAULA MCLAIN, *The Paris Wife*

I looked off at the blue forms of the mountains, growing less transparent and cloudlike, shifting their positions, rolling from side to side off the road, coming back and centering in our path, and then sliding off the road again, but strengthening all the time. We went through some brush and then out across a huge flat field that ran before us for miles, going straight at the bulging range of hills, which was now turning mile by mile from blue to a light green-gold, the color of billions of hardwood leaves.

—James Dickey, *Deliverance*

Instead of the shades of pink and peach that I would have expected—Rubens has a lot to answer for—her body displayed, disconcertingly, a range of muted tints from magnesium white to silver and tin, a scumbled sort of yellow, pale ochre, and even in places a faint greenishness and, in the hollows, a shadowing of mossy mauve.

—John Banville, *Ancient Light*

The pink dusty road before us, the scrub and the dark pines, lay always between these depths of blue. The sea was calm; as one looked down, it drowned the eye like a second zenith, but bluer still; bluer than lapis, or sapphire, or whatever flower is bluest; and then again, in the dark clear shadows round the deep roots of the rocks, green and grape-purple, like the ring-dove's sheen.

—Mary Renault, *The King Must Die*

The light fell upon the pages of his coloring book, across his child's hands. Coloring excited him, not the act of filling in space, but choosing colors that no one else would select. In the green of the hills he saw red. Purple snow, green skin, silver sun. He liked the effect it had on others, that it disturbed his siblings. He discovered he had a talent for sketching. He was a natural draftsman and secretly he twisted and abstracted his images, feeling his growing powers. He was an artist, and he knew it. It was not a childish notion. He merely acknowledged what was his.

—Patti Smith, *Just Kids*

Weighing only about seven pounds, the southern gray fox is smaller than the better-known red fox. Its grizzled, salt-and-pepper-gray body, with rusty red along the sides and neck, is about two feet long; the black-tipped bushy gray tail, with a black streak along its top, adds another twelve or fourteen inches to the fox's length. He stands not much more than a foot above the ground at the shoulders, and when he trots, his paw marks along his trail are about eleven inches apart.

—John K. Terres, *From Laurel Hill to Siler's Bog: The Walking Adventures of a Naturalist*

I have depended on Central Park for its usefulness, but its incidental beauty has often taken my breath away. I may look up from catching the flash of a scarlet tanager out of the corner of my eye, a tanager perched in the high branches of one of the huge cherry trees on the West Side, and my eyes hit the shimmering towers of midtown—the Plaza Hotel and the General Motors Building floating just above the Sheep Meadow.

—Susan Cheever, "My Little Bit of Country," *Central Park: An Anthology* (Andrew Blauner, ed.)

Caracals flicking their long sharp-tipped and slender ears are a delight to watch. They are often pitch-black with a long tassel of hair. The outside of the ears is covered with silver hair while the inside is light grey. A black spot on either side of the face near the muzzle, and a black line from the eye to the nose, with some white on the chin and at the base of the ear, make the caracal's face one of the most beautiful of the African felines.

—VIVIAN J. WILSON, *Orphans of the Wild: An African Naturalist in Pursuit of a Dream*

Mother's yellow station wagon slid like a Monopoly icon along the gray road that cut between fields of Iowa corn, which was chlorophyll green and punctuated in the distance by gargantuan silver silos and gleaming, unrusted tractors glazed cinnamon red.

—MARY KARR, *Lit: A Memoir*

Like a woman's wispy dress that has slipped off its hanger, the city shimmered and fell in fantastic folds, not held up by anything, a discarnate iridescence limply suspended in the azure autumnal air. Beyond the nacrine desert of the square, across which a car sped now and then with a new metropolitan trumpeting, great pink edifices loomed, and suddenly a sunbeam, a gleam of glass, would stab him painfully in the pupil.

—VLADIMIR NABOKOV, *King, Queen, Knave*

He has saved up enough money to go anywhere he wants, and there is no question that he has had his fill of the Florida sun—which, after much study, he now believes does the soul more harm than good. It is a Machiavellian sun in his opinion, a hypocritical sun, and the light it generates does not illuminate things but obscures them—blinding you with its constant, overbright effulgences, pounding on you with its blasts of vaporous humidity, destabilizing you with its miragelike reflections and shimmering waves of nothingness. It is all glitter and dazzle, but it offers no substance, no tranquillity, no respite.

—Paul Auster, *Sunset Park*

Off to my left, in that vast bowl of stillness that contains the meandering river, tens of square miles of tundra browns and sedge meadow greens seem to snap before me, as immediate as the pages of my notebook, because of unscattered light in the dustless air. The land seems guileless. Creatures down there take a few steps, then pause and gaze about. Two sandhill cranes stand still by the river. Three Peary caribou, slightly built and the silver color of the moon, browse a cutbank in that restive way of deer. Tundra melt ponds, their bright dark blue waters oblique to the sun, stand out boldly in the plain. In the center of the large ponds, beneath the surface of the water, gleam cores of aquamarine ice, like the constricted heart of winter.

—Barry Lopez, *Arctic Dreams: Imagination and Desire in a Northern Landscape*

A riot of color in one, very clean but tight packed. Tufted hot pink bedspread such as it was inconceivable Martha would buy, with many figural wildly colored pillows in a similar vein heaped on top, posters as from a travel agency hung on the walls, bedside table bristling with photographs of grinning toothy children in imitation metal frames. The other room used such a different palette as to seem a different planet. Robin's-Egg Blue, Cappuccino, and Leaf would have been fitting names for the paint.

—SUSAN CHOI, *My Education*

The houses of the central village were quite unlike the casual and higgledy-piggledy agglomeration of the mountain villages he knew; they stood in a continuous row on either side of a central street of astonishing cleanness; here and there their parti-coloured façade was pierced by a door, and not a solitary window broke their even frontage. They were parti-coloured with extraordinary irregularity; smeared with a sort of plaster that was sometimes grey, sometimes drab, sometimes slate-coloured or dark brown. . . .

—H. G. WELLS, "The Country of the Blind," *The Country of the Blind and Other Stories*

Ahead, the shadowed purple line of the Ballon d'Alsace, highest point in the Vosges, was hidden in mist. Patrols who ventured to the top could see down below the red-roofed villages of the lost territory, the gray church spires, and the tiny, gleaming line of the Moselle where, young and near its source, it was narrow enough to be waded. Squares of white potato blossom alternated with strips of scarlet-runner beans and gray-green-purple rows of cabbages. Haycocks like small fat pyramids dotted the fields as if arranged by a painter.

—BARBARA W. TUCHMAN, *The Guns of August*

STRUCTURES AND SPACES

TYPES OF BUILDINGS AND DWELLINGS

urban multistory dwelling typically of reddish brown sandstone and usually having front steps
brownstone

urban multistory dwelling typically with a facade of limestone and usually having front steps
greystone

outbuilding, originally for a horse-drawn carriage, typically converted for residential use
carriage house

small cottage or house of one story with no basement
bungalow

house whose rooms are at different one-, two-, or half-story levels (and built on slanted or hilly land)
split-level

luxurious one-family city house of several stories (and often of brick) and usually one of several in a row
town house

building or dwelling with a steeply triangular front and rear with walls reaching to the ground
A-frame

small rural or resort-area house
cottage, cabin

simple one-story dwelling built of logs
log cabin

large private dwelling (usually on spacious property)
mansion, estate, château, country house, palace, manor, manor house, family home, ancestral home, plantation, homestead, hacienda, demesne, stately home

pretentiously large, often shoddily constructed house in poor taste
McMansion

additional or minor building
outbuilding, outhouse

freestanding bell tower
campanile

grounds of a country house or mansion
demesne

primary house on an estate or plantation
great house

impressive public or private dwelling
palace, palazzo

round and often domed building
rotunda

farmhouse with outbuildings
grange

large farm for raising horses and/or other animals, esp. in the western U.S.
ranch, spread

large or impressive building or buildings
pile

dwelling raised, as protection against flooding, on a pile-supported platform near or over a body of water
stilt house, pile dwelling, palafitte

country estate or retreat
villa (Russia: dacha)

home of prebuilt sections or units
prefab, modular home, modular

tunnel-shaped prefabricated shelter of corrugated metal (and concrete floor)
Quonset hut, Nissen hut

house whose rooms lie in a line front to back
shotgun house

apartment extending from the front to the rear of a building
floor-through

poor or shabby dwelling
hut, shack, hovel, shanty, shed, hutch, cottage, cabin, crib

rudimentary platform shelter with a simple sloping roof
lean-to

house or apartment needing repair or renovation
fixer-upper

cabin with an open breezeway
dogtrot house

primitive (Eskimo) dome-like dwelling usually made of blocks of snow
igloo

primitive circular (Mongol) tent-like hut of hides with a conical top
yurt

primitive (Native American) conical animal-skin tent
tepee

primitive (Native American) matted oval or rounded hut of bark or hides
wigwam

primitive (Native American) tepee-like hut of brushwood or mats
wickiup

primitive (Native American) mud-covered log building of various shapes

hogan

communal terraced adobe (Native American) dwelling

pueblo

primitive (Native American) bark-and-wood communal dwelling of great length

longhouse

house with a widely overhanging roof as well as decoratively carved supports and balconies

chalet

house having a timber framework

frame house

house (with two entrances) designed vertically or horizontally for two families but having a common side wall and usually separate entrances

two-family house, duplex, semidetached

small house connected to an apartment building

maisonette

house similar to others in a development

tract house

house that is one of a continuous line of houses usually all of the same general appearance

row house

one-story house with a low-pitched roof

ranch house, ranch, rambler

house high up on a hill or mountain

aerie, eyrie

apartment above the ground floor in a building having no elevator

walk-up

apartment suite with connecting rooms on two floors
duplex apartment, maisonette

apartment with rooms in more or less a straight line
railroad flat, railroad apartment

roof-level or special (and usually luxurious) upper-level apartment
penthouse

apartment in a low-rise complex that has landscaped grounds
garden apartment

apartment with one main room (often with a high ceiling) but with kitchen and bathroom facilities
studio apartment, studio

small apartment (often furnished) with a bathroom and kitchenette
efficiency apartment, efficiency

building's upper story converted for use as an artist's studio or apartment
loft, atelier

temporary, secondary, or occasional lodgings
pied-à-terre

multiple dwellings
apartment house, tenement, residential building, high-rise, cooperative apartment house, co-op building, co-op, condominium, condo, multiple-unit dwelling

residential building of many stories in height and having elevators
high-rise

residential building of few stories in height
low-rise

structure where lodging and usually meals are provided
boardinghouse, guesthouse, pension, rooming house

overnight lodging place

hotel, motel, inn, hostelry, caravansary, lodge, bed-and-breakfast

cheap lodging place

hostel, flophouse, dosshouse, fleabag, cold-water flat

low-rent, usually urban apartment dwelling meeting at best minimum legal standards

tenement

establishment providing food and housing for people in need (or animals)

shelter

apartment house in which indigent tenants live in single rooms

SRO (single-room occupancy)

PARTS OR FEATURES OF BUILDINGS AND DWELLINGS

surface space occupied by a building

footprint

building plot or lot

plat

building's upper or visible part

superstructure

building's lower or unseen part

understructure

external supporting structure for a building

exoskeleton

section of or addition to a building often projecting laterally

wing, annex, pavilion

space or set of rooms between (horizontal) floor levels

story, storey

main story of a house

bel étage

ground floor

rez-de-chaussée

intermediary and often balcony-like story

mezzanine, entresol

supportive wall built to resist lateral pressure, as from advancing earth or water

retaining wall

protective cellar accessible in case of tornadoes or other violent weather

storm cellar

pit or cellar used to store root crops

root cellar

crude, shallow space beneath the first floor or the roof for access to plumbing

crawlspace

platform outside or around a house

deck

covered or arched and usually columned walkway open on at least one side

gallery, arcade, loggia, cloister

small or blind (decorative rather than structural) arcade

arcature

columns in a row and usually supporting a roof or wall

colonnade

colonnade encircling an open space or building

peristyle

roofed outdoor passageway between buildings

breezeway, (of a cabin) dogtrot

long walkway within a structure or between buildings
passageway
depressed open area at cellar or basement level
areaway
level space that encompasses a building site
parterre
central interior area or lobby with a high ceiling
rotunda
interior open space several stories high and usually having a skylight
atrium
roofed entrance structure
porch, portico, lanai
roofed and railinged platform fronting or around part of a house
porch, veranda
small porch or entrance stairway
stoop
screen-walled or roofed driveway (along a house entrance or to an interior courtyard) for vehicles
porte cochere, carriage porch
roofed, open-sided shelter for a motor vehicle or vehicles
carport
front wall
facade, face
protective or ornamental covering on the front of a building
facing
protective or ornamental covering on the side or sides of a building
siding

one of many floor- or ceiling-supporting parallel beams of wood, metal, or reinforced concrete
 joist, rafter
projecting brace supporting a building externally
 buttress
low protective wall along a roof or platform
 parapet
defensive or decorative notched parapet topping a wall
 battlement
building's external angle or corner, or the stone forming it
 quoin, cornerstone
triangular part of a roof's end or building's projection (sometimes with a window)
 gable
above-the-roof gable with "steps" or setbacks
 crowstep gable, corbiestep
structurally recessed or steplike feature of a building's exterior, esp. of a skyscraper
 setback
small sloping-roof or attic gable often with a window (all in all like a miniature house)
 dormer
low or small dormer over which the roofing curves
 eyebrow
horizontal structural supporting brace spanning a door or other opening
 lintel
horizontal frame-like (and often decorative) projection all along the top of a wall
 cornice

projecting block (one of many) beneath a cornice

dentil

part (lower) of roof overhanging the wall

eave

rounded vertical support

pillar, column

simple fluted column with no base and a saucer-shaped capital (simplest of the three orders of columns in classical Greek architecture)

Doric column

more refined fluted column with two opposed volutes in the capital (intermediate order of column in classical Greek architecture)

Ionic column

slender, finely fluted column with ornate capital of sculpted acanthus-leaves (most decorative order of column in classical Greek architecture)

Corinthian column

square or rectangular vertical support

pier

rectangular vertical support not freestanding but projecting from part of a wall

pilaster

scroll-like or spiral ornamental feature

volute

wall's clamp-like support (beneath a roof or overhang)

bracket, corbel

ornamental scroll-like projection beneath a cornice

modillion

projecting curved or foliage-like ornament high up on a building
crocket
rounded (part of a sphere) rooftop structure
dome, cupola
rooftop structure for observation or decoration
cupola, lantern, belfry, belvedere
opening at the top of a dome
oculus
Russian-style (ogival) bulbous dome that comes to a point
onion dome, imperial dome, imperial roof
pointed tower-like construction rising from a roof
spire, flèche, steeple
small spire-like ornament topping a feature of a building
pinnacle, finial
octagonal spire
broach spire
topmost structure housing bells
bell tower, belfry
sculptural relief whose projection is slight
bas relief
triangular gable-like fronting of a classical roof (or an ornamental version of this)
pediment
crown-like upper end of a column, pier, or pilaster
capital
supporting block at the base of a column, pier, or pilaster
plinth
wedge-shaped piece at the top of an arch
keystone

wedge-shaped piece in an arch or vault
voussoir
ornamental part of a wall adjoining an arch or below an upper-level window
spandrel
decorative work
strapwork
carved or otherwise shaped or designed ornamentation
fretwork
any construction or feature pierced or perforated with openings in its design
openwork
decorative grating-like features or ornamentation
grille, grill, grillwork
decorative work with coiled forms
scrollwork
intricate or very fine ornamental pattern
filigree
circular or oval decorative element
medallion
decorative molding with a design alternating oval and arrow- or tongue-like figures
egg and dart
building features of iron or cast iron
ironwork
arched ceiling
vaulted ceiling
in a dwelling a high, often slanted ceiling like that of many a church
cathedral ceiling

ceiling with paint-on or spray-on spongy material to deaden sound

popcorn ceiling, acoustic ceiling

recessed or inverted ceiling

tray ceiling

concave ceiling edge, molding, or other architectural surface

cove

roof peaking at a high angle

steep-pitched roof

roof peaking at a low angle

low-pitched roof

conventional ridged roof with the same angle of slope on either side

gable roof, saddle roof, saddleback roof

roof with a third face sloping down before where the two main slopes meet

hip roof, hipped roof

roof having not one but two slopes (or angles of slope) on either side of its ridge

curb roof

roof only part of which is hipped (so that part of the main gable is "blunted" or truncated)

jerkinhead roof, hipped-gable roof

curb roof with the lower of its two slopes the steeper one

gambrel roof, mansard roof, dual-pitched roof

roof with four faces or slopes that rise to a point

pyramidal roof

roof with a single downward or upward slope

lean-to roof, shed roof, penthouse roof, half-gabled roof, pent roof

roof that is a double-gable or ridged roof (with the lowest part or "valley" in the center)

M roof

roof with broad parallel indentations across its top

saw-tooth roof

roof tiled in the southwestern U.S. style

Spanish-tiled roof, mission-tiled roof

raised construction with windows or louvers straddling the ridge of a roof

monitor

railed platform on a coastal house

widow's walk

vertical post or support framing an opening such as a door or window

jamb, reveal

conventional wooden-frame (stile-and-rail) door with panels

panel door

conventional door without panels or moldings

flush door

door with some glass in its construction

sash door

slatted door

louvered door

slatted door on tracks that folds up or out horizontally

accordion door

door composed of glass panes (usually one of a pair)

French door, casement door

door of glass that opens or closes along horizontal tracks

sliding glass door

door with two sides that open or close

double door

door hinged to swing in or out
double-swing door

crude cellar or shed door
batten door

horizontally divided door with both the upper and the lower part separately able to open and close
dutch door

outer (second) door used as protection against inclement weather
storm door

paneling or other border-like features around a door
surround

design or arrangement of windows and doors in a structure
fenestration

framework with a pane or panes of glass in a window or door
sash

window that does not open
fixed window

standard window with raisable upper and lower sashes
double-hung window

window with a sash that moves right or left
sliding window

window that opens on hinges
casement window

pair of casement windows reaching to the floor and opening in the middle
French window

window with adjustable horizontal slat-like glass panes (or louvers)
jalousie

large fixed window dominating a room
picture window
window or windows projecting or curving outward from a wall
bay window
curved bay window
bow window
window above a door or other window
transom window
bay window supported by a bracket (corbel)
oriel
semicircular fixed window, above a door, like a fan (or half a lemon slice), with radiating muntins (sash bars)
fanlight, fan window
fixed fan-like window with muntins in the form of concentric semicircles
circle-head window
window with a sash sliding left or right
sliding window
window that (hinged at the top) opens out (sometimes with a crank mechanism)
awning window
window that (hinged at the top) opens in or is like an upside-down awning window
hopper window
window that (hinged at the top) opens in
basement transom window
window with a sash anchored at the center of the frame that swings around perpendicularly
center pivot window, pivot window
window in a ceiling or roof
skylight

window with small panes separated by lead

leaded window

window like an archway with a lower side-window on either side (the whole looking like the frontal outline of a domed building)

Palladian window, Diocletian window, Venetian window

tall and narrow pointed-arch window

lancet window

wall opening with (usually wooden) adjustable slats for ventilation

louver

small round opening or window

bull's-eye, oeil-de-boeuf, oxeye, oculus

horizontal ledge or member beneath a window

sill

vertical dividing member in the middle of a window (particularly of a large Gothic window)

mullion

horizontal part of a classical building above the columns and below the eaves

entablature

part of an entablature resting directly on the capital over a column

architrave

sculptured or in-relief band along the top of a classical building

frieze

strip-like horizontal decorative feature around a room or along a wall

molding

decorative external horizontal band or molding
stringcourse
decoratively carved board along a projecting roof
bargeboard, vergeboard
molding between an internal wall and the ceiling
crown molding
wooden paneling applied to the lower part of an interior wall
wainscot, wainscoting

ROOMS AND INTERIOR SPACES

room in a house for the occupants' social activities and leisure
living room, family room, parlor, great room
large formal room for receiving and entertaining guests
drawing room
entrance hall between the front door and a house's interior
vestibule, hall, hallway, entry hall, foyer
outer room, often used as a waiting room
anteroom, antechamber
room in a usually rural house for occupants to remove muddy boots and wet or damp garments
mudroom
room or sleeping room for the use of young children
nursery
entrance room in a hotel, building, or headquarters
lobby
interior walkway or passage among rooms
corridor, hallway, hall, passageway
(chiefly British) one-room apartment serving as both a living room and a bedroom
bed-sitter, bed-sitting room, bed-sit

room, often book-lined, for studying, letter writing, or literary work

study

room in which books, video recordings or films, and other items are collected and arranged

library

somewhat private or secluded room for relaxation or informal pursuits

den

room or space just below the roof

attic, garret

spare room, usually without a closet, that can be used as a den, office, TV room, or any of various other purposes

bonus room

usually glass structure for the cultivation or display of special plants

greenhouse, conservatory, hothouse

compact, typically longitudinal kitchen (without a table) on a ship, train, or plane or its equivalent in an apartment or small house

galley kitchen, galley

room in a house, hotel, or other establishment in which meals are eaten

dining room

room, off a kitchen, for tableware, dishware, linens, and other items

pantry

small room near a kitchen for dishwashing and other meal-related chores

scullery

small area adjoining a kitchen for informal meals

dinette

glass or multi-windowed porch or room for enjoying maximum sunlight

sun porch, solarium, sun parlor, sunroom

space smaller than a conventional room

alcove, compartment, cubicle, niche, carrel

shaped, often vaselike supporting post or leg for a handrail or staircase

baluster

rail-topped row of vertical supports

balustrade

handrail

banister

vertical support for handrail at landing or at bottom of staircase

newel post

central vertical support from which the steps of a winding or circular staircase radiate

newel

COMMON CONSTRUCTION MATERIALS

earth and grass

sod, turf

poles with interwoven branches, reeds, twigs, or the like used in primitive dwellings

wattle

framework of woven rods, twigs, or the like plastered with clay

wattle and daub

straw, rushes, or the like used for roofing

thatch

lengths of unshaped timber

log

strips of wood used for flooring or, nailed, to reinforce siding boards

batten

bonding mixture (lime or cement or both with sand and water) used between stones or bricks

mortar

clay bricks, tiles, stones, or concrete or glass blocks usually bonded with mortar or cement

masonry

craft of construction through joining pieces of wood

joinery

pulverized clay and limestone mixture

cement, Portland cement

stone-like mixture of Portland cement with water and an aggregate (pebbles, shale, gravel, etc.)

concrete

concrete strengthened with embedded metal (usually steel) strands or mesh

reinforced concrete

translucent blocks used chiefly in walls

glass block

red brick

redbrick

glazed or baked brick

fired brick

bricks of sun-dried clay and straw

adobe, unfired brick

lime-water or other mixture used to whiten surfaces

whitewash

raw or unfinished pieces of stone

fieldstone

hewn or squared masonry stone

ashlar

broken stone

riprap, rubble, revetment

stone made (dressed) smooth

cut stone

burnt or baked thin or curved slab or various building materials used mostly for roofs

tile, tiling

fired waterproof ceramic clay used esp. ornamentally in roofing and facing

terra-cotta

mixture of gypsum or limestone with sand and water and sometimes hair used primarily for walls and ceilings

plaster

material of bonded wood fragments pressed into sheets

particle board, particleboard

boards of fiberboard, felt, or the like used in place of plaster

plasterboard, Sheetrock, drywall, gypsum board

covering or overlay of one material over another in a wall

cladding

weatherproof boards, sheets, or shingles used for the exposed facing of a frame building

siding

construction of siding using vertical wide boards and narrower strips

board-and-batten, board-and-batt

exterior plaster finish (usually of Portland cement and sand)

stucco

wall exterior of mortar and pressed-in pebbles
pebble-dash, rock-dash, roughcast

long and thin horizontal boards (with one edge thinner) used overlappingly with others for siding
clapboard, weatherboard

sawed thin oblongs of wood, slate, or other building material used overlappingly as roofing or siding
shingle

split-log shingles (commonly of cedar)
shake

polished mosaic or chip-like flooring usually of marble and stone
terrazzo

hard, slab-like stone whose flat pieces are used for a path or terrace
flagstone, flag

ridged steel rods used in reinforced concrete
rebar

EXTERIOR STRUCTURES AND OUTDOOR SPACES

ornamental garden with paths
parterre

garden decoratively interspersed with rocks
rock garden, rockery

platform-like and usually paved open recreational area alongside a house
terrace, patio

structure for swimming pool equipment near such a pool or a secondary dwelling near a pool
pool house

roofed, usually open structure in a garden or with a pleasant view

belvedere, gazebo, summerhouse, pavilion

walkway or arbor with vine-covered posts and trelliswork

pergola

beach or swimming pool shelter or hut

cabana

level open grassy or paved area for walking

esplanade

interior open area

courtyard, court, cloister

area designated to protect game or other wildlife or natural resources

preserve, reserve

federally designated tract of land, esp. one for Native American people

reservation

cultivated area of particular trees and shrubs designated for educational purposes

arboretum

garden, often with greenhouses, for the exhibition and study of selected or special plants

botanical garden

public walkway or area for strolling

promenade

extensive bridge-like walkway, between observation platforms, built high up in a canopy of tall trees, as in a rainforest

canopy walkway

communal square or park of grassy land in a town or city

green, common, commons

sizable open public space in a town or city

square, plaza, piazza

very small urban park or courtyard area, as between buildings and with benches and a fountain or artificial waterfall, for public relaxation

pocket park, vest-pocket park

grounds and buildings of a university, college, hospital, corporation, or other organization

campus

rectangular or square space surrounded by buildings, as on a college campus

quadrangle, quad

enclosed open space, as on religious property or near a cathedral

close

building or freestanding wall, using structural support and often hydroponics, covered with vegetation

green wall, vertical garden, living wall, biowall

roof covered with vegetation to absorb rainwater, filter air pollutants, and provide insulation

green roof, eco roof, living roof, vegetative roof, oikosteges

level area used for troop formations or recreationally

parade ground

COMMUNITIES WITH BUILDINGS AND DWELLINGS

publicly funded development usually for low-income families

housing project, housing development, projects

walled or fenced-in area of buildings

compound, enclave

group of similar or interrelated buildings

colony, complex, installation, facility, base

often rural settlement where residents have communal responsibilities

commune

collective farm in modern-day Israel

kibbutz

semi-communal settlement combining private housing and shared facilities

cohousing

temporary settlement for a particular group

camp, encampment

area of land apportioned or divided into lots for real estate development

subdivision

usually affluent, restricted residential complex with protected access by private security personnel and a gatehouse or barrier

gated community

area with impoverished residents and crudely built houses

shantytown, favela

ARCHITECTURAL STYLES

Greek Revival

Commonly classical-temple-like rectangular blocks with a full-width front or entry portico with rounded or square columns and a flat or low roof above a wide band of trim. Usually no arches, no roof balustrade, no dormers, and no wings or projections on the building. Front door usually surrounded by narrow sidelights. Windows are small and inconspicuous.

Gothic Revival

Church-like steeply pitched roofs and cross gables, pointed (Gothic) arches, and gables with decorative vergeboards. Sometimes flat roofs with castle-like parapets and usually a one-story full-width or entry porch. Structure basically of one color.

Romanesque Revival

This pre-Gothic style, based on medieval and Roman architecture, is characterized by thick walls and a generally massive look, simple and symmetrical floor plan, and above all the repetition of semicircular or rounded arches over doors and windows. Many examples are chiefly of brick.

High Victorian Gothic

An eclectic variation of Gothic Revival, differing in being of many colors (polychrome), having details that are heavy rather than delicate or fragile in appearance, and having many overhanging or "top-heavy" gables and towers.

Queen Anne

An asymmetrical hodgepodge style of house, usually with a preeminent front-facing gable, a steeply pitched but irregular roof with numerous gables or turrets, any kind of window except a pointed-arch one, and a porch that extends to at least one side wall. Upper stories commonly project over the lower ones.

Italian Villa

An asymmetrical dwelling, and a square or octagonal, off-center or corner tower is typical, as are eaves projecting considerably, roofs that are flat or not steep, a veranda, and windows grouped in twos or threes.

Second Empire

A high mansard (double-sloped on all sides) roof is the giveaway, as are varied dormer windows, chimneys, and ornamental brackets beneath the eaves. Sometimes there is a central cupola or off-center tower.

Colonial Revival

There are many subtypes, and roofs vary, but common to most examples is a prominent, pedimented front porch and door with columns or pilasters and a fanlight or sidelights. The double-hung windows have many panes. Most but by no means all houses have symmetrical facades.

Regency

A simple, informal variety of Colonial Revival, typically a symmetrical, white-painted-brick, two- or three-story house with a hip roof, double-hung windows (and shutters of the same size), and a chimney on one side; lacks the classical lines of the Georgian style.

Federal (Adam)

A semicircular fanlight over the front door and windows with small panes are characteristic. Decorative moldings usually highlight the cornice. The house is most commonly a simple box, but it may also have curved or polygonal projections at the side or rear.

Saltbox Colonial

A simple shingle or clapboard rectangular house with a steep, lean-to-like roof (showing no windows) extending far down its rear, and with a large central chimney. The double-hung windows are small-paned.

Dutch Colonial

A one-story (or, occasionally, one-and-a-half-story) dwelling with a side-gabled or side-gambreled roof that does not overhang far at the sides and small-paned double-hung windows. The entrance door is usually a two-halved Dutch door unless replaced by a conventional door, and often with an unsupported hood or roof over the entrance door.

Tudor

Usually a fortress-like stone-and-brick house with semi-hexagonal bays and turrets, high chimneys, tall leaded-glass casement windows (with stone mullions), and the well-known decorative half-timbering.

Spanish Colonial

Stucco-protected adobe brick or rubble stone is the distinctive material, and the flat or low-pitched red-tile roof is also distinctive. Small window openings have or originally had grilles and inside shutters. One or two stories. Elaborate ornamentation is sometimes found around openings, and a two-story building may have a pergola.

Mission

A stucco style, lacking the sculptural ornamentation of the Spanish Colonial, with balconies, towers or turrets, and tiled roofs being common. Eaves have a wide overhang, and square piers support porch roofs.

American Craftsman

Varied style of architecture, interior design, furniture, and so on (a British-inspired reaction against the dehumanizing structures of the Industrial Revolution and the opulent aesthetic of the Victorian Age), developed at the end of the nineteenth century and popular into the 1930s, created to serve and ennoble the American middle class with family-oriented structures—notably affordable bungalows—evincing simplicity of form, use of local materials, and palpably visible craftsmanship and decorative elements of woodwork as well as stained glass. Typified by an open floor plan, low-pitched roofs, prominently overhanging eaves, extensive porches, exposed beams and rafters, dormer windows, and exterior stone chimneys.

Prairie
Two-story dwellings with low, hipped roofs, widely overhanging eaves, one-story porches or wings, and no ornamentation—the emphasis or feeling being distinctly horizontal. The porch supports are often massive, and ribbon windows with dark-wood stripping are common.

Stick (Carpenter Gothic)
Accenting the vertical, these buildings have a steep gabled roof, large verandas, and boldly projecting eaves. The main and other gables often have near the top an ornamental truss. Other characteristics are vertical, horizontal, or diagonal stick-work (boards) overlaid on the wall surface, to suggest exposed structural framing, and gingerbread trim.

New England Farm House
A simple box-shaped house of (usually) white clapboard, with a steep-pitched roof and central chimney.

Cape Cod
A simple rectangular, one-and-one-half-story house of clapboard, shingles, brick, or other material, with a low central chimney and a steep, shingled roof.

Beaux-Arts

Double or coupled columns are the telltale feature of these imposing symmetrical buildings, which often have monumental (impressive) steps; wall surfaces with pilasters, columns, or decorative features; and sometimes sculpted classical figures at the top of the edifice.

Georgian Revival

Most commonly a boxlike house of one or two stories whose doors, windows, and chimney or chimneys are strictly symmetrical. The roof may have a centered gable or side gables or be either hipped or gambrel, but the cornice usually has a decorative molding of toothlike dentils. Usually a paneled front door framed by pilasters and an entablature. The double-hung windows usually have small panes and are always symmetrically positioned, never paired.

Shingle

The ground stories are sometimes of stones, but the upper stories are always clad in shingles. Roofs are often of the gambrel type with moderate steepness ending in a broad gable, and there are generally several chimneys, extensive porches, and multilevel eaves. The windows have small panes.

Modernistic

Sleekly asymmetrical. In the Art Moderne style, wall surfaces (usually of stucco) are smooth, and there is a generally horizontal emphasis accented by lines or grooves in the walls and horizontal balustrades. In the earlier and rarer Art Deco style, on the smooth stucco wall surfaces there are zigzag and other geometric designs and, above the roof line, tower-like projections.

International Style

Asymmetrical but unlike parts are carefully balanced. There is absolutely no ornamentation around walls or windows, with surfaces smooth and uniform and roofs flat. The windows, of the metal casement type, are flush or blended into the walls and sometimes "turn the corner." Balconies and other projections are often cantilever supported.

Postmodern Style

An eclectic, late-twentieth-century reaction to the functional severity of modern (or International Style) architecture, an embracing of invention or fantasy, complexity, use of traditional materials, and allusions to or elements of previous historical styles and forms.

COMMON ARCHITECTURAL MODIFIERS

arranged or proportioned equivalently from the center
symmetrical

not symmetrical
asymmetrical, irregular

having a middle or central emphasis
centralized

configured like rays or spokes from a center
radial

standing alone or unsupported
freestanding

impressively broad and sizable
expansive, sweeping

very small
matchbox

irregular in layout or spread
rambling

thrust forward
projecting

constructed lower than surrounding floor levels
sunken

set back
recessed

being of the usual or typical style
vernacular

serving a single purpose without elaboration
functional, utilitarian

stately and sober in effect
formal

suggestive of a past style or nostalgically old-fashioned
retro

showing or using different elements or styles
eclectic

unoriginal, typical, or too much like others
cookie-cutter

imposingly massive or grandiose
monumental, grand, stately

suggestive of ancient Greece or Rome
classical, neoclassical

in three parts or divisions
tripartite

in four parts or divisions
quadripartite

in six parts or divisions
sexpartite

impressively bulky or dense in construction

massive

lengthened or notably long

elongated

curved or opening outward

flared

curved in a semicircular way

arched

arched and rounded

domed

stressing line or elongated contour

streamlined, sleek

relatively low or close to the ground

low slung

having different horizontal levels

terraced

paved with flagstones

flagged

seemingly shortened or cut off (at the top or an end)

truncated, stunted

relatively small and square

boxlike, boxy

extending around a corner or corners

wraparound

showing decorative features

ornamental, embellished

showing elaborately fanciful or ornate but superfluous ornamentation

gingerbread, wedding-cake

bearing shapes or decoration representing leaves

foliated

checkered or mosaic-like

tessellated

having a netlike pattern

reticulated

having sunken (usually) square or octagonal panels (lacunars or lacunaria) in the ceiling

coffered, lacunar

showing segments (as of a circle) as constructional pieces

segmental

having columns

columniated

having columnar grooves

fluted

without columns

astylar

having a colonnade

colonnaded

having a colonnade on all sides

peripteral, peristylar

having or painted in several colors

polychrome, multicolor

having stone rough-surfaced masonry whose edges or joints are accentuated (by beveling or rebating the blocks)

rusticated

consisting of or framed by exposed wooden beams

timbered

having a wall surface of wooden beams with masonry between them

half-timbered

sloping backward vertically or upward (as a wall)

battered

built or supported with horizontal beams
trabeated

projecting horizontally beyond its stabilizing or anchoring support
cantilevered

left visible although a supporting feature
exposed

arched or hollowed (as a ceiling)
vaulted

having a vaulted ceiling like a tunnel or half-cylinder
barrel-vaulted

having a ceiling of intersecting vaults
groin-vaulted

in disrepair, crumbling, or abandoned
dilapidated, ramshackle, rickety, tumbledown, disused, run down, derelict, squalid

painted as an architectural likeness so as to give the illusion of being real
trompe l'oeil

molding, surmounted by the lower half of the facade, which is in turn composed of three rows of mask panels running across the front of the building. Above an elaborate medial molding there are again three rows of mask panels, the topmost being surmounted by a terminal molding.

—Sylvanus G. Morley and George W. Brainerd, *The Ancient Maya*

When I'm walking its stone-cobbled streets, catching glimpses here and there of the bordering Tejo River, or taking in, from a vista on one of the city's hills, the glorious staggered topography of the white buildings and their salmon-colored tile roofs, I feel that I'm also traveling some interior landscape, that those streets are leading to a place inside myself I haven't yet located.

—Philip Graham, *The Moon, Come to Earth: Dispatches from Lisbon*

The house he lived in was a nondescript affair called the San Bernardino Arms. It was an oblong three stories high, the back and sides of which were of plain, unpainted stucco, broken by even rows of unadorned windows. The facade was the color of diluted mustard and its windows, all double, were framed by pink Moorish columns which supported turnip-shaped lintels.

—Nathanael West, *The Day of the Locust*

In a rush, a *high*, the bus breaks out after three minutes into the esplanade des Invalides, the huge, flat, officially forbidden lawn—though, on a Wednesday afternoon, I once did see two brave and determined Americans playing Frisbee there (you could tell they were Americans because they looked thirty and were dressed like six-year-olds). The golden covered dome of the church stands straight up behind, not looming but preening, and the Invalides itself sits below, an old military hospital with the two horses incised on its front, combining splendor with the old barrackslike solidity, the bureaucratic confidence, of the architecture of the *grand siècle*.

—ADAM GOPNIK, *Paris to the Moon*

Yes, there it was, the Manderley I had expected, the Manderley of my picture post-card long ago. A thing of grace and beauty, exquisite and faultless, lovelier even than I had ever dreamed, built in its hollow of smooth grass-land and mossy lawns, the terraces sloping to the gardens, and the gardens to the sea.

—DAPHNE DU MAURIER, *Rebecca*

There was the road below the window, with its blueberry-blue tarmac, and, nearer in, a shiny black hump that was part of the roof of our car, and the single silver birch across the way, slim and shivery as a naked girl, and beyond all that the bay, pinched between the finger and thumb of its two piers, the north one and the south, and then the distant, paler azure of the sea, that at the invisible horizon became imperceptibly sky.

—JOHN BANVILLE, *Ancient Light*

The sweet old farmhouse burrowed into the upward slope of the land so deeply that you could enter either its bottom or middle floor at ground level. Its window trim was delicate and the lights in its sash were a bubbly amethyst.

—ERIC HODGINS, *Mr. Blandings Builds His Dream House*

The detached houses were stuccoed and washed in shades of yellow, salmon, and blue. Some still had their pointed fifties roofs with decorative beams in the shape of a half sun; others had slate-clad loft extensions; one had been completely rebuilt in the style of a Swiss chalet.

—RACHEL JOYCE, *The Unlikely Pilgrimage of Harold Fry*

Yetta Zimmerman's house may have been the most open-heartedly monochromatic structure in Brooklyn, if not in all of New York. A large rambling wood and stucco house of the nondescript variety erected, I should imagine, sometime before or just after the First World War, it would have faded into the homely homogeneity of other large nondescript dwellings that bordered on Prospect Park had it not been for its striking—its overwhelming—pinkness. From its second-floor dormers and cupolas to the frames of its basement-level windows the house was unrelievedly pink.

—WILLIAM STYRON, *Sophie's Choice*

As if purposely living the cliché of a New York writer, I rented a cramped one-room studio, where I slept on a pullout sofa. The apartment, eerily quiet, overlooked the courtyard of several tenements, and I often awoke not to police sirens and grumbling garbage trucks but to the sound of a neighbor playing the accordion on his balcony. —SUSANNAH CAHALAN, *Brain on Fire: My Month of Madness*

Above the treetops, the structure raised, clear against the sky's hot haze, a small dome. The dome was surmounted by a pillared cupola in whose round base four faces of the court-house clock were set. Crowning the cupola, stiffly poised on the summit, stood a bronze effigy—Justice. The copper carbonates of time had turned this effigy greenish-blue. The epicene figure's verdigrised hands held the verdigrised sword and balance.

—JAMES GOULD COZZENS, *By Love Possessed*

But it will all be worth it, to get our house. It sounds, from Beth's description, as though it has everything that I look for in a house: (1) a basketball hoop and (2) a fiberglass backboard. I understand it also has rooms.

—DAVE BARRY, "The House of the Seven Figures," *Dave Barry's Greatest Hits*

We found ourselves in a vast patio or court, one hundred and fifty feet in length, and upwards of eighty feet in breadth, paved with white marble, and decorated at each end with light Moorish peristyles, one of which supported an elegant gallery of fretted architecture. Along the mouldings of the cornices and on various parts of the walls were escutcheons and ciphers, and cufic and Arabic characters in high relief, repeating the pious mottoes of the Moslem monarchs, the builders of the Alhambra, or extolling their grandeur and munificence.

—WASHINGTON IRVING, "The Alhambra," *Washington Irving: Bracebridge Hall, Tales of a Traveller, The Alhambra*

It had been handsome once, beneath the streaks of wiring and soot. I could even make out limestone and ironwork and some fancy nymphs. The balconies, it seems, had fallen off at about the time of Suez, followed shortly afterwards by the corbels and most of the shutters. The owner, Fumel, hardly seemed to notice.

—JOHN GIMLETTE, *Panther Soup: Travels Through Europe in War and Peace*

The private houses of long-dead bankers or shipowners, Gothic, Neo-classic or defiantly eclectic, stand on advantageous corners in glorious grandiloquence. Exercises in Art Nouveau, called here the Liberty Style, display gigantic bare-busted ladies guarding doorways or precariously ornamenting ledges. What's this, now? A Roman amphitheatre. Who's that? Verdi, composing, on a plinth in a garden. Which way are we going? Search me.

—JAN MORRIS, *Trieste and the Meaning of Nowhere*

Wigbaldy had begun by erecting single houses, mostly bungalows, on vacant street lots. Now he had acquired backing for a twenty-acre development of thirty or so medium-priced "homes" to be disposed with conscious rusticity among winding roads and named Green Knoll—though no relief of the flat terrain was apparent to justify this designation. The pilot house was up by early spring and was instantly furnished for display as a Model Home and thrown open for public inspection one Saturday morning. —PETER DE VRIES, *The Blood of the Lamb*

The canopies over the many gas-pump islands were sleek stainless-steel ovals trimmed with neon tubing that, at night, would lend them a flying-saucer feel, and the pumps looked like platoons of robots at parade rest. The facade of the huge building was clad in stainless steel—probably a convincing plastic imitation of stainless—with the lines and the details of a classic Art Deco diner, but that didn't give it the appeal its architect most likely intended; because of its size, the place had an ominous military quality, as if it must be the headquarters of the extraterrestrial overlord of an invading force from another planet.

—DEAN KOONTZ, *Deeply Odd (Odd Thomas)*

The sitting-room, beside it, was slightly larger, and they both commanded a row of tenements no less degenerate than Ransom's own habitation—houses built forty years before, and already sere and superannuated. These were also painted red, and the bricks were accentuated by a white line; they were garnished, on the first floor, with balconies covered with small tin roofs, striped in different colours, and with an elaborate iron lattice-work, which gave them a repressive, cage-like appearance, and caused them slightly to resemble the little boxes for peeping unseen into the street, which are a feature of oriental towns.

—Henry James, *The Bostonians*

Whenever you turned at a road sign that had "Farm" in the title, you weren't sure what you might find—a house that looked like a function center or a small castle or a Mediterranean villa—but you knew you wouldn't find a farm.

—Sarah Payne Stuart, "Pilgrim's Progress," *The New Yorker*, July 30, 2012

The Tassel House is not imposing (the facade measures 25 feet), but its design is characterized by a rhythmic fluidity which has a majesty of its own. The consoles flanking the entrance way support a corbeled loggia which links the ground and parlor floors. The completely glazed, curved bay window is supported by visible iron framework. The only ornamentation is the wrought-iron balustrade of the bay window.

—Bernard Champigneulle, *Art Nouveau*

By way of recreation at the end of the day, he is looking into Katherine's land holdings and judging what he can redistribute. Sir Nicholas Carew, who does not like him and does not like Anne, is amazed to receive from him a package of grants, including two fat Surrey manors to adjoin his existing holdings in the county.

—Hilary Mantel, *Wolf Hall*

The entrance to this ancient place of devotion was under a very low round arch, ornamented by several courses of that zig-zag moulding, resembling sharks' teeth, which appears so often in the more ancient Saxon architecture.

—Sir Walter Scott, *Ivanhoe*

Crispin's magnetic personality and Joely's natural charm attracted other political drifters, and soon they had become a commune of twenty-five (plus ten cats, fourteen dogs, a garden full of wild rabbits, a sheep, two pigs, and a family of foxes) living and working from a Brixton bedsit that backed on to a large expanse of unused allotment. —Zadie Smith, *White Teeth*

Yet we knew another New Orleans existed. We saw that when we piled into my mother's car and rode past the red brick projects scattered through New Orleans, two-story buildings with sagging iron balconies, massive old trees standing like sentinels at each side of the buildings, women gesticulating and scratching their heads, small dark children playing angrily, happily, sulking on the broken sidewalks. I eyed the young men through the car window. Men in sagging pants with their heads bent together, murmuring, ducking into corner stores that sold POBOYS SHRIMP OYSTER. I wondered what the men were talking about. I wondered who they were. I wondered what their lives were like. I wondered if they were murderers. —Jesmyn Ward, *Men We Reaped: A Memoir*

The lodge, unlike the castle, had been built in an age in which symmetry was regarded as the only means to elegance, and it consisted of four diminutive rooms, each in a kind of pygmy Gothic, disposed two on one and two on the other side of the drive. —MICHAEL INNES, *Lord Mullion's Secret*

Brunelleschi's magnificent cupola on the Duomo, the city's vast cathedral—the first large dome constructed since Roman antiquity and to this day the principal feature of the city's skyline—did not yet exist, nor did his elegantly arched loggia of the Foundling Hospital or his other projects carefully constructed on principles derived from antiquity. The cathedral's baptistery lacked the famous classicizing doors designed by Ghiberti, and the Church of S. Maria Novella was without Leon Battista Alberti's harmonious, gracefully symmetrical facade. The architect Michelozzi had not designed the beautiful, austere buildings for the Convent of San Marco. The wealthiest families of the city—the Medici, the Pitti, the Rucelli—had not yet built their grand palaces, whose columns, arches, and carved capitals conspicuously emphasize classical order and proportion.

—STEPHEN GREENBLATT, *The Swerve: How the World Became Modern*

Stretching out of sight on either side of the road were identical semidetached houses, each with a path running down the side. They might, she thought, be architecturally undistinguished, but at least they were on a human scale. The gates and railings had been removed and the front gardens were bounded with low brick walls. The front bay windows were square and turreted, a long vista of ramparted respectability. —P. D. JAMES, *Innocent Blood*

It is an impressive house—not a true mansion, like the one Isaac de Pinto built for himself across the street, but even so it is a stately place. The three-story facade is made of brick with inlaid stone. It is quite wide, thirty-two feet across. Its tall front windows are topped by half-moon arcs of brick and stone. Above the roofline rise two thin dormer windows, each with a beam and pulley-hook sticking straight out into the street. The only way to move things to the upper floors of these narrow Dutch houses is to hoist them up and through the windows. In the center above the uppermost row of windows, crowning it all, is a decorative stone relief. —STEVEN NADLER, *Rembrandt's Jews*

The house itself looked, more than anything else, like an English country house. Family descended from the Normans. There was an enormous terrace skirting the tall square fieldstone house with a mansard roof. At each corner there were small round towers with tall narrow windows in them. —ROBERT B. PARKER, *A Catskill Eagle*

Spanish Harlem was worthless property in the seventies and early eighties. Many property owners burned their own buildings down and handed the new immigrants a neighborhood filled with hollow walls and vacant lots. Urban Swiss cheese. The city would then place many of us in the projects, creating Latino reservations.

—ERNESTO QUIÑONEZ, *Chango's Fire*

I found the place within a couple of minutes: a big, old, twenties Victorian with a lot of gingerbread trim on the front porch and windows that had leaded-glass borders.

—BILL PRONZINI, *Bindlestiff*

As the cave became important, the village built a portico to define the entrance, and over the next three centuries the cave was expanded by sacred spaces of advancing size, chronologically growing through several styles into a hexagonal dome terminating in an unusual nineteenth-century forecourt portico.

—HAL BOX, *Think Like an Architect*

Compared to the Whiting mansion in town, the house Charles Beaumont Whiting built a decade after his return to Maine was modest. By every other standard of Empire Falls, where most single-family homes cost well under seventy-five thousand dollars, his was palatial, with five bedrooms, five full baths, and a detached artist's studio. C. B. Whiting had spent several formative years in old Mexico, and the house he built, appearances be damned, was a mission-style hacienda. He even had the bricks specially textured and painted tan to resemble adobe. A damn-fool house to build in central Maine, people said, though they didn't say it to him. —RICHARD RUSSO, *Empire Falls*

It was the damndest-looking house I ever saw. It was a square gray box three stories high, with a mansard roof, steeply sloped and broken by twenty or thirty double dormer windows with a lot of wedding cake decoration around them and between them. The entrance had double stone pillars on each side but the cream of the joint was an outside spiral staircase with a stone railing, topped by a tower room from which there must have been a view the whole length of the lake.

—RAYMOND CHANDLER, *The Long Goodbye*

When Michael and Christine bought the house on Hazelhurst Drive, in 1985, northwest Austin had not yet been bisected by toll roads or swallowed up by miles of unbroken suburban sprawl. The real estate busts had brought construction to a standstill, and the half-built subdivision where they lived, east of Lake Travis, was a patchwork of new homes and uncleared, densely wooded lots.

—PAMELA COLLOFF, "The Innocent Man, Part One," *Texas Monthly*, November 2012

Because it was a remnant, soon to be swept away, it was greatly favored by railway buffs. Their interest always seemed to me worse than indecent and their joy-riding a mild form of necrophilia. They were on board getting their last looks at the old stations, photographing the fluting and floriation, the pediments and bargeboards and pilasters, the valencing on the wooden awnings, the strapwork, and—in architecture every brick has a different name—the quoins.

—PAUL THEROUX, *The Kingdom by the Sea: A Journey Around the Coast of Great Britain*

The apartments which Alexander has taken for himself are made up of a string of first- and second-floor chambers at the corner of the existing palace, alongside a blunt, workmanlike new tower, mostly built, save for its crenellated battlements. When finished, there will be both intimate and public spaces.

—SARAH DUNANT, *Blood and Beauty: The Borgias*

Everything about the front was irregular, but with an irregularity unfamiliar to him. The shuttered windows were very tall and narrow, and narrow too the balconies, which projected at odd angles, supported by ornate wooden brackets. One corner of the house rose into a tower with a high shingled roof, and arched windows which seemed to simulate the openings in a belfry. A sort of sloping roof over the front door also rested on elaborately ornamented brackets, and on each side of the steps was a large urn of fluted iron painted to imitate stone, in which some half-dead geraniums languished.

—EDITH WHARTON, *Hudson River Bracketed*

I can still see the hole like it was yesterday, and it was. Life is a perpetual yesterday for us. It was the size of a small room, the mud room in our house, say, where we kept our boots and slickers and where Mom had managed to fit a washer and dryer, one on top of the other.

—ALICE SEBOLD, *The Lovely Bones*

The Radley Place jutted into a sharp curve beyond our house. Walking south, one faced its porch; the sidewalk turned and ran beside the lot. The house was low, was once white with a deep front porch and green shutters, but had long ago darkened to the color of the slate-gray yard around it. Rain-rotted shingles drooped over the eaves of the veranda; oak trees kept the sun away.

—Harper Lee, *To Kill a Mockingbird*

Fashionable districts developed along High and State Streets, and a new Capitol, nearly as big as the United States Capitol, opened its doors in January 1857. Built in Greek Revival style, with tall Doric columns defining each of the entrances and a large cupola on top, the magnificent structure, which housed the governor's office as well as the legislative chambers, was proclaimed to be "the greatest State capitol building" in the country.

—Doris Kearns Goodwin, *Team of Rivals: The Political Genius of Abraham Lincoln*

There was a drive, always covered with gravel, that swept around in a beautiful curve and brought you up under a big porte-cochere, which reminded you of horses with fly-nets, and shiny and black closed carriages; and the house, which was yellow and covered with shingles that overlapped with rounded ends like scales, was an impressive though rather formless mass of cupolas with foolscap tops, dormers with diamond panes, balconies with little white railings and porches with Ionic columns, all pointing in different directions.

—Edmund Wilson, *Memoirs of Hecate County*

Duke reached beneath his seat and nipped from the flask. He followed the canal, the engine humming in his ears. The shantytown spread across an acre of raw black earth along the water's banks. He made his way down toward the sheet-iron houses and canvas canopies. The fire pits were still smoldering from the night before, and all through the camp, he could see braids of smoke washing skyward. —BILL CHENG, *Southern Cross the Dog*

Ocean Street is five minutes from the motel, an extension of Sea Street, profuse with weathered shingles and blue shutters. Shepard's house was no exception. A big Colonial with white cedar shingles weathered silver, and blue shutters at all the windows. It was on a slight rise of ground on the ocean side of Ocean Street.

—ROBERT B. PARKER, *Promised Land*

Drewsboro owed something to the stylish houses my mother had seen in America. There were ornamental piers on the gateway, bay windows and a tiled porch that was called a vestibule opening into a tiled hallway. No other house around there had bay windows or a vestibule. The lawn had many trees, not planted in succession as in a demesne, but each tree in its own massive empire, leaves stirring and drowsing in summer and in winter, the boughs groaning and creaking, as if they were about to expire. —EDNA O'BRIEN, *Country Girl: A Memoir*

The university capped a then bleak hill, its buildings evoking the cultural aspirations of a faraway Europe of a distant past. The centerpiece was the baroque Hall of Languages, built of stones of two colors and partly covered with ivy. Behind it, a bit to the west, stood the gymnasium, as Gothic as a temple of sweat could hope to be, of dark brick, with high windows. Also to the west was the university library, later to become the administration building. Farther still to the west and south, on another rise overlooking the city, was the dark Gothic cathedral-like spire of Crouse College, in which Fine Arts were housed. Wooden walkways, some of them dilapidated, ran between these buildings.

—John Hersey, *The Call: An American Missionary in China*

My father was all but undone by my mother's death. In the evening after supper he walked the floor and I walked with him, with my arm around his waist. I was ten years old. He would walk from the living room into the front hall, then, turning, past the grandfather's clock and on into the library, and from the library into the living room. Or he would walk from the library into the dining room and then into the living room by another doorway, and back to the front hall. Because he didn't say anything, I didn't either. I only tried to sense, as he was about to turn, which room he was going to next so we wouldn't bump into each other.

—William Maxwell, *So Long, See You Tomorrow*

It sat on a shelf between our lane and the creek, a little higher than the rest of the bottomland. Its board-and-batten sides and its shake roof were weathered silvery as an old rock. To me it has an underwater look—that barnacled silveriness, the way three big live oaks twisted like seaweed above the roof, the still, stained, sunken light.

—Wallace Stegner, *All the Little Live Things*

But constructing a riprap river wall and leveling the flinty rock surface to lay gradeless track was an engineering challenge, not an operating one, and within two years the trains were running north past Peekskill from a terminal at West 32nd Street and Ninth Avenue (a route that would extend downtown to Chambers Street on Ninth Avenue, paralleling in some places the former elevated freight tracks that were transformed into what is now the High Line park).

—Sam Roberts, *Grand Central: How a Train Station Transformed America*

At the far end of a scrubby courtyard was a sooty brick building, the shape of Monticello on the back of the nickel, a domed roof but with one difference: this one had a chimney at the rear belching greasy smoke. It was too squat, too plain, too gloomy for a church.

—Paul Theroux, "A Real Russian Ikon," *Commentary*, December 1969

The outlines of the house of Dr. Trescott had faded quietly into the evening, hiding a shape such as we call Queen Anne against the pall of the blackened sky. The neighborhood was at this time so quiet, and seemed so devoid of obstructions, that Hannigan's dog thought it a good opportunity to prowl in forbidden precincts, and so came and pawed Trescott's lawn, growling, and considering himself a formidable beast. Later, Peter Washington strolled past the house and whistled, but there was no dim light shining from Henry's loft, and presently Peter went his way.

—Stephen Crane, "The Monster," *The Monster and Other Stories*

It was a Gothic Revival eyesore of decaying brick, flaking paint, and narrow windows, with spiky gables that gave it a menacing upward thrust—a vulgar aberration on a street lined with square-built structures that were fully restored. In place of the front porch there was a ladder to be climbed, and in the entrance hall a massive chandelier lay on its side. The front room, a vaultlike space with an implausibly high ceiling, featured heaps of rubble and dangling wires. —A. S. A. Harrison, *The Silent Wife*

The houses on either side were high and large, but very old; and tenanted by people of the poorest class: as their neglected appearance would have sufficiently denoted, without the concurrent testimony afforded by the squalid looks of the few men and women who, with folded arms and bodies half doubled, occasionally skulked along. A great many of the tenements had shop-fronts; but these were fast closed and mouldering away: only the upper rooms being inhabited. Some houses which had become insecure from age and decay, were prevented from falling into the street, by huge beams of wood reared against the walls, and firmly planted in the road; but even these crazy dens seemed to have been selected as the nightly haunts of some houseless wretches; for many of the rough boards, which supplied the place of door and window, were wrenched from their positions, to afford an aperture wide enough for the passage of a human body.

—Charles Dickens, *Oliver Twist*

A badge of grass, a green brooch pinned at the collarbone of a mountain to a vast black cloak of fir trees. At the center of the clearing, a handful of buildings clad in brown shakes radiate from a circular fountain, linked by paths and separated by quilted patches of lawn and gravel.

—Michael Chabon, *The Yiddish Policemen's Union*

She was right about the guest house: it wasn't to everyone's taste. It was stubby and ill-proportioned, made of stucco in a pale shade of pinkish-gray, with the wooden trim and shutters at its windows painted lavender. Upstairs, at one end of it, French doors led out onto an abbreviated balcony that was overgrown with leafy vines, and from the balcony a frivolous vine-entangled spiral staircase descended to a flagstone terrace at what proved to be the front door. If you stepped back on the grass to take it all in with a single searching glance, the house had a lopsided, crudely fanciful look, like something drawn by a child with an uncertain sense of the way a house ought to be. —Richard Yates, *Young Hearts Crying*

She was in the inner yard now, moving as if in a trance toward the door, which even from this distance she could see had been sloppily cut and hung so that there was a wide gap running across the doorstep like a black horizontal scar. The windowsills were blistered, the panes gone milky with abrasion. A jagged line of dark nailheads ran the length of the clapboard, climbing crazily to the eaves and back down again as if they'd been blown there on the wind, the boards themselves so indifferently whitewashed they gave up the raised grain of the cheap sea-run pine in clotted skeins and whorls that looked like miniature faces staring out at her—or no, leering at her.

—T. C. Boyle, *San Miguel*

MacGregor rebuilt the singer's house more than a hundred years ago on the decayed princely foundations, with money got, it was rumoured, from bribes. Foursquare, there is a flagged inner courtyard; on the outer aspect, verandahs with rounded arches shading the upper as well as the ground floor rooms. The brickwork is stuccoed and painted cream that always dries yellow. Stone steps lead from the gravel driveway to the front entrance.

—Paul Scott, *The Jewel in the Crown*

I came to on the loggia—the only question was whose loggia? There was the Cavanaghs' loggia, designed by that famous and locally celebrated architect whom I once met. The name is gone. The Cavanaghs' loggia faced the backyard, and they had a splendid garden with unusual varieties of rosebushes.

—Rick Moody, "The Omega Force," *Right Livelihood: Three Novellas*

Then suddenly the car plunged into a tunnel and emerged into another world, a vast, untidy suburban world of filling stations and billboards, of low houses in gardens, of vacant lots and waste paper, of occasional shops and office buildings and churches—primitive Methodist churches built, surprisingly enough in the style of the Cartuja at Granada, Catholic churches like Canterbury Cathedral, synagogues disguised as Hagia Sophia, Christian Science churches with pillars and pediments, like banks.

—Aldous Huxley, *After Many a Summer Dies the Swan*

Seventy-seventh Street was very wide at the point. On one side was the museum, a marvelous Romanesque Revival creation in an old reddish stone. It was set back in a little park with trees. Even on a cloudy day like this the young spring leaves seemed to glow. *Verdant* was the word that crossed his mind. On this side of the street, where he was walking, was a cliff of elegant apartment houses overlooking the museum. There were doormen. He got glimpses of marbled halls. And then he thought of the girl with the brown lipstick. . . .

—Tom Wolfe, *The Bonfire of the Vanities*

In the spring and summer, boxes of brilliant flowers and strange plants crowd almost every apartment window, some with leaves so large they look tropical. Clover, wood-sorrel, crab grass, and violets sprout from the sidewalk cracks that are off to the side, and there's always a sweet perfume that comes from either wisteria, pine, or honeysuckle. Steam rises from the manholes like water escaping from a pot. Branches from each side of the street reach across, forming awnings overhead whose leaves sound like hundreds of tiny drums whenever it rains. In the winter, holiday decorations pick up where nature leaves off and the color comes from tasteful wreaths hanging on the windows and doors, and garlands of pine and Christmas lights winding down the wrought iron gates, railings, and balustrades.

—Stacy Horn, *Imperfect Harmony: Finding Happiness Singing with Others*

The grassy track ran level, curved and dipped a little, emerged from the trees. The house, dazzlingly white where the afternoon sun touched it, stood with its shadowed back to me. It had been built on the seaward side of a small cottage that had evidently existed before it. It was square, with a flat roof and a colonnade of slender arches running round the south and east sides. Above the colonnade was a terrace. I could see the open french windows of a first-floor room giving access to it.

—John Fowles, *The Magus*

Rudyard was a small town like many others in the Middle West, its core a few dark buildings, still smudged with coal soot, and several tin hangars with corrugated plastic roofs that housed various farm services. At the outskirts, a kind of mini-suburbanization was under way, with strip malls and tract homes, the result of the economic security afforded by an unusual anchor industry—the prison.

When they turned a corner on a movie-set neighborhood of maple trees and small frame houses, the facility suddenly loomed at the end of the block, like a horror-flick monster jumping out of a closet, a half-mile continuum of randomly connected yellow-brick buildings, notable for the narrowness of the few windows. Those structures in turn surrounded an old stone edifice stout enough to have survived the Middle Ages.

—SCOTT TUROW, *Reversible Errors*

The night sky was clear. The air was faintly scented with the aroma of flowers which grew in such profusion inside the walled gardens that belonged to the rich families in our neighborhood. Often I had climbed those walls and peered through the black iron grillework into the great rooms of their houses or looked down into the gardens where, among the beds of flowers, a stone hut had been piled up to shelter the house slaves.

—PAULA FOX, *The Slave Dancer*

A square smug brown house, rather damp. A narrow concrete walk up to it. Sickly yellow leaves in a window with dried wings of box-elder seeds and snags of wool from the cottonwoods. A screened porch with pillars of thin painted pine surmounted by scrolls and brackets and bumps of jigsawed wood. No shrubbery to shut off the public gaze. A lugubrious bay-window to the right of the porch.

—SINCLAIR LEWIS, *Main Street*

I like my bedroom, too. I've had a lot of bedrooms in my life—twenty-seven, if you count every room change at boarding school and college—but never one quite like this. High ceilings, windows looking out over the front stoop, wall-to-wall mirrored closets. Okay, the mirrors are yellowed and the wallpaper is a faded rosebud print that looks like something out of an old movie. It just *feels* right. Like this is how it's supposed to look.

—Gemma Burgess, *Brooklyn Girls*

The church was a Gothic monument of shingles painted pigeon blue. It had stout wooden buttresses supporting nothing. It had stained-glass windows with heavy traceries of imitation stone. It opened the way into long streets edged by tight, exhibitionist lawns. Behind the lawns stood wooden piles tortured out of all shape; twisted into gables, turrets, dormers; bulging with porches; crushed under huge, sloping roofs. —Ayn Rand, *The Fountainhead*

Beyond the security gate at the Johnson Space Center's 1960s-era campus here, inside a two-story glass and concrete building with winding corridors, there is a floating laboratory. —Danny Hakim, "Faster than the Speed of Light?" *New York Times*, July 22, 2013

The building was of gray, lichen-blotched stone, with a high central portion and two curving wings, like the claws of a crab, thrown out on each side. In one of these wings the windows were broken and blocked with wooden boards, while the roof was partly caved in, a picture of ruin. The central portion was in little better repair, but the right-hand block was comparatively modern, and the blinds in the windows, with the blue smoke curling up from the chimneys, showed that this was where the family resided. —Arthur Conan Doyle, "The Adventure of the Speckled Band," *The Extraordinary Cases of Sherlock Holmes*

Life radiated out from the club to the "cottages" on West and Eden Streets, large shapeless shingle structures, sometimes brightly painted, with well-mowed emerald lawns, to the cozy shops on Main Street with windows invitingly full of imported luxuries, to the woods and the long blue driveways of the more distant villas concealed by spruce and pine, yet all familiar to us, including stone castles, Italian palazzos, Georgian red brick villas, but still for the most part shingle habitations, with dark proliferating turrets and porches.

—LOUIS AUCHINCLOSS, *Honorable Men*

The Ansonia, the neighborhood's great landmark, was built by Stanford White. It looks like a baroque palace from Prague or Munich enlarged a hundred times, with towers, domes, huge swells and bubbles of metal gone green from exposure, iron fretwork and festoons. Black television antennae are densely planted on its round summits.

—SAUL BELLOW, *Seize the Day*

Now's the time to gaze across all those red-grooved roof-waves oceaning around, all the green-tarnished tower-islands rising above white facades which grin with windows and sink below us into not yet completely telephone-wired reefs; now's the time to enjoy Europe Central's café umbrellas like anemones, her old grime-darkened roofs like kelp, her hoofbeats clattering up and bellnotes rising, her shadows of people so far below in the narrow streets.

—WILLIAM T. VOLLMANN,
Europe Central

Behind the farm the stone mountains stood up against the sky. The farm buildings huddled like little clinging aphids on the mountain skirts, crouched low to the ground as though the wind might blow them into the sea. The little shack, the rattling, rotting barn were grey-bitten with sea salt, beaten by the damp wind until they had taken on the color of the granite hills.

—JOHN STEINBECK, "Flight," *The Long Valley*

All started well. The bus was old, with cracked armrests, and it smelled of urine, but was freshly swept, and I had an aisle seat with no one next to me. And the road, it turned out, had been paved in December, two lanes of smooth blacktop snaking up the Andes into a cold, largely treeless world of llamas and adobe houses with smoke pouring from chimneys in thatch roofs.

The clouds were ominous, though. And a couple of hours out, as we started descending the Andes' eastern flanks, everything changed: the pavement ended. Harsh white lightning ripped through the skies and torrential rains poured down. The bus filled; the air turned humid and thick.

—CARL HOFFMAN, *The Lunatic Express: Discovering the World . . . via Its Most Dangerous Buses, Trains, and Planes*

It was set on a little rise, a biggish box of a house, two-story, rectangular, gray, and unpainted, with a tin roof, unpainted too and giving off blazes under the sun for it was new and the rust hadn't bitten down into it yet, and a big chimney at each end.

—ROBERT PENN WARREN, *All the King's Men*

This last sign pointed toward a wide pair of doors at the end of the alley. It was all marvelously pompous and silly. And yet . . . as he walked along, Vendacious took a long look at the crenellations above him. Surely that was plaster over wood. But if it was real stone, then this was a fortified castle hidden right in the middle of East Home commercialism. —VERNOR VINGE, *The Children of the Sky (Zones of Thought)*

On the opposite side of the house, the living room fronts on a spectacular canyon view, breaking open with glass walls and a deep porch, recessed, however, to keep the taut wall line and provide shelter in any weather. Most striking of all is what has happened to the hipped roof, made unfamiliar by an oversized monitor skylight which creates a silhouette like a farmer's broad-brimmed hat.

—MARY MIX FOLEY, *The American House*

He loved letting himself in at the three-locked green front door, and locking it again behind him, and feeling the still security of the house as he looked into the red-walled dining room, or climbed the stairs to the double drawing room, and up again past the half-open doors of the white bedrooms. The first flight of stairs, fanning out into the hall, was made of stone; the upper flights had the confidential creak of oak. —ALAN HOLLINGHURST, *The Line of Beauty*

Composite ranches feature irregular perimeter outlines. Thus they are characterized by degrees of irregular mass-ing with L- and T-shapes the most prevalent forms. . . . Like other ranches, roofs are low-pitched except that multiple-gables, multiple-hip, and combined gable and hip roofs predominate.

—John A. Jakle, Robert W. Bastian, and Douglas K. Meyer, *Common Houses in America's Small Towns*

The suffused light I had detected seconds before goes out in a flicker, while a second, brighter alpenglow leaks through three sets of wooden shutters. There is no glass. I stare at a room unlike any I have seen. Thirty feet above the ground floor, mountain views all around. Crafted with fancy handiwork, Tibetan dragons, filigree, and crenellation. —Michael Tobias, *Voice of the Planet*

By the early fall, Deb had finally reached a fancy corbelled top of the chimney. And Eantha launched into Judith Jones' series of duck recipes. There were many steps, each one dependent on the before. First the chimney, then the roof, thought Eantha, rendering cracklings for the next night's cassoulet.

—Bailey White, "The Second Hand or the Roach," National Public Radio, November 22, 2012

The ceiling design is in large coffered bays corresponding to the buttresses, which are emphasized by the *pietra serena* pilasters resting on a string-course above the tops of the desks and supporting a narrow architrave below the ceiling. —Linda Murray, *Michelangelo*

Inside the carriage house, there was one cavernous room and a loft under thick cedar beams. Encompassed by slabs of hewn wood, the air was hushed. It held promise. One corner was rounded into a turret shape; the roof was a series of intersecting gambrels, one for the turret, one for the carriage room, one for the owl's nest that peeked up over the loft. Outside, the shingles were white on the siding, dove gray on the roof, weathered by decades of wind. —LOUISA HALL, *The Carriage House*

For just a moment I linger at the carriageway. The shroud, the pall, the unspeakable, clutching emptiness of it all. Then I walk quickly along the gravel path near the wall, past the arches and columns, the iron staircases from one quadrangle to the other. Everything is locked tight. Locked for the winter. I find the arcade leading to the dormitory. A sickish light spills down over the stairs from the grimy, frosted windows.

—HENRY MILLER, *Tropic of Cancer*

I have thirteen wives. We all live together in a sprawling Queen Anne house with half a dozen gables, two round towers, and a wraparound porch, not far from the center of town. Each of my wives has her own room, as I have mine, but we gather for dinner every evening in the high dining room, at the long table under the old chandelier with its pink glass shades. Later, in the front room, we play rummy or pinochle in small groups, or sit talking in faded armchairs or couches.

—STEVEN MILLHAUSER, "Thirteen Wives," *The New Yorker*, May 27, 2013

The flat roofs, *azoteas*, were protected by stone parapets, so that every house was a fortress. Sometimes these roofs resembled parterres of flowers, so thickly were they covered with them, but more frequently these were cultivated in broad terraced gardens, laid out between the edifices. Occasionally a great square or marketplace intervened, surrounded by its porticos of stone and stucco; or a pyramidal temple reared its colossal bulk, crowned with its tapering sanctuaries, and altars blazing with inextinguishable fires. The great street facing the southern causeway, unlike most others in the place, was wide, and extended some miles in nearly a straight line, as before noticed, through the centre of the city.

—William H. Prescott, *History of the Conquest of Mexico*

Number 5 is a low, two-story brick interruption after the wall with an airport orange wooden door and a bronze plaque the size of an Etch A Sketch that reads École Primaire. Primary school. But this can't be a school anymore, can it? Unless I've been sent to the wrong place? Two bow windows sit on either side of the door like eyes on a face, and the door itself is like a mouth that might try and eat you.

—Susan Conley, *Paris Was the Place*

He walked up toward the Kingsbrook bridge past the Georgian house that was now the Youth Employment Bureau, past the Queen Anne house that was now a solicitor's office, and entered a newly opened shop in a block with maisonettes above it. It was bright and clean, with a dazzling stock of pots and jars and bottles of scent.

—RUTH RENDELL, *From Doon with Death*

The houses that adjoined this row of shops were small terraced cottages with front doors that opened straight into the front rooms, and a bare yard of space between the windows and the pavement. Their own house, though not much bigger, was more modern and semi-detached, with a pebble-dash façade and some decorative woodwork which his father, like their neighbours, kept brightly painted in two colours, green and cream.

—DAVID LODGE, *Out of the Shelter*

Harry and Ron looked at each other, then leaving Wormtail's body on the floor behind them, ran up the stair and back into the shadowy passageway leading to the drawing room. Cautiously they crept along it until they reached the drawing room door, which was ajar.

—J. K. ROWLING, *Harry Potter and the Deathly Hallows*

Imagine to yourself, my dear Letty, a spacious garden, part laid out in delightful walks, bounded with high hedges and trees, and paved with gravel; part exhibiting a wonderful assemblage of the most picturesque and striking objects, pavilions, lodges, groves, grottoes, lawns, temples and cascades; porticoes, colonades [*sic*], and rotundos; adorned with pillars, statues, and painting. . . .

—TOBIAS SMOLLETT, *The Expedition of Humphry Clinker*

He'd grown up in an old house on San Francisco's Russian Hill, and spent a lot of time in the impressive old homes of Presidio Heights, and the suburbs of San Francisco, including Berkeley, where he'd gone to school, and Hillsborough, where his late grandfather's half-timbered mansion had been the holiday gathering place for many a year.

—ANNE RICE, *The Wolf Gift*

It is one of two evidently designed by the same architect who built some houses in a characteristic taste on Beacon Street opposite the Common. It has a wooden portico, with slender fluted columns, which have always been painted white, and which, with the delicate moldings of the cornice, form the sole and efficient decoration of the street front; nothing could be simpler, and nothing could be better.

—WILLIAM DEAN HOWELLS, *The Rise of Silas Lapham*

My grandfather told me these stories about himself while sitting on the roof of the storm cellar, a dank cell to which we often repaired at inconvenient times—both my mother and my grandmother were paranoid about tornadoes. Any dark cloud might send us scuttling downward, into a place that, as I discovered early, was not scorpion free.

Our ranch house, which my father and my grandfather built from plans purchased from Montgomery Ward—usually the supplier was just called Monkey Ward—was a simple shotgun house, three bedrooms and a bath on the south side, simple hall, kitchen, dining room, living room on the north side. We rarely used the living room, although my grandfather was laid out in it, once he died. It did have a fireplace, into which my grandfather, before his death, often spat copiously.

As a very small child I was awed by the amount of spit he could summon—I didn't realize that most of it was tobacco juice. —LARRY MCMURTRY, *Books: A Memoir*

The pretty Queen Anne house, with its pitted rosy-red bricks and its blunted grey stonework, stretched its bland length with a certain luxuriant confidence, surrendering itself to the garden whose proportions were perfectly attuned to its own. —IRIS MURDOCH, *An Unofficial Rose*

He went into the scullery at the back of the house. He dipped a tin bowl into the water barrel, washed his face and hands, and poured the water away in the shallow stone sink. The scullery had a copper with a fire grate underneath, but it was used only on bath night, which was Saturday. —KEN FOLLETT, *Fall of Giants*

It was long and low built, with a pillared veranda and balcony all the way round. The soft white bulk of it lay stretched upon the green garden like a sleeping beast.

—KATHERINE MANSFIELD,
"Prelude," *The Best Short Stories of Katherine Mansfield*

Then, having previously studied the map and committed the route to memory, he set off across the Pont au Double and entered the medieval maze of the Île de la Cité. After getting lost in the cul-de-sacs and the chapel closes, he found the other bank and threaded his way through the crowded streets to the east of the Louvre.

—Graham Robb,
Parisians: An Adventure History of Paris

Derricks swung steel girders into place 18 hours after they left the furnaces in Pittsburgh and just hours after they had been numbered for assembly in an empty lot in New Jersey. The building's skeleton marched upward at a rate of four and a half floors a week. In June, 290 bricklayers and 384 carriers left the ground, chasing the steelworkers into the sky as they ate into a lode of 10 million bricks. Following them, stoneworkers clad the building in a thin layer of Indiana limestone, 200,000 cubic feet in all. Onto this gray skin workers bolted 300 tons of polished chrome-nickel alloy fashioned into shining vertical spandrels. Red metal window frames were laid into 6,400 holes in the tower.

—Mitchell Pacelle, *Empire: A Tale of Obsession, Betrayal, and the Battle for an American Icon*

. . . I escaped to the open country and fearfully took refuge in a low hovel, quite bare, and making a wretched appearance after the palaces I had beheld in the village. This hovel, however, joined a cottage of a neat and pleasant appearance, but after my late dearly bought experience, I dared not enter it. —Mary Shelley, *Frankenstein*

That night Razor Blade Baby and I left the party and started our walk back to 315 Lake. It had been raining heavily up in the Sierras for two days straight, and the Truckee was raging—the highest I'd ever seen it. The water was milky and opaque, and in it tumbled massive logs that had probably lain on the river's bed for years. Across the bridge two concrete stumps with rebar worming out the tops stood on either side of the street like sentinels, all that was left of the original arch.

—CLAIRE VAYE WATKINS,
"Ghosts, Cowboys," *Battleborn: Stories*

And if you look at the marble walls, the cathedral ceiling we recovered, you can piece together this really narrow, sharply defined V pattern, with the apex pointing somewhere in the middle of the floor, most likely where the rug was, meaning the fire developed really fast and hot in that one spot. —PATRICIA CORNWELL, *Point of Origin*

I've wanted to live on a farm ever since I was a little girl and my upwardly mobile parents moved my brother and me from one apartment, duplex, and bi-level to the next, finally settling down for good in a "ranch"-style house in "Country Estates." But real farms were where you had gardens. Real farms were where you had space. Best of all, real farms, and not subdivisions, were where you had *horses*.

—MARDI JO LINK, *Bootstrapper: From Broke to Badass on a Northern Michigan Farm*

It was a great barn of a room. A tall four-post bed, hung with faded tapestries of Love and War, was set off by oak chests-of-drawers and Court cupboards. The floor was uneven, strangely out of keeping with the rose-infested Brussels carpet so vividly new. Most of the windows, latticed and small, were set flush with the floor; but high up in a dormer was a large window with diamonded panes, uncurtained, black and ominous. A couple of tall cheval-glasses added to the mystery of the room with their reduplication of shadowy corners.

—COMPTON MACKENZIE, *Carnival*

Of all the streets that meet the circle, P is by far my favorite. As it heads west toward Dupont and Georgetown, it only grows prettier and wider, with the houses increasingly grand and luxurious, as if each step forward were a step toward paradise. Men with matching dogs walk along P Street. Half a mile away are sidewalk cafes and restaurants, three used-book stores, wine shops, flower shops, and cheese shops. And the farther up P you move, the better life gets. From Dupont the street proceeds to Georgetown, where the road narrows and the sidewalks become a quaint uneven brick bordered by nineteenth-century colonial mansions bearing Ionic columns. The trees form a canopy over the cobblestone road, still lined with the metal tracks of the trolley cars that stopped running decades ago.

—DINAW MENGESTU, *The Beautiful Things That Heaven Bears*

Next morning Johnny got up early and went round to the office of the Ocean City Improvement and Realty Company that was in a new greenstained shingled bungalow on the freshly laid out street back of the beach. There was no one there yet, so he walked round the town. It was a muggy gray day and the cottages and the frame stores and the unpainted shacks along the railroad track looked pretty desolate. —JOHN DOS PASSOS, *The Morning of the Century*

A stretch now without a quay, just a shoulder, no other pedestrians, but cars seemed to stream past without noticing them. Then they were in Arnavutköy, a line of waterside *yalis* with elaborate fretwork, and streets behind to wind through, a maze for anyone following.

—JOSEPH KANON, *Istanbul Passage*

This house was the pride of the town. Faced with stone as far back as the dining-room windows, it was a house of arches and turrets and girdling stone porches: it had the first portcochere seen in that town. There was a central "front hall" with a great black walnut stairway, and open to a green glass skylight called the "dome," three stories above the ground floor. A ballroom occupied most of the third story; and at one end of it was a carved walnut gallery for the musicians. Citizens told strangers that the cost of all this black walnut and wood-carving was sixty thousand dollars.

—BOOTH TARKINGTON, *The Magnificent Ambersons*

It is Orlando's most exclusive gated community. Homes sell there for millions of dollars, though the land—your typical lakeside lots—and the houses—McMansions ranging from the merely huge to the stupendously gargantuan—account for neither the prices nor the prestige.

—T. D. ALLMAN, "The Theme-Parking, Megachurching, Franchising, Exurbing, McMansioning of America," *National Geographic*, March 2007

The cottages were mostly rambling, shingled affairs, gabled, dormered, and turreted, with screened porches and wooden walls on the inside and big stone fireplaces. Each cottage was different, yet one seemed much like another. The Aldrich cottage, where the McGhees always stayed, was one of Tommy's two favorites; it was a big log cabin—the only log cabin on the Island—with a Dutch door. The Farnsworth cottage, his other favorite, was a shingled house weathered to a silver sheen with blue trim and a round room in a high turret that Mrs. Farnsworth sometimes used to take him up to. You could see way up the river from that room.

—WILLIAM MCPHERSON, *Testing the Current*

The north side of Washington Square Park is lined with Greek Revival mansions built in the 1830s. Henry James's novel *Washington Square* is set in one of these houses, one that belonged to his grandmother and that was part of a group called the Rhinelander houses, which were torn down in the early 1950s to make way for a high-rise apartment building. Village pressure prevented the erection of the tall building directly on the square. Number 2 Fifth Avenue came in two parts, therefore; one towering and cream-colored, set back from the square, the other five-storied and red brick, a mock-Georgian structure on the spot where the five-story Rhinelander houses had stood.

—GRACE MARMOR SPRUCH, *Squirrels at My Window: Life with a Remarkable Gang of Urban Squirrels*

When we finally made it home, Robbie climbed out, and I slithered after him on wobbly legs. Mom had already leaped out, slamming the door behind her. We followed her into the house, a small rancher with cedar-shake siding, a sloping floor, and so many leaks we had buckets all over the house when it rained.

—CHEVY STEVENS, *Always Watching*

He cared nothing for the lives enclosed within a set of walls and was excited only by the character of *the house itself*. A circular porch lent this one a jovial air, a double row of open-work bricks rendered another spiteful, while a third, *an upstairs house*, situated deep in a treed garden, exuded a sinister charm. Ravi's imagination worked to penetrate the enigma of each dwelling: the brilliance and dark within, the disposition of rooms, the dusty places where dead flies collected.

—MICHELLE DE KRETSER, *Questions of Travel*

Through my glasses I saw the slope of a hill interspersed with rare trees and perfectly free from undergrowth. A long decaying building on the summit was half buried in the high grass; the large holes in the peaked roof gaped black from afar; the jungle and the woods made a background. There was no enclosure or fence of any kind; but there had been one apparently, for near the house half-a-dozen slim posts remained in a row, roughly trimmed, and with their upper ends ornamented with round carved balls.

—JOSEPH CONRAD, *Heart of Darkness*

I never get tired of gazing from the back seats of buses at the stone eagles . . . and the cast-iron rosettes and the cast-iron medallions and the clusters of cast-iron acanthus leaves bolted to capitals of cast-iron Corinthian columns and the festoons of cast-iron flowers and the swags of cast-iron fruit and the zinc brackets in the shape of oak leaves propping up the zinc cornices of brownstone houses and the scroll-sawed bargeboards framing the dormers of decaying old mansard-roofed mansions and the terra-cotta cherubs and nymphs and satyrs and sibyls and sphinxes and Atlases and Dianas and Medusas serving as keystones in the arches over the doorways and windows of tenement houses.

—JOSEPH MITCHELL, "Street Life," *The New Yorker*, February 11 and 18, 2012

Around the time that Junior was born, we moved to a newly constructed public housing project in Soundview, just a ten-minute drive from our old neighborhood. The Bronxdale Houses sprawled over three large city blocks: twenty-eight buildings, each seven stories tall with eight apartments to a floor. My mother saw the projects as a safer, cleaner, brighter alternative to the decaying tenement where we had lived.

—SONIA SOTOMAYOR, *My Beloved World*

There was always a little grey street leading to the stage-door of the theatre and another little grey street where your lodgings were, and rows of little houses with chimneys like the funnels of dummy steamers and smoke the same colour as the sky; and a grey stone promenade running hard, naked and straight by the side of the grey-brown or grey-green sea. . . .

—JEAN RHYS, *Voyage in the Dark*

Two doors from Henry's was the abandoned house. It wore cinderblock bandages over the windows and doorway like a mummy with blanked eyes and stilled howling mouth, and had a blasted yard with no fence or gate. The stoop was barren too, no rail. Possibly someone had taken the ironwork for scrap. The mummy house was a flat surface with no windows, so it made a high wall for wallball, a game where a spaldeen was bounced high against the wall by a thrower and caught by a catcher standing in the field of the street, zipping between the cars to make the catch.

—JONATHAN LETHEM, *The Fortress of Solitude*

He lived alone in this deteriorating, blind building of a thousand uninhabited apartments, which like all its counterparts, fell, day by day, into greater entropic ruin. Eventually everything within the building would merge, would be faceless and identical, mere pudding-like kipple piled to the ceiling of each apartment. And, after that, the uncared-for building itself would settle into shapelessness, buried under the ubiquity of the dust. By then, naturally, he himself would be dead, another interesting event to anticipate as he stood here in his stricken living room alone with the lungless, all-penetrating, masterful world-silence.

—PHILIP K. DICK, *Do Androids Dream of Electric Sheep?*

I've been working on the window series for over two years, rummaging around the city with my sketchbook and Nikon. Church windows, reflective windows, Boston's ubiquitous bays. Large, small, old, broken, wood- and metal-framed. Windows from the outside in and the inside out. I especially like windows on late winter afternoons before anyone inside notices the darkening sky and snaps the blinds shut. —B. A. SHAPIRO, *The Art Forger*

We lived on the first floor of a three-story brownstone house that stood on a quiet street just off busy Lee Avenue. The brownstone row houses lined both sides of the street, and long, wide, stone stairways led from the sidewalks to the frosted-glass double doors of the entrances.

—CHAIM POTOK, *The Chosen*

The house is narrow and quite distinctive, with pilasters and spandrel panels and a keystone above the parlor floor window in the shape of a bearded man. The brownstones looked much as they do today, though their facades were worn, and many hid rooming houses within. The day the Mieles moved in, Mr. Miele first unpacked a shotgun that he left sitting on the stoop for all to see.

—WENDELL JAMIESON, "The Crime of His Childhood," *New York Times*, March 2, 2013, Metropolitan

Judge Tyler's house was one of the brick ones, with a Mansard roof and patterns in the shingles. There were dormer windows. It was three stories high, with a double-decker veranda, and with white painted stonework around all the windows, which were high and narrow. The whole house looked too high and narrow, and there were a lot of steps up to the front door. There was a lawn, and lilac bushes, and out back a long, white carriage house and stable. It was a new place, and the brick looked very pink and the veranda and stonework very white. It looked more than ever high and narrow because there weren't any big trees around it yet, but only some sapling Lombardies, about twice as high as a man, along the drive.

—Walter Van Tilburg Clark, *The Ox-Bow Incident*

The elevated trains provided a rather unexpected benefit to passengers: They were fun. The height of the cars, at sixty feet above ground along some sections of track, allowed relatively unobstructed, expansive views. Towering over church steeples, the city's tallest structures, the elevated cars allowed New Yorkers to discover aspects of the city they had never seen before. Predating the roller coaster, the elevated trains coiled through space at relatively high speeds. Adults and children alike would clamor to get a space at the front of the first car.

—Tracy Fitzpatrick, *Art and the Subway: New York Underground*

The houses of the central village were quite unlike the casual and higgledy-piggledy agglomeration of the mountain villages he knew; they stood in a continuous row on either side of a central street of astonishing cleanness; here and there their parti-coloured façade was pierced by a door, and not a solitary window broke their even frontage. They were parti-coloured with extraordinary irregularity; smeared with a sort of plaster that was sometimes grey, sometimes drab, sometimes slate-coloured or dark brown. . . .

—H. G. Wells, "The Country of the Blind," *The Country of the Blind and Other Stories*

The beauty of the campus, an acquired taste, certainly, lay in its stalwart understatement, its unapologetic capitulation to the supremacy of line over color, to the artistry of repetition, and the lyrics of a scrupulous unsentimental vision. The four barracks and all the main academic buildings on campus faced inward toward the parade ground, a vast luxurious greensward trimmed like the fairway of an exclusive golf course.

—Pat Conroy, *The Lord of Discipline*

I drove on past the curve that goes down into the Strip and stopped across the street from a square building of two stories of rose-red brick with small white leaded bay windows and a Greek porch over the front door and what looked, from across the street, like an antique pewter doorknob. Over the door was a fanlight and the name Sheridan Balou, Inc., in black wooden letters severely stylized.

—Raymond Chandler, *The Little Sister*

The temple, made of sandstone, was a massive pyramid-like structure in the shape of a chariot. It was dedicated to the great master of life, the sun, which struck three sides of the edifice as it made its journey each day across the sky. Twenty-four giant wheels were carved on the north and south sides of the plinth. The whole thing was drawn by a team of seven horses, speeding as if though the heavens.

—JHUMPA LAHIRI,
Interpreter of Maladies

Most of the cottages were built of Cotswold stone and were roofed by split-stone tiles. The tiles grew a kind of golden moss which sparkled like crystallised honey. Behind the cottages were long steep gardens full of cabbages, fruit-bushes, roses, rabbit-hutches, earth-closets, bicycles, and pigeon-lofts. In the very sump of the valley wallowed the Squire's Big House—once a fine, though modest sixteenth-century manor, to which a Georgian façade had been added.

—LAURIE LEE, *Cider with Rosie*

EARTH AND SKY

TERRAIN AND LANDSCAPE

LAND AND WATER

aspect or conformation of land
landscape
particular extensive locale of land
area, region, tract, expanse
area of land with respect to its physical features
terrain
detailed description or representation of a region with respect to relative locations or elevations
topography
long strip of terrain
swath, swathe
relating to or of the earth, or relating to land or ground as opposed to sea or air
terrestrial
on or close to the earth's surface
subaerial

extensive area of uncultivated, little-populated, and often uncharted terrain

wilderness, the wild, the wilds, the bush, backcountry, hinterland (Australia: outback)

region or demarcation at the edge of settled or known territory

frontier

area of unclaimed or uninhabited land or one not suitable for either

no-man's-land

country that is level and low in altitude

lowland, lowlands

country that is elevated or mountainous

highland, highlands, upland, uplands

country's or region's central or interior part

midland, midlands

country having few or no trees

open country

region abounding in trees

forest, woods, wood, woodland, forestland

mature woodland ecosystem having old trees, shrubs, and long-present wildlife

old growth forest

corridor-like strip of forest near a river or wetland in an area otherwise having few trees

gallery forest, fringing forest

wet tropical forest with constant cloud cover throughout the year, usually at the canopy level

cloud forest, fog forest

open space in woodland or a forest

clearing, glade

extensive tropical wet woodland with tall trees that form a light-blocking canopy

rain forest

tropical terrain overgrown or thick with vegetation

jungle

describing a tree or forest with foliage that falls off annually rather than with needles or scales

deciduous, broad-leaf, broad-leaved

describing a tree or forest with foliage that stays and remains green throughout the year

evergreen, coniferous (for the most part)

small group or grouping of trees (usually without undergrowth)

grove

patch of thick or twisted growth

tangle

grove or thicket of small trees

copse, coppice, arbustum (British: spinney)

leafy tree-enclosed nook or recess

arbor, bower

dense thicket of shrubs or dwarf trees

chaparral

growth or array of one type of tree (shrub, or plant) in an area

stand

uncultivated land covered with stunted vegetation

scrub, scrubland

cluster of shrubs or small trees

shrubbery, thicket

loss of leaves

defoliation

large-scale loss or clearing of trees

deforestation

something, as a branch or ripened fruit, blown down by the wind

windfall

plant growth or life

vegetation, flora, foliage

green plant life or trees

greenery, verdure

clump of grass

tussock

grass-covered tract of level land

meadow

land constituting or used as a meadow

meadowland

grassland for grazing

pastureland, pasturage

greenery as cover or food for deer

vert

thicket where game hide

covert

small trees, bushes, or shrubs that are part of a forest

underbrush, brush, undergrowth

decaying leaves, twigs, and other organic matter covering a forest floor

duff

grassy (or non-woody) vegetation

herbage

green tract of grassland

sward, greensward, turf

extensive area of treeless grassland (with tall grasses)

prairie, plain, champaign, campagna, pampa (South America)

extensive area of treeless grassland (with short grasses) and less rainfall than a prairie

steppe

steppe with scattered trees and shrubs (esp. in Africa)

veld, veldt

extensive grazing grassland with scattered trees and shrubs

savanna, savannah, campo

extensive treeless plain in the southeastern U.S.

savanna, savannah

extensive plain with few trees in the southwestern U.S.

llano

extensive northern (subarctic) evergreen forest that is moist

taiga, boreal forest

extensive northern (arctic and subarctic) treeless plain with mucky soil

tundra

tundra treeless because of elevation (rather than latitude)

alpine tundra

barren, erosionally "sculpted" region with picturesque or fantastic formations, hills, or mesas

badlands

alpine forest having stunted trees

krummholz, elfinwood

level area of terrain

flatland, flats

area of burned terrain

burn

tract of open and rolling land with poor soil

moor, heath, moorland

high moor or barren field

fell

barren land

waste, wasteland, barren, barrens

tract of sandy ground where topsoil has been blown away by the wind

sandblow

extensive area of barren and arid land

desert

desert at high elevation (2,000 feet or more above sea level)

high desert

broad desert area of wind-blown sand

erg, sand sea, dune sea

flat-bottomed desert basin that at times becomes a shallow lake

playa

illusory optical phenomenon, as experienced at a distance in the desert, in which one sees a body of water or reflected inverted objects, caused by distortion of light rays in alternate layers of hot and cold air

mirage, fata morgana

opening or recession in terrain

hole, cavity, depression, hollow, basin, pan

open longitudinal depression

trench, ditch, cut

valley

vale, dale

small and nestled (usually wooded) valley

dell, glen, dingle

deep and narrow valley

hollow, combe, comb, coombe

deep and steep-sided valley (often with a river)

canyon, cañon

small steep-walled canyon to which access is possible only through its mouth

box canyon

small and narrow steep-sided valley (often with a stream)

gorge, ravine, flume, gulch, barranca, barranco, clough, quebrada (South Africa: kloof)

geological fracture in the earth's crust

fault, rift

uplift of the earth's crust

upthrust

deep, elongated valley between two roughly parallel faults

rift valley

pass between mountains

notch, gap

place suitable for crossing or zigzagging

traverse

divide between valleys or side of a valley

coteau

small ravine sometimes having rainwater flowing in it

gully, clough, draw, coulee, nullah, wash, wadi (South Africa: donga)

flat-bottomed gulch or gully sometimes having rainwater flowing in it

arroyo

long hollow or depression

trough

deep drop or hollow

gulf, chasm, abyss

chasm formed by receding ice

randkluft

underground or rock-walled chamber
cave, cavern, grotto
icicle-like calcium carbonate formation hanging in a cave
stalactite, dripstone
irregular, convoluted stalactite
helictite
icicle-like calcium carbonate deposit on the floor of a cave
stalagmite, dripstone
drainage depression or hollow
sinkhole, sink, swallow, swallowhole, dolina, doline
limestone sinkhole with a pool or deep natural well
cenote
extensive or deep mucky or mossy basin
mudhole, muskeg
level area covered by shallow water at high tide
mudflat
high point
elevation, eminence
top of a hill
hilltop, rise
elevated place affording an extensive or scenic view
overlook
projection at the top of a hill
brow
small and rounded hill
knoll, hillock, hummock, monticule, monticle, mound (England: barrow)
hill with a broad top
loma
lower hills beneath mountains
foothills

narrow or oval hill
drumlin
rounded elevation
swell
rounded solitary hill usually with steep sides
knob
steep bare slope
cutbank
mound in permafrost terrain
pingo
African veld's small and scrubby hill
kopje, koppie
ground that slants upward or downward
slope, incline, grade
upward slope
acclivity, rise
downward slope
declivity
gentle slope
glacis
precipitous slope
steep
hill steep on one side but with a gentle slope on the other
cuesta
open upland of rolling hills or open country
wold
rolling grassy upland with few trees
down, downs
one of successive indentations (from slumping soil) on a hillside
catstep, terracette

tree deformed by wind
wind cripple
parapet-like natural formation atop a wall
battlement
projecting or support-like natural formation
buttress
extensive flat-topped land elevation that rises steeply on at least one side
plateau, table, tableland
small and isolated plateau
mesa
small mesa
mesilla
isolated steep hill or small mountain (flat, rounded, cone-like, or pointed)
butte
solitary and fragmentary mountain
inselberg
series of mountains
range, chain
system of mountain chains (sometimes parallel)
cordillera
chain of mountains with sawtooth-like peaks
sierra
chain of hills or mountains
ridge, chine
ridge dividing drainage directions and regions
watershed, divide
area at the foot of a mountain range
piedmont

side of a formation or mountain
flank

top of a mountain
peak, summit, pike, crest

long and narrow crest-like elevation
ridge

exposed rock surface
face

rugged and sharp-crested mountain ridge
arête, hogback

pyramidal peak usually with concave faces (where three or more arêtes meet)
horn

elevation overlooking other terrain
heights

elevated place
aerie, eyrie

high and rugged mountain
alp

mountain range section or mass
massif

projection laterally or on an angle from a mountain
spur

mountain or hill protuberance
buttress

area near the top or to the side of a mountain
shoulder

short mound or ridge
kame

winding ridge that is gravelly or sandy
esker

cliff formation or line of cliffs
scarp, escarpment, palisade, palisades

jagged glacial ridge or pinnacle (as in an icefall)
serac

steep vertical facing
wall, cliff, bluff, crag, face

precipitous place
steep, precipice

very steep descent or wall
drop-off

small space like a recess in a wall
niche

projection of rock
outcrop, outcropping

steep and bare rocky outcrop or cliff
scar

flat layer of rock
shelf

narrow level space along or projecting from a cliff or slope
ledge, shelf

cliff or wall projection viewed from below
overhang

pointed rock formation
pinnacle

long narrow opening
fissure, cleft, rift, crevice

channel or scoop-like depression between mountains
pass, col, saddle

narrow pass between hills or cliffs
defile, gorge

mountainside gorge or gully
couloir
cleft that is steep and narrow in a cliff or mountain face
chimney
bowl-like mountain basin with steep walls
cirque, cwm, corrie, corry
steep wall of a cirque
headwall
roughly circular or oval flat area enclosed at one end by a curve of higher ground
amphitheater
high and craggy hill or rocky peak
tor
colossal single rock or rock formation
monolith
oddly or fantastically shaped (eroded) rock column
hoodoo
single rock or boulder carried to where it lies by a glacier
erratic
rounded or hump-like natural formation
dome
notably arched or bridge-like formation
natural bridge, arch
smooth and slippery rock
slickrock
downward slide of earth or rocks
landslide, slump, rockfall
swift, massive, and overwhelming fall of ice, snow, earth, rocks, or other material down a mountainside
avalanche

rocky detritus (debris) on a mountain slope
scree, talus

glacial deposit of boulders and stones
moraine

wall-like ridge of rocks, ice, or other debris
rampart

volcanic activity
volcanism, vulcanism

mountain (with a crater) formed by ejected material
volcano

bowl-like depression at the top of a volcano or (from an impact) in the earth's surface
crater

wide volcano crater (formed by eruptions or rim collapse)
caldera

moving mass of volcanic debris and water or resultant deposit from such a landslide or mudflow
lahar

fast-moving downhill current of hot gas and rock resulting from a volcanic eruption
pyroclastic flow, pyroclastic density current

volcanic vapor hole
fumarole, vent

spring that at times throws up jets of hot water or steam
geyser

extinct volcano crater often containing a lake or marsh
maar

molten rock that issues from a volcano or other surface fissure
lava

molten rock material beneath the earth's crust that, when cooled, forms igneous rock
magma

solid matter ejected into the air by a volcanic eruption
tephra

underground layer containing and yielding water
aquifer

upper limit of an underground area saturated with water
water table, water level

ledge-like plain above a river or body of water
terrace

moist land
wetland, wetlands

low terrain along a watercourse
bottom, bottomland

tract of low-lying soggy soil
morass

tract of low and wet or spongy ground
marsh, marshland, bog, fen, swamp, swampland, wash, slough, slew, slue

swampy grassland with branching waterways
everglade

low land subject to flood tides
tideland, tidelands

flat and usually muddy tideland
tidal flat, mud flat

body of water, subject to tides, whose water level is controlled artificially
tidal basin

creek affected by ocean tides
tidal creek

high wave in an estuary caused by colliding tidal currents or an upstream flood surge

bore, eagre

flat land having brackish water

salt marsh

body of water separate, held back, or immured from the main current of a larger body

backwater

rough or marshy tract of land with one kind of vegetation (shrubs or ferns)

brake, bracken

sunken and wet tract of land

swale

marshy sluggish or stagnant creek or body of water

bayou

moist low-lying land (usually pineland)

flatwoods

continent or appreciable part of it, as opposed to an extension of it or an island

mainland

land body surrounded by water

island, isle

large group or chain of islands (or their ocean area)

archipelago

small island

islet, ait, eyot

low coral island or visible reef

cay, key

ringlike coral island or reef surrounding a lagoon

atoll

long sandy island parallel to the mainland's shore and protective against erosion or tides adversely affecting that coastline

barrier island

land arm almost completely surrounded by water

peninsula, chersonese

land formation jutting into the sea or other large body of water

cape

narrow projection of land

tongue

narrow stretch or connecting piece of land

neck

land tip or projection

point

crescent-shaped arm of land

horn

elevated land area jutting over the sea or other large body of water

headland, promontory, ness, naze

neck or strip joining two larger masses of land

isthmus

land inland from the coast

hinterland

strip of land (sometimes prehistoric or submerged) between two relatively large landmasses

land bridge

land along the sea temporarily covered by tides or saturated during floods

tideland

tract or region drained by a river or river system

basin

land along a river subject to flooding
floodplain
flat area encrusted with salt
salt flat
river mouth's (debouchment's) often fan-shaped sedimentary plain
delta, alluvial plain
river (alluvial) land between a levee and its lower-water stage
batture
sandbar connecting two islands or an island and its mainland
tombolo
small jutting of sand or gravel at water's edge
spit, sandspit
area suitable for landing goods from a boat
landing
land border along water
coast, coastline, shore, shoreline, seaboard, littoral
sandy margin along water
beach, strand, lido
pebbled or stony beach
shingle
swampy coastline
maremma
mound of accrued or windblown sand
dune
crescent-like dune that shifts
barchan, barchane, barkhan
ocean, sea
the deep, the briny deep, blue water
ocean beyond territorial waters
high seas, main, open sea, international waters

connecting passage between two large bodies of water
strait, narrows
wide strait or navigable connecting waterway
channel
narrow passage or channel
gut
sea inlet that is extensive
gulf
sea inlet that is long or separates an island from a mainland
sound
sea inlet smaller than a gulf
bay, embayment
bay at a coastal bend
bight
usually sheltered coastal area suitable as an anchorage or port
harbor
shoreline indentation that is sheltered
cove, creek, hole, basin
shallow pond near a body of water
lagoon
long lagoon near the sea
haff
sea inlet or arm
estuary, firth, frith
sea inlet that is narrow and has steep slopes or cliffs
fjord, fiord
sea inlet or creek shallower inland
ria
arm of the sea or of a river
wash

sea's juncture with a river's mouth
estuary
channel or passage that runs beneath cliffs from the shore inland
gat
pool of water left after the tide recedes
tidal pool, tide pool
pool of water between two beaches
beach pool
body of shallow water
shallows
dangerously cross-currented or turbulent patch of water
rip, riptide, rip current
submerged (or partly so) bank of sand or gravel obstructive to navigation
bar, sandbar, sandbank, shoal
coral ridgelike growth usually near the surface in warm seas
reef
sea rock opening through which water intermittently spouts
blowhole, gloup
giant circular rotating system of surface currents in the ocean
gyre
water moving in an inward (centripetal) circle
whirlpool, maelstrom, gurge, vortex
small whirlpool
eddy
submarine (undersea) mountain
seamount
flat-topped seamount
guyot

lengthy shallow depression in the ocean floor
trough
lengthy deep, usually steep-walled depression in the ocean floor
trench
any flowing line of fresh water
watercourse, course, channel, waterway, stream (archaic: freshet)
junction of two rivers
watersmeet
inland-flowing course of fresh water smaller than a river
stream, brook, creek, kill, run, quebrada
dry bed of an intermittent stream
dry wash, wash, streambed
small stream
streamlet, brooklet, rivulet, rill, runnel, burn, bourn, bourne
winding stream
meander, serpentine
winding stream dividing around a neck of land
oxbow
river or stream feeding a larger river
tributary, feeder
open stretch of river
reach
river's source or upper tributary
headwaters, headwater
onrushing or raging stream
torrent
turbulent and rock-obstructed part of a river
rapid, rapids

steep rapids
cataract
turbulent frothy water
white water
abrupt or steep river descent
chute
waterfall
cataract, cascade
narrow channel or strait with swift and dangerous waters
euripus
river or stream channel in a mountain ridge gap
water gap
trough for water
run
shallow area of water that can be waded across
ford
inland body of (usually) fresh water
lake, loch, mere
small lake or standing body of water
pond, lakelet, pondlet, pool, water hole
small mountain lake with steep banks
tarn
artificial pond subject to the tides of a river or stream
tidal basin
stagnant pool
stagnum
dam in a stream
weir
vast moving or spreading mass of ice
glacier

mantle of perennial ice and snow, as at the earth's two poles
ice cap, ice sheet

extensive area of floating (sea) ice
ice field

floating extension of an ice sheet beyond coastal waters
ice shelf, shelf ice

sheet of floating ice smaller than an ice field
floe

hill in an ice field
hummock

mountain-like mass of floating ice
iceberg

massed array of ice formations at sea
ice pack, pack ice

narrow path of open water through sea ice helpful to wildlife and vessels
lead

path of open water through sea ice, larger and more uniform in size than a lead
polynya

sloping area of jumbled glacial ice blocks, or an avalanche that produces such a perilous area
icefall

glacial fissure or crevice that is deep
crevasse

series of crevasses
bergschrund

granular or ice-like mountain (glacial) snow
névé, firn

permanently frozen subsurface layer in polar or frigid regions
permafrost, pergelisol

thin coating of ice, as on rock
verglas
runoff of water from melted snow
snowmelt
oldest and densest ice, pale blue in color, in a glacier
blue ice
vertical shaft (worn by falling surface water through a crack) in a glacier
moulin
elongated mound or ridge of glacial drift
drumlin
mass of floating ice fragments
brash
fragment of thin ice near shore
pan
fog composed of ice particles
ice fog
pertaining to or like the ocean
oceanic, marine, pelagic, thalassic, maritime
pertaining to the ocean depths or bottom
benthic, benthonic
pertaining to or like a lake
lacustrine
pertaining to or like a river
riverine, fluvial, amnic
pertaining to or like a riverbank
riverain
pertaining to or like a shore
littoral, riparian
pertaining to or like a swamp
swampy, marshy, quaggy, boggy, paludal

pertaining to or like a plain or field
campestral

pertaining to or like a mountain
montane

pertaining to or like an island
insular

pertaining to a shore region moist but always above water
supralittoral

pertaining to a shore region between the high-water and low-water line
littoral

pertaining to an ocean zone from the low-water line to the edge of the continental shelf
sublittoral, neritic

pertaining to an ocean zone from the continental shelf to a depth of some 13,000 feet (4,000 meters)
bathyal, bathypelagic

pertaining to an ocean zone from some 13,000 feet (4,000 meters) to 20,000 feet (6,500 meters)
abyssal

pertaining to an ocean zone deeper than 20,000 feet (6,500 meters)
hadal

CULTIVATED AREAS AND MAN-MADE STRUCTURES

land covered by grass
grassland, parkland

public or park-like promenade bordered with trees
alameda

planned or mall-like alley whose trees are at least twice as high as the route's width

allée

narrow tree- or branch-covered pathway

tunnel

tree-bordered or hedged and park-like walk

alley

country route or path

trail, lane, track

zigzagging path or road

switchback

grassland tract for grazing or hay

pasture, lea

hedge-forming line of bushes or small trees that separate or enclose fields

hedgerow

enclosed field or pasture for animals, esp. racehorses

paddock

group of planted fruit or nut trees

orchard

thicket of cane

canebrake

wet land cultivated for growing rice

paddy, padi

yard or field used as a household kitchen garden or for a few farm animals

croft (British)

artificial lake often maintained as a water supply

reservoir

artificial waterway for navigation or irrigation

canal

embankment to prevent river or sea flooding

levee, dike

beach- or harbor-protective structure offshore

breakwater, mole, seawall

excavated earthen construction, as for protection or a fortification

earthwork, embankment

Common Modifiers for Terrain or Landscape

impenetrable
tropical
varied
broken
pastoral
bucolic
bleak
panoramic
fertile
intimidating
scorched-earth
stunted
vast
arid
featureless
gentle
idyllic
majestic
scenic
stark

unearthly
unrelieved
decaying
pristine
verdant
lush
sylvan
virgin
arcadian
icy
magical
uncharted
weed-choked
beautiful
overgrown
rolling
wild
blighted
parched
impassable
towering
familiar
rugged
daunting
primordial
colorless
dense
forbidding
intransigent
pitiless
ravaged

scrubby
surreal
fantastical
ruined
austere
mountainous
uniform
colorful
hard
picturesque
stony
unspoiled
variegated
ancient
harsh
luxuriant
unchanging
unworldly
barren
elysian
off the beaten track
rough
frozen
spectacular
craggy
primeval
unreal
desolate
dreamlike
rocky
insular

unchanged
variable
inhospitable
unbroken
windswept
sun-drenched
blasted
flat
lofty
withered
remote
serene

QUOTATIONS

Then they crossed a stone stile on to the moor, and followed a pony-trail northwards, with the screes of the mountain rising steeply on the left. Beyond a spinney of birches, they came to a barn and longhouse, standing amid heaps of broken wall.

—BRUCE CHATWIN, *On the Black Hill*

I moved to Beaufort, South Carolina, in the early sixties, a town fed by warm salt tides and cooled by mild winds from the sea; a somnolent town built on a high bluff where a river snaked fortuitously.

—PAT CONROY, *The Water Is Wide*

We now come abreast of the gap on the right, and it ends the tedium of the reach upriver. It is a broad window into stands of cypress, their wide fluted bases attached to their reflections in still, dark water. "How I love them," says Houck, who is a conservationist of the sunset school, with legal skills adjunct to the force of his emotion. Pointing into the beauty of the bayous, he informs General Sands, "That's what it's all about."

—JOHN MCPHEE, *The Control of Nature*

The fields and hedgerows, once tended by medieval peasants and eighteenth-century laborers, still visibly patterned the land in irregular quadrilaterals, and every brook, fence, and pigsty, virtually every tree, was known and probably named in the Domesday Book after all-conquering William in 1085 conferred with his advisers and sent his men all over England. —IAN MCEWAN, *Solar*

An immediate result of this self-inflicted ecological disaster was that the islanders no longer had the logs needed to transport and erect statues, so carving ceased. But deforestation also had two indirect consequences that brought starvation: soil erosion, hence lower crop yields, plus lack of timber to build canoes, hence less protein available from fishing. As a result, the population was now greater than Easter could support, and island society collapsed in a holocaust of internecine warfare and cannibalism.

—JARED DIAMOND, *The Third Chimpanzee: The Evolution and Future of the Human Animal*

The coast for the fifty miles west of Bognor was full of pleats and tucks—harbors, channel, inlets, and Southampton Water, and the bays of Spithead. The coastal footpath around Selsey Bill gave out at one of the two Witterings. Beyond it were inconvenient islands and not enough causeways and a path made impossible by the scoops and cuts of all this water. There were no walkers here. This territory was for sailors—full of fine bays, friendly harbors, and the waterlogged geography of the Solent; all the blowing boats.

—Paul Theroux, *The Kingdom by the Sea: A Journey around the Coast of Great Britain*

Boardwalks skirt the edge of the marsh, rough-hewn planks of silvered cedar spiked together only a few inches above the water: I set out on one of them. The occasional catfish swifted itself into the depths. A quarter mile behind me a crowd of mourners was still about, but from the trough where I walked I could see none of it; I crossed the central bog, hidden to shoulder height by cattails, then climbed to the ridge that runs above the creek.

—Ethan Canin, *America America*

Even though he was relatively safe up there in the Chittagong Hills, the highest point of that low-lying, flatland country, still she hated the thought that Magid should be as she had once been: holding on to a life no heavier than a paisa coin, wading thoughtlessly through floods, shuddering underneath the weight of black skies. . . .

—Zadie Smith, *White Teeth*

The traveler from the coast, who, after plodding northward for a score of miles over calcareous downs and corn-lands, suddenly reached the verge of one of these escarpments, is surprised and delighted to behold, extended like a map beneath him, a country differing absolutely from that which he has passed through. Behind him the hills are open, the sun blazes down upon fields so large as to give an unenclosed character to the landscape, the lanes are white, the hedges low and plashed, the atmosphere colourless. Here, in the valley, the world seems to be constructed on a smaller and more delicate scale; the fields are mere paddocks, so reduced that from this height their hedgerows appear a network of dark green threads overspreading the paler green of the grass.

—THOMAS HARDY, *Tess of the D'Urbervilles*

There was not much work to be got out of Duny. He was always off and away; roaming deep in the forest, swimming in the pools of the River Ar that like all Gontish rivers runs very quick and cold, or climbing by cliff and scarp to the heights from which he could see the sea, that broad northern ocean where, past Perregal, no islands are.

—URSULA K. LE GUIN, *A Wizard of Earthsea*

Near to the foot of the hill arose the short spiky spears of a sweet chestnut plantation, and beyond it a little patch of woodland, where the wild cherry was but lately over, half veiled a group of conical oast houses in a blur of green.

—IRIS MURDOCH, *An Unofficial Rose*

To level out the meadow, they crimped blasting caps to fuses, shattered boulders with dynamite, leveled walls and fences, removed hillocks. It was summertime but still there was a chill in the air. Flocks of birds moved fluidly across the sky. —COLUM MCCANN, *TransAtlantic*

In the middle of what's known as Far West Texas, there is Marfa: a hardscrabble ranching community in the upper Chihuahuan desert, sixty miles north of the Mexican border, that inhabits some of the most beautiful and intransigent countryside imaginable: inexhaustible sky over a high desert formed in the Permian period and left more or less alone since. It's situated in one of the least populated sections of the contiguous United States, known locally as el despoblado (the uninhabited place), a twelve-hour car-and-plane trip from the east coast, and seven from the west. —SEAN WILSEY, "The Republic of Marfa," *McSweeney's*, March 1999

Behind and over us towered Sheba's snowy breasts, and below, some five thousand feet beneath where we stood, lay league on league of the most lovely champaign country. Here were dense patches of lofty forest, there a great river wound its silvery way. To the left stretched a vast expanse of rich, undulating veldt or grass land, on which we could just make out countless herds of game or cattle, at that distance we could not tell which.

—H. RIDER HAGGARD, *King Solomon's Mines*

Now, as they came out of the hills, they faced the plain and the far wall of the Gila Mountains. Mauve and yellow cliffs. A volcanic cone called Raven's Butte that was dark, as if a rain cloud were hovering over it. It looked as if you could find relief on its perpetually shadowy flanks, but that too was an illusion. Abandoned army tanks, preserved forever in the dry heat, stood in their path, a ghostly arrangement that must have seemed like another bad dream. Their full-sun 110-degree nightmare.

—Luis Alberto Urrea, *The Devil's Highway: A True Story*

We defended the city as best we could. The arrows of the Comanches came in clouds. The war clubs of the Comanches clattered on the soft, yellow pavements. There were earthworks along the Boulevard Mark Clark and the hedges had been laced with sparkling wire. People were trying to understand. I spoke to Sylvia. "Do you think this is a good life?" The table held apples, books, long-playing records. She looked up. "No."

—Donald Barthelme, *"The Indian Uprising," Sixty Stories*

Stepping ever so carefully, edging forward in the dark, I make my way across the narrow creek bed. With no recent rain, it's almost dry, apart from a thin trickle down the center, the sound of which is all that's to be heard—that, and the rustling of Geert settling into his sleeping bag behind me.

My bare feet probing forward, I pull back from contact with the cool moss tempting me to slide across its surface, and search instead for dry rock before shifting my weight forward. A few more steps and I'm across, reaching out in the dark for the granite bank I need to climb if I'm going to get any distance from this creek. This is turning into a bit of a mission just to go for a leak, but having had more than one dose of giardia, I'm not about to break the golden rule and urinate anywhere near the water. —WARREN MACDONALD, *A Test of Will: One Man's Extraordinary Tale of Survival*

At the foot of the palatial facade was strewn, with careful art and ordered irregularity, a broad and broken heap of massive rock, looking as if it might have lain there since the deluge. Over a central precipice fell the water, in a semicircular cascade; and from a hundred crevices, on all sides, snowy jets gushed up, and streams spouted out of the mouths and nostrils of stone monsters, and fell in glistening drops. . . . —NATHANIEL HAWTHORNE, *The Marble Faun*

There are a few "hidden forests" where the topography allows mostly scrub oaks. It resembles southern Scotland more than it does the neighboring island of Martha's Vineyard or the mainland. It is best explored on foot, off the roads, in September and October, when the moors change colors, veering toward purple, and the sunlight turns winey. Some find it too bleak, but many, like myself, do not. —FRANK CONROY, *Time and Tide: A Walk Through Nantucket*

So we went along by the hurrying brook, which fell over little cascades in its haste, never looking once at the primroses that were glimmering all along its banks. We turned aside, and climbed the hill through the woods. Velvety green sprigs of dog-mercury were scattered on the red soil. We came to the top of a slope, where the wood thinned. . . . There was a deep little dell, sharp sloping like a cup, and a white sprinkling of flowers all the way down, with white flowers showing pale among the first inpouring of shadow at the bottom.

—D. H. LAWRENCE, *The White Peacock*

Going up, the day was fine but the trail deep-drifted and slopping wet at the margins. They left it to wind through a slashy cut, leading the horses through brittle branchwood, Jack, the same eagle feather in his old hat, lifting his head in the heated noon to take the air scented with resinous lodgepole, the dry needle duff and hot rock, bitter juniper crushed beneath the horses' hooves. Ennis, weather-eyed, looked west for the heated cumulus that might come up on such a day but the boneless blue was so deep, said Jack, that he might drown looking up.

—ANNIE PROULX, "Brokeback Mountain,"
Close Range: Wyoming Stories

I followed a cattle path through the thick underbrush until I came to a slope that fell away abruptly to the water's edge. A great chunk of the shore had been bitten out by some spring freshet, and the scar was masked by elder bushes, growing down to the water in flowery terraces.

—WILLA CATHER, *My Ántonia*

For the present generation of battlefield tourists, the most important hill on the battlefield is the cone-shaped moraine known as Little Round Top. Oddly, this was not the name by which it was known at the time of the battle. People referred to it variously as Wolf's Hill, Sugar Loaf, or simply the "rocky hill," and after the battle, John B. Bachelder (who set himself up almost at once as the official chronicler of Gettysburg) tried to fix the name "Weed's Hill" to it, in honor of the most senior Union officer killed there during the battle, Stephen Weed.

—ALLEN C. GUELZO, *Gettysburg: The Last Invasion*

In order to get the Project, the beachfront owners would have to sign easements giving the government the rights to build the dunes on their property. The landward toe of the dune would sit on the non-buildable, riparian portion of their real estate, and the crest of the dune would block their view of the ocean from the main floor, unless the house was elevated.

—JOHN SEABROOK, "The Beach Builders," *The New Yorker*, July 22, 2013

But above all it is the fantastic colouring of the beaches that as an image overpowers the minutiae. Above the tide-line the grey rocks are splashed gorse-yellow with close-growing lichen, and with others of blue-green and salmon pink. Beneath them are the vivid orange-browns and siennas of wrack-weeds, the violet of mussel-beds, dead-white sand, and water through which one sees down to the bottom, as through pale green bottle-glass, to where starfish and big spiny urchins of pink and purple rest upon the broad leaves of the sea-tangle.

—GAVIN MAXWELL, *Ring of Bright Water*

The Vosges massif loomed like a granite glacis thirty miles deep and seventy miles wide; cleft by few passes, the range was so thickly wooded that a Guadalcanal veteran like Patch was reminded of jungle fighting.

—RICK ATKINSON, *The Guns at Last Light: The War in Western Europe, 1944–1945*

She had not been beyond the town hitherto; very soon she discovered that a road was where the car drove across country. The land was parched and dry with the heat of summer, covered with thin tufts of scorched grass. It was a wooded land, covered thinly with spindly, distorted eucalyptus trees averaging twenty to thirty feet in height; these trees were fairly widely spaced so that it was possible for a car or truck driven across country to find a way between them. This was the road, and when the surface of the earth became too deeply pitted and potholed with traffic the cars and trucks would deviate and choose another course. —NEVIL SHUTE, *A Town Like Alice*

It was mid-day when I emerged from the forest into an open space at the foot of the peninsula. A broad lake of beautiful curvature, with magnificent surroundings, lay before me, glittering in the sunbeams. It was full twelve miles in circumference. A wide belt of sand formed the margin which I was approaching, directly opposite to which, rising seemingly from the very depths of the water, towered the loftiest peak of a range of mountains apparently interminable. The ascending vapor from innumerable hot springs, and the sparkling jet of a single geyser, added the feature of novelty to one of the grandest landscapes I ever beheld.

—TRUMAN EVERTS, *Thirty-Seven Days of Peril—from Scribner's Monthly Vol III Nov. 1871*

For a while the country was much as it had been; then, climbing all the time, we crossed the top of a Col, the road winding back and forth on itself, and then it was really Spain. There were long brown mountains and a few pines and far-off forests of beech-trees on some of the mountainsides. The road went along the summit of the Col and then dropped down. . . . We came down out of the mountains and through an oak forest, and there were white cattle grazing in the forest. Down below there were grassy plains and clear streams.

—ERNEST HEMINGWAY, *The Sun Also Rises*

Sonam Kesang pointed his driver at the blue sky. He explained that the course remained green and soft until mid-October because the monsoon season usually extends until the middle of September and there is plenty of runoff after that. By early fall, the temperatures begin to cool, dropping into the low sixties during the day, and it hardly rains again until late the following spring, so the grass begins to wither and the fairways become rock hard. "We used to try to fertilize the course in winter to keep it green and playable," Sonam Kesang said. "But that didn't work. The only fertilizer we could get was cow manure, but that brought up cloves, so we gave up. Now we just don't play in January and February."

—RICK LIPSEY, *Golfing on the Roof of the World*

The DC-8 took off again and the sea fell away behind it; it climbed over a floor of rain forest and cleared the wall of the cordillera—range after range broken by sunless valleys over which the clouds lowered, brown peaks laced with fingers of dark green thrust up from the jungle on the lower slopes. And in less than an hour—in a slender valley refulgent and shimmering—the white city of Compostela, on twin hills, walled in by snow peaks and two spent volcanoes. —ROBERT STONE, *A Flag for Sunrise*

In the years that followed, one version or another of his rapacious fantasy was pursued by legions of avaricious speculators—land developers, bankers, railroad barons, real-estate promoters, citrus growers, cattle ranchers, sugar tycoons and, last but not least, the politicians they owned.

Those wetlands that could not be dried, paved or planted were eventually trenched out and diked into vast reservoirs by the U.S Army Corps of Engineers. Billions of gallons of freshwater that for eons had flowed freely as a broad marshy river toward Florida Bay was now held captive for siphoning by agriculture, industry and burgeoning municipalities. First one cross-state highway and then another transected the southern thumb of the peninsula, fatally interrupting the remaining southbound trickle from Lake Okeechobee.

—CARL HIAASEN, *Skinny Dip*

Tuesday morning: the country east of Heber was a desert of sagebrush and globe-shaped junipers and shallow washes with signs warning of flash floods. I turned north at Snowflake, founded by Erastus Snow and Bill Flake, and headed toward the twenty-five thousand square miles of Navajo reservation (nearly equal to West Virginia) which occupies most of the northeastern corner of Arizona. The scrub growth disappeared entirely and only the distant outlines of red rock mesas interrupted the emptiness. But for the highway, the land was featureless.

—WILLIAM LEAST HEAT-MOON, *Blue Highways: A Journey into America*

He slowed down to make the road last longer. He had passed the big pines and left them behind. Where he walked now the scrub had closed in, walling in the road with dense sand pines, each one so thin it seemed to the boy it might make kindling by itself. The road went up an incline. At the top he stopped. The April sky was framed by the tawny sand and the pines.

—MARJORIE KINNAN RAWLINGS, *The Yearling*

On these days of winter I climb to the top of a sky-raking spine of sandstone and sit beside a juniper tree. The ridge runs from a crumpled mountain range in southern Utah to the Arizona desert, jumping a river along its way. It is an elongated, asymmetrical reef of Mesozoic sandstone with a face and a flank, two sides so different you think that you are somewhere else when you are in the same place. The face rises brick-red from a broad wash, nearly vertical but for a skirt of boulders along its talus. The flank is the crazy side: an abruptly sloped flexure of ancient rock beds tilted upward into a jagged crest.

—ELLEN MELOY, *The Anthropology of Turquoise: Meditations on Landscape, Art, and Spirit*

We traveled on, past the settlement that lay behind Santa Rosa, the sloping shacks and the huts on stilts and the rows of overturned canoes on the riverbank. We passed the gate-like entrance of a green lagoon, and pushed on, struggling in the river that brimmed at our bow. It was hotter here, for the sun was above the palms and the storm clouds had vanished inland. There were no mountains or even hills. There was nothing but the riverbank of palms and low bushes and yellow-bark trees, and the sky came down to the treetops. The high muddy river had flooded the bushes on the bank.

—Paul Theroux, *The Mosquito Coast*

In other places, scraps of life are frozen in death at mid-stride, as Lot's wife was petrified to salt while fleeing to higher ground. Here is a wood-framed shack buried by sand, with only the roof joists still visible. In the distance is a copse of skeletal trees, the bones of orchards dried to a brittleness like charcoal. And is that a schoolhouse, with just the chimney and two walls still standing?

—Timothy Egan, *The Worst Hard Time: The Untold Story of Those Who Survived the Great American Dust Bowl*

The sun fell behind the right side of the gorge, and the shadow of the bank crossed the water so fast that it was like a quick step from one side to the other. The beginning of darkness was thrown over us like a sheet, and in it the water ran even faster, frothing and near-foaming under the canoe. —James Dickey, *Deliverance*

On the far side of the river valley the road passed through a stark black burn. Charred and limbless trunks of trees stretching away on every side. Ash moving over the road and the sagging hands of blind wire strung from the blackened lightpoles whining thinly in the wind. A burned house in a clearing and beyond that a reach of meadowlands stark and gray and a raw red mudbank where a roadworks lay abandoned.

—Cormac McCarthy, *The Road*

It's summer, and when it's summer, there's always a hurricane coming or leaving here. Each pushes its way through the flat Gulf to the twenty-six-mile manmade Mississippi beach, where they knock against the old summer mansions with their slave galleys turned guesthouses before running over the bayou, through the pines, to lose wind, drip rain, and die in the north.

—Jesmyn Ward, *Salvage the Bones*

It lay in the blue Pacific like a huge left-handed gauntlet, the open wristlet facing westward toward the island of Oahu, the cupped fingers pointing eastward toward Maui. The southern portion of Molokai consisted of rolling meadow land, often with gray and parched grasses, for rainfall was slight, while the northern portion was indented by some of the most spectacular cliffs in the islands.

—James A. Michener, *Hawaii*

Chee left his hiding place, and walked back to the arroyo where he had left his patrol car. He drove it, with no effort at all at concealment, up the wash to the crash location. He parked it beside the basalt upthrust. His shovel was in his pickup truck but he didn't really need it. He dug with his hands, exposing the two suitcases, and pulled them out. They were surprisingly heavy—each sixty to seventy pounds. —TONY HILLERMAN, *The Dark Wind*

At our backs rose the giant green and brown walls of the sierras, the range stretching away on either hand in violet and deep blue masses. At our feet lay the billowy green and yellow plain, vast as ocean, and channeled by innumerable streams, while one black patch on a slope far away showed us that our foes were camping on the very spot where they had overcome us.

—W. H. HUDSON, *The Purple Land*

Three men were standing in the narrow opening of the bush. One of them was the man with the huge gilded palm hat. They stood for a while rather bewildered, seeing the place bare and no sign of a human being near. They called back to the other men coming into the clearing. It seemed they had left their horses on a little plateau, located some hundred and fifty feet below on the road, where there was a bit of thin pasturage.

—B. TRAVEN, *The Treasure of the Sierra Madre*

The chain is a place renowned for its winter fisheries: from January to April the best cod on earth comes from the Lofoten waters. The seas off the archipelago are exceedingly complex, with black deeps and sudden shallows, weird currents and dense fogs. The seamen who occupy their business here are skilled, wary, courageous. And they know full well the dangers of the whirlpool that rages between Lofoten Point and the tiny off-island called Værøy. Not for nothing, they say, is the long-abandoned village that overlooks the swirling torrents called Hell.

—SIMON WINCHESTER, "In the Eye of the Whirlpool," *Smithsonian*, August 2001

Winged by her own impetus and the drying breeze, the *Casco* skimmed under cliffs, opened out a cove, showed us a beach and some green trees, and flitted by again, bowing to the swell. The trees, from our distance, might have been hazel; the beach might have been in Europe; the mountain forms behind modelled in little from the Alps, and the forest which clustered on their ramparts a growth no more considerable than our Scottish heath. Again the cliff yawned, but now with a deeper entry; and the *Casco*, hauling her wind, began to slide into the bay of Anaho.

—ROBERT LOUIS STEVENSON, *In the South Seas*

I am interested enough in that whopping statistic to spend most of the day being driven around the immense battlefield. Interested enough to walk down a spur on Little Round Top to see the monument to the 20th Maine, where a bookish but brave college professor named Joshua Lawrence Chamberlain ran out of ammo and ordered the bayonets that held the Union's ground. Interested enough to stop at the Copse of Trees—where the Confederate General George Pickett aimed his thousands of soldiers who were mowed down at the climax—and sit on a rock and wonder how many Southern skulls were cracked open on it. —SARAH VOWELL, "What He Said There," *The Partly Cloudy Patriot*

High up on the plateau at the foot of the Blue Ridge Mountains, she saw rolling red hills wherever she looked, with huge outcroppings of the underlying granite and gaunt pines towering somberly everywhere. It all seemed wild and untamed to her coast-bred eyes accustomed to the quiet jungle beauty of the sea islands draped in their gray moss and tangled green, the white stretches of beach hot beneath a semi-tropic sun, the long flat vistas of sandy land studded with palmetto and palm.

—MARGARET MITCHELL, *Gone with the Wind*

Once the team arrived at Base Camp, they had to contend with the Khumbu Icefall, a half-mile-wide glacier flowing down from Everest's Western Cwm and blocking the path to Camp I. The mess of constantly shifting and teetering blocks, which moves some four feet every day, has killed more than two dozen climbers over the years. Nowadays, the icefall is tamed each climbing season with aluminum ladders placed by a group of Sherpas whose sole job is to maintain a safe passage through it.

—GRAYSON SCHAFFER, "Lost on Everest," *Outside*, April 2013

A world of uneven ground, of treeless hills and mist-filled hollows, of waterlogged paths and heather-clad slopes, of high tors capped with broken granite, of hut circles and avenues of stones left by ancient peoples, Dartmoor extends over an area of between 200 and 300 square miles.

—EDWIN WAY TEALE, *Springtime in Britain*

Tenzin Taklha walked me to a spacious waiting room adjacent to the Dalai Lama's reception hall, up a hillock. Around the knoll were dramatic views of the valley dropping sharply below and the seventeen-thousand-foot peaks behind. Crows cawed from the wooded thickets around the complex, and hawks soared in the sky overhead, gliding on summer thermals. Tall, thin evergreens, known as deodars, cloaked the hill.

—TIM JOHNSON, *Tragedy in Crimson*

Then, as the midday sun withdraws from the gulf the shadow of the mountains the clouds begin to roll out of the lower valleys. They swathe in sombre tatters the naked crags of precipices above the wooded slopes, hide the peaks, smoke in stormy trails across the snows of Higuerota. The Cordillera is gone from you as if it had dissolved itself into great piles of grey and black vapours that travel out slowly to seaward and vanish into thin air all along the front before the blazing heat of the day.

—JOSEPH CONRAD, *Nostromo*

Nantucketers had good reason to be superstitious. Their lives were governed by a force of terrifying unpredictability—the sea. Due to a constantly shifting network of shoals, including the Nantucket Bar just off the harbor mouth, the simple act of coming to and from the island was an often harrowing and sometimes catastrophic lesson in seamanship.

—Nathaniel Philbrick, *In the Heart of the Sea: The Tragedy of the Whaleship* Essex

Viewed from the seaward scarp of the moors, the marsh takes form as the greener floor of a great encirclement of rolling, tawny, and treeless land. From a marsh just below, the vast flat islands and winding rivers of the marsh run level to the yellow bulwark of the dunes, and at the end of the vista the eye escapes through valleys in the wall to the cold April blue of the North Atlantic plain.

—Henry Beston, *The Outermost House*

Cyberspace was born where the laurel grows lush and verdant; where the dogwoods blossom and the whip-poorwills cry in the wind-whipped limbs of the tulip tree. It was born between the ridges, deep in the glades where streams rush cold along their limestone courses; born high on the mountainsides not yet strip-mined for their coal, atop the lone green knobs of Mars. The Southern Highlands, this region was once called; we now call it Appalachia. —William Gibson, *Neuromancer*

The glen of Tior will furnish a curious illustration of this. The inhabited part is not more than four miles in length, and varies in breadth from half a mile to less than a quarter. The rocky vine-clad cliffs on one side tower almost perpendicularly from their base to the height of at least fifteen hundred feet; while across the vale—in striking contrast to the scenery opposite—grass-grown elevations rise one above another in blooming terraces.

—HERMAN MELVILLE, *Typee*

It was dark by the time I hobbled with the last of my gear up the steep, narrow path to the top of the headland. My feet were swollen. Like an idiot, I'd left my sandals on Bob and Tanya Lamb's porch. I slumped in the windswept grass, utterly spent, head lolling against a leathery tussock. The Southeast Trade Winds hushed to a whisper, and droves of mosquitoes appeared from nowhere, zinging in my ears. I had no intention of sleeping. Far below, glowing orange in the beam of my headlamp, a pair of sleepless eyes patrolled back and forth.

—JASON LEWIS, *Dark Waters: True Story of the First Human-Powered Circumnavigation of the Earth* (The Expedition trilogy, Book 1)

Following the ridge, which made a gradual descent to the south, I came at length to the brow of that massive cliff that stands between Indian Cañon and Yosemite Falls, and here the far-famed valley came suddenly into view throughout almost its whole extent. The noble walls—sculptured into an endless variety of domes and gables, spires and battlements and plain mural precipices—all a-tremble with the thunder tones of the falling water. The level bottom seemed to be dressed like a garden—sunny meadows here and there, and groves of pine and oak; the river of Mercy sweeping in majesty through the midst of them and flashing back the sunbeams.

—JOHN MUIR, *My First Summer in the Sierra*

Forty-two miles south of the Sitka city limits, a house crafted from salvage planks and gray shingles teeters on two dozen pilings over a slough. A nameless backwater, riddled with bears and prone to methane flatulence. A graveyard of rowboats, tackle, pickup trucks, and, somewhere deep down, a dozen Russian fur hunters and their Aleut dog-soldiers. —MICHAEL CHABON, *The Yiddish Policemen's Union*

They were in the hills now, among pines. Although the afternoon wind had fallen, the shaggy crests still made a constant murmuring sound in the high sere air. The trunks and the massy foliage were the harps and strings of afternoon; the barred inconstant shadow of the day's retrograde flowed steadily over them as they crossed the ridge and descended into shadow, into the azure bowl of evening, the windless well of night; the portcullis of sunset fell behind them. —WILLIAM FAULKNER, *The Hamlet*

To the east, under the spreading sunrise, are more mesas, more canyons, league on league of red cliff and arid tablelands, extending through purple haze over the bulging curve of the planet to the ranges of Colorado—a sea of desert. —EDWARD ABBEY, *Desert Solitaire*

Some of the blocks can be as big as footballs, some as big as refrigerators or cars or houses. The blocks drop fast, bouncing, grinding, colliding down the cliff or slope like rocks in a rockfall. (Glacial ice is a type of metamorphic rock.)

The icefall is pursued by a turbulent dust cloud hundreds of feet high. The cloud can have a runout miles past where the icefall stops.

The most prominent hanging glacier on K2 is the one that sits brooding over the Bottleneck. It is a serac—defined, in the dictionary, as an irregular-shaped pinnacle of ice on a glacier, formed by the intersection of crevasses, or deep-running fissures.

—GRAHAM BOWLEY, *No Way Down: Life and Death on K2*

This regarded the request of the academy to widen the saltwater river and dredge a deeper low-tide channel at a point in the Squamscott that would improve the racing course for the academy crew; several shells had become mired in the mud flats at low tide. The part of the river the academy wished to widen was a peninsula of tidewater marsh bordering the Meany Granite Quarry; it was totally unusable land, yet Mr. Meany owned it and he resented that the academy wanted to scoop it away—"for purposes of recreation!" he said.

—JOHN IRVING, *A Prayer for Owen Meany*

On either side rocks, cliffs, treetops and a steep slope: forward there, the length of the boat, a tamer descent, tree-clad, with hints of pink: and then the jungly flat of the island, dense green, but drawn at the end to a pink tail. There, where the island petered out in water, was another island; a rock, almost detached, standing like a fort, facing them across the green with one bold, pink bastion. —WILLIAM GOLDING, *The Lord of the Flies*

It was another glaring day. The arid hills loomed desolate on every side while to the north the white cone of Etna shimmered in distant splendour. The road looped and labored over a wild landscape. Villages of prehistoric origin hung on their pinnacles of sun-blasted rock. Decaying fortresses—relics of war that had raged through Sicily for three millennia—looked down upon yet one more invading army. Brown fields burned under the smoking dust stirred by our column, and here and there little groups of desiccated peasants straightened backs and stared impassibly at our military might as they probably had at the guns and armour of the retreating Germans short hours earlier.

—FARLEY MOWAT, *And No Birds Sang*

A part of the land towards the north rises more than a thousand feet perpendicularly from the sea. A tableland at this height extends back nearly to the center of the island, and from this tableland arises a lofty cone like that of Teneriffe. The lower half of this cone is clothed with trees of good size, but the upper region is barren rock, usually hidden among the clouds, and covered with snow during the greater part of the year. There are no shoals or other dangers about the island, the shores being remarkably bold and the water deep. On the northwestern coast is a bay. . . . —EDGAR ALLAN POE, *The Narrative of Arthur Gordon Pym of Nantucket*

The island in sight was Flores. It seemed only a mountain of mud standing up out of the dull mists of the sea. But as we bore down upon it, the sun came out and made it a beautiful picture—a mass of green farms and meadows that swelled up to a height of fifteen hundred feet, and mingled its upper outlines with the clouds. It was ribbed with sharp, steep ridges, and cloven with narrow cañons, and here and there on the heights, rocky upheavals shaped themselves into mimic battlements and castles; and out of rifted clouds came broad shafts of sunlight, that painted summit, and slope, and glen, with bands of fire, and left belts of sombre shade between.

—MARK TWAIN, *Roughing It*

What is most striking in the Maine wilderness is the continuousness of the forest, with fewer open intervals or glades than you had imagined. Except for the few burnt lands, the narrow intervals on the rivers, the bare tops of the high mountains, and the lakes and streams, the forest is uninterrupted.

—HENRY DAVID THOREAU, *The Maine Woods*

Sharp hills rose immediately behind the town. The town is in a saddle of the hills, slipping down to the river in terraces of white, chrome, and blue houses. The Rio Tapajos, a black water tributary and a noble river, enters the main stream by Santarem, its dark flood sharply contrasted with the tawny Amazon. But the Amazon sweeps right across its mouth in a masterful way. There is a definite line dividing black from yellow water, and then no more Tapajos.

We passed numerous floating islands (Ilhas de Caapim) and trees adrift, evidence, the pilots said, that the river was rising. These grass islands are a feature of the Amazon. They look like lush pastures adrift. Some of them are so large it is difficult to believe they are really afloat till they come alongside. Then, if the river is at all broken by a breeze, the meadow plainly undulates.

—H. M. Tomlinson, *The Sea and the Jungle*

With a jerk the cart moved off, gathering speed: They hurtled past Travers, who was wriggling into a crack in the wall, then the cart began twisting and turning through the labyrinthine passages, sloping downward all the time. Harry could not hear anything over the rattling of the cart on the tracks: His hair flew behind him as they swerved between stalactites, flying ever deeper into the earth, but he kept glancing back.

—J. K. Rowling, *Harry Potter and the Deathly Hallows*

It was an impressive lookout point. To the eastward the main valley lay outspread. On the opposite side the land fell away in gullies and precipitous ravines to the sea. Several small cascades, the result of recent heavy rains, streamed down the rocky walls, arching away from them, in places, as they descended. Small as the island was, its aspect from that height had in it a quality of savage grandeur, and the rich green thickets on the gentler slopes, lying in the full splendour of the westering sun, added to the solemnity of narrow valleys already filling with shadow, and the bare precipices that hung above them.

—CHARLES NORDHOFF AND JAMES NORMAN HALL, *Pitcairn's Island*

Odell suffered terribly, and Mallory took note of it, but eventually he and Lhakpa joined the others, and they continued on, traversing the face and straddling, at one point, a narrow ridge of ice that fell away on one side to the blackness of a fathomless crevasse and on the other to open space and the head of the glacier, thousands of feet below.

—WADE DAVIS, *Into the Silence: The Great War, Mallory, and the Conquest of Everest*

The chief feature of the landscape, and of your life in it, was the air. Looking back on a sojourn in the African highlands, you are struck by your feeling of having lived for a time up in the air. The sky was rarely more than pale blue or violet, with a profusion of mighty, weightless, ever-changing clouds towering up and sailing on it, but it has a blue vigour in it, and at a short distance it painted the ranges of hills and the woods a fresh deep blue. In the middle of the day the air was alive over the land, like a flame burning: it scintillated, waved and shone like running water, mirrored and doubled all objects, and created great Fata Morgana.

—ISAK DINESEN, *Out of Africa*

There is no trail up this gray valley, only dim paths that lose themselves in bogs and willow flats and gravel streams. Several hours pass before we come to the rock outwash of a chasm in the northern walls where the torrent comes down from the ice fields of Kang La. Even at midday the ravine is dark, and so steep and narrow that on the ascent under hanging rocks the torrent must be crossed over and over. —PETER MATTHIESSEN, *The Snow Leopard*

To truly grasp what this sea journey meant, what bravery and audacity it required, one must understand how the world was seen and known at that time. Though George Ashby and his contemporaries had been born in the Age of Discovery (1500–1700), most of the world was still terra incognita for Europeans. Maps were often sketchy and inaccurate. Two continents, Australia and Antarctica, had not been traced at all, and vast areas were still blank. The interiors of South America, Africa and Asia had scarcely been explored. Beyond the eastern fringe of North America, which George's fellow pioneers had begun to document, were millions of square miles of uncharted wilderness. —ANDREA STUART, *Sugar in the Blood: A Family's Story of Slavery and Empire*

This solitary stone peak overlooks the whole of my childhood and youth, the great Salinas Valley stretching south for nearly a hundred miles, the town of Salinas where I was born now spreading like crab grass toward the foothills. Mount Toro, on the brother range to the west, was a rounded benign mountain, and to the north Monterey Bay shone like a blue platter.

—JOHN STEINBECK, *Travels with Charley: In Search of America*

He looked at the miles of ocean between the boat and the beach at the foot of the mountains. Far off to the right he could see white water, the current running swiftly over the top of a reef that extended southwesterly, at a 45-degree angle to the beach. Beyond the reef was a sand-spit where the island tapered to its narrow southern end. On their left, the base of the mountains extended to the edge of the sea, forming a rock wall against which the waves broke. According to the charts, the wall plunged to a depth of ten fathoms, and the ocean concealed a network of submarine caves and grottoes in the volcanic rock of which the Pitons were composed. Across the towering ridge, completely out of sight, was the celebrated resort.

—ROBERT STONE, "Under the Pitons," *Bear and His Daughter*

There were miles of pastures and tens of miles of wasted, washed-out land abandoned to the hardier weeds. The train cut through deep green pine forest where the ground was covered with the slick brown needles and the tops of the trees stretched up virgin and tall into the sky. And farther, a long way south of the town, the cypress swamps—with the gnarled roots of the trees writhing down into the brackish waters, where the gray, tattered moss trailed from the branches, where tropical water flowers blossomed in dankness and gloom. Then out again into the open beneath the sun and the indigo-blue sky.

—Carson McCullers, *The Heart Is a Lonely Hunter*

He crawled up a small knoll and surveyed the prospect. There were no trees, no bushes, nothing but a gray sea of moss scarcely diversified by gray rocks, gray lakelets, and gray streamlets. —Jack London, "Love of Life," *Love of Life, and Other Stories*

A film of mist hung over the inlet. A family of red-fronted geese rippled the water, and at the first gate more geese stood by a puddle. I passed along the track that led up into the mountains. Ahead was Harberton Mountain, black with trees, and a hazy sun coming over its shoulder. This side of the river was rolling grass country, burned out of the forest and spiked with charred trees.

—Bruce Chatwin, *In Patagonia*

Overall, leaf quality is an important influence in recruitment and harvesting intensity in leaf-cutting ants. Its parameters include leaf tenderness, nutrient contents, and the presence and quantity of secondary plant chemicals. In one experiment, harvest preference in *Atta cephalotes* was tested by offering the ants fresh leaves of forty-nine plant species from a tropical deciduous forest in Costa Rica. —Bert Hölldobler and Edward O. Wilson, *The Leafcutter Ants*

Above the tongue is North Otter Bay, which is deep; below it is South Otter Bay, so shoal as to be dangerous, in spots, to anything but a canoe. It was through the shallows of South Otter Bay that we dragged our boats ashore on the tongue of land along which the river pours itself into the lake; and it was across this tongue of land that we were obliged to carry the boats in order to get to the northward of the French. —KENNETH ROBERTS, *Northwest Passage*

The river was squeezed into a twisty crevice between high bluffs, and the wind, thickened with sand from the bars, went scouring into every cranny and backwater. The forest came down sheer into the water on both sides, broken by outcrops of ribbed limestone, staring out of the solid cliffs of green like the faces of Easter Island statues.

—JONATHAN RABAN, *Old Glory*

Now, after fourteen hours in the stream, a night of naps, and a soaking rain, we stand in the outlet of Allagash Lake. The most distant point we can see is perhaps four miles away—a clear shot down open water past a fleet of islands. The lake is broad in all directions, and is ringed with hills and minor mountains. Its pristine, unaltered shoreline is edged with rock—massive outcroppings, sloping into the water, interrupting the march of the forest.

—JOHN MCPHEE, *The Survival of the Bark Canoe*

The magnitude of this calamity was so far beyond anything I'd ever imagined that my brain simply shorted out and went dark. Abandoning my hope of comprehending what had happened, I shouldered my backpack and headed down onto the frozen witchery of the Icefall nervous as a cat, for one last trip through the maze of decaying seracs. —JON KRAKAUER, *Into Thin Air: A Personal Account of the Mt. Everest Disaster*

As Ice Ages came and went and glaciers repeatedly advanced and retreated, a distinctive, fiercely-glaciated landscape was created. Valley troughs were deepened, smoothed and straightened; at the heads of the valleys, basin-like corries—the lofty nurseries of the glaciers—were slowly scooped out; knife-sharp aretes were honed as the steep corrie backwalls retreated and met; hummocks of ground-up rock debris were then dumped as moraine when the glaciers began to recede; and in the aftermath of glaciation, lakes formed in the hollows which the ice had gouged in the valley bottoms. Gradually, the deposition of river silts is filling up the lake basins, and eventually the lakes will disappear.

—RICHARD MUIR, *The Stones of Britain*

The path unfurls through a rolling broad-leaf forest peppered with Siberian stone pines, larches, and silver fir and inhabited, Andrei says, by at least several hundred sables, those bearers of the golden fleece, still hanging on in these old woods. The air is as clear and dry and sweet and warm as a June day in Maine, and it fills every few minutes with the distant rumble of a train clattering along the Trans-Siberian tracks down by the lake, a couple of kilometers away.

—PETER THOMSON, *Sacred Sea: A Journey to Lake Baikal*

The sheer flanks of the cañon descended in furrowed lines of vines and clinging bushes, like folds of falling skirts, until they broke again into flounces of spangled shrubbery over a broad level carpet of monkshood, mariposas, lupines, poppies, and daisies.

—BRET HARTE, *The Youngest Miss Piper*

The mountains of the Pennines are not particularly tall and by some definitions not even mountains, Cross Fell being the highest at just short of 3,000 feet, and are often referred to as fells, pikes, or simply hills. . . . Their unique characteristic is that of moorland, and I say unique because for all my wanderings, I have never come across anywhere in the world which resembles the moors of my own country. These are wide and undulating expanses of high altitude, treeless hillsides, often boggy, usually with very poor or "peat" soil, incapable, on the face of it, of sustaining anything but the hardiest of grasses or the most adaptive of species.

—SIMON ARMITAGE, *Walking Home*

The path, a rather dubious and uncertain one, led us along the ridge of high bluffs that border the Missouri; and by looking to the right or to the left, we could enjoy a strange contrast of opposite scenery. On the left stretched the prairie, rising into swells and undulations, thickly sprinkled with groves, or gracefully expanding into wide grassy basins, of miles in extent; while its curvatures, swelling against the horizon were often surmounted by lines of sunny woods. . . .

—FRANCIS PARKMAN, *The Oregon Trail*

The Klamath tribe of Native Americans who witnessed the eruption believed it was a fierce battle between Llao, the spirit of the underworld, and Skell, the spirit of the sky. When the battle was over, Llao was driven back into the underworld and Mount Mazama had become an empty bowl. A caldera, it's called—a sort of mountain in reverse. A mountain that's had its very heart removed. Slowly, over hundreds of years, the caldera filled with water, collecting the Oregon rain and snowmelt, until it became the lake that it is now. Reaching a maximum depth of more than 1,900 feet, Crater Lake is the deepest lake in the United States and among the deepest in the world.

—CHERYL STRAYED, *Wild: From Lost to Found on the Pacific Crest Trail*

WEATHER, FORCES OF NATURE, AND THE SOLAR SYSTEM

WEATHER AND FORCES OF NATURE

characterized by good weather

fair, clear, pleasant, lovely, balmy, halcyon, temperate, springlike, summer-like, summery

characterized by bad weather

nasty, foul, inclement, wintery, winter-like, smoggy

sunny

bright, cloudless, glorious, sunshiny

intensely bright

glary, glaring, dazzling, blinding

cloudy

cloud-covered, nebulous, partly sunny

covered or blanketed with clouds

overcast, lowering, gray, gloomy, clouded up

foggy

misty, thick, murky, vaporous, brumous

permeated by a heavy haze of fog mixed with smoke and atmospheric chemical pollutants
smoggy

windy
breezy, gusty, blowing, blowy, howling, roaring, turbulent, blustery, zephyrous

stormy
tempestuous, raging, angry, dirty

threatening
lowering, darkening, looming, black

damp
humid, muggy, dank, steamy, moist

rainy or wet
precipitating, drizzly, drippy, torrential, showering, pouring

dewy
roric, roriferous

wet and cold
raw, bleak

wet and messy underfoot
slushy, sloppy

dry
arid, parched, desiccated, bone-dry, waterless

very warm
hot, torrid, burning, blazing, scorching, blistering, broiling, baking, searing, roasting, tropical, pitiless

hot and humid
sultry, steamy, sweltering, stifling

cool
chill, chilly

refreshingly cool or chill

crisp, bracing, brisk, autumnal, fall-like

cold

chilly, nippy, sharp, algid

very cold

biting, piercing, bone-chilling, freezing, numbing

snowing

snowy, niveous, nival

frosty

rimy, hoary

icy or frozen

frigid, freezing, gelid

multi-colored (red, orange, yellow, green, blue, indigo, violet) arc of light (on the side of the sky opposite to the sun—the higher the sun, the lower the arc) produced when sunlight is reflected inside raindrops

rainbow

visibly dense mass or stratum of fog seen from a distance formed above the sea

fog bank

rainbow-like arc of diffracted white light sometimes visible in fog

fogbow, fogdog, fogeater, seadog

hazy glow of light sometimes visible just before dawn or just after sunset

zodiacal light

visible coronal (electrical) discharge, during a thunderstorm, seen on a pointed object, such as part of the tip of a tree, the wing of a plane, or the mast of a ship

St. Elmo's fire, St. Elmo's light, corposant

transitional zone between two air masses differing in temperature or density

front

edge of a warm air mass that is advancing

warm front

rising current of warm air (used by birds, balloonists, and glider pilots to gain altitude)

thermal

brief spell of briskly cold weather

cold snap

edge of a cold air mass that is advancing

cold front

mixed front occurring when a cold front overtakes a warm front and lifts the warm air

occluded front

transitional zone between two differing air masses, neither of which is forceful enough to replace the other

stationary front

elongated area having low barometric pressure

trough

ocean low-pressure area near the equator having characteristic calms, light winds, and squalls

doldrums

two regions or belts, at about 30° North and 30° South, known for having high pressure, calms, and baffling winds

horse latitudes

predominant, continual wind of the tropics and subtropics blowing toward the equator from the northeast (between the doldrums and the northern horse latitudes) or the southeast (between the doldrums and the southern horse latitudes)

trade wind, trade

narrow band of high-speed winds 10 to 15 miles (the upper atmosphere) above the earth from a generally westerly direction
jet stream

marked shift in wind speed and direction over a short area
wind shear

rising current of air
anabatic wind

downward-flowing current of air
katabatic wind

lying on or coming from the other side of a mountain range
tramontane

brief, violent downdraft over a small area
microburst, downburst

strong wind
gale

brief, violent windstorm, often bringing rain or snow
squall

storm of wind-borne clouds of sand, as in a desert
sandstorm

wall of dust resulting from a microburst
haboob

cold and dry northerly wind of southern France
mistral

hot, dry, dust-laden wind from the deserts of Libya that reaches the northern Mediterranean coast
sirocco, scirocco

moist, warm wind in the coastal Pacific Northwest from the southwest; also, a warm dry wind blowing down the eastern slopes of the Rocky Mountains
Chinook

warm, dry, dusty wind along the west coast of Africa in some seasons

harmattan

warm, dry wind coming off the northern slopes of the Alps

foehn, föhn

southerly hot Saharan wind that blows across Egypt from March to May

khamsin

hot, dry Southern California wind from inland deserts to the Pacific coast

Santa Ana

strong, hot, sand-laden wind of the Sahara and Arabian deserts

simoom, simoon, samiel

small, rotating windstorm

whirlwind

small, usually brief whirlwind bearing sand, dust, or debris

dust devil

brief rainstorm with thunder and lightning

thundershower

sudden, heavy rainstorm

cloudburst

sometimes violent storm of thunder and lightning often accompanied by rain or hail

thunderstorm

periodic, seasonal change in wind direction that brings heavy rainfall to areas of southern Asia

monsoon

tropical cyclone of the western Pacific Ocean or the Indian Ocean

typhoon

broad and deep undulation of the ocean caused by an earthquake or distant storm

groundswell

giant fast-advancing ocean wave caused by an underwater earthquake or volcanic eruption

tsunami, tidal wave, seismic sea wave

THE SOLAR SYSTEM

lunar phase when the moon is between the earth and the sun, making it visible at sunset only as a narrow crescent

new moon, dark of the moon

lunar phase when the entire disk of the moon is illuminated

full moon

the coinciding of a full moon or new moon with its nearest orbital position to the earth

supermoon

second full moon occurring within a single month

blue moon

lunar phase of a full moon closest in time to the autumnal (September) equinox

harvest moon

lunar phase showing half of an illuminated moon (first quarter or last quarter)

half-moon

lunar phase showing more than half of the moon illuminated

gibbous moon

lunar phase (waxing or waning) when less than half of the moon is illuminated

crescent moon

lunar phase when the visible moon is becoming gradually larger (between a new moon and a full moon)

waxing moon, increscent moon

lunar phase when the visible moon is becoming gradually smaller (between a full moon and a new moon)

waning moon, decrescent moon

in an orbit, the nearest point of the moon from the earth

perigee

in an orbit, the farthest point of the moon from the earth

apogee

either of two lunar orbital points (as during a solar or lunar eclipse) when the moon lies in a straight line with the sun and the earth

syzygy

the envisioned or imaginary sphere having earth as its center

celestial sphere

on the celestial sphere, the great circle midway between the celestial poles or envisioned as on the same plane as the earth's equator

celestial equator

the mean plane of earth's orbit when it meets the celestial sphere, or the sun's apparent path against the background of the sky

ecliptic

either of two points on the ecliptic when its distance is maximal from the celestial equator, reached by the sun about June 22 (summer solstice) or about December 22 (winter solstice)

solstice

either of two points on the celestial sphere when the celestial equator intersects the ecliptic (about March 21, the vernal equinox, and September 23, the autumnal equinox), when everywhere on earth day and night are of approximately equal duration

equinox

partial or total obscuring of one celestial body by another, as of the sun by the moon or the moon by the earth
eclipse
reddish moon associated with a total lunar eclipse
blood moon
eclipse when the moon is between the earth and the sun and, appearing smaller than the sun, has a bright ring around it
annular eclipse
area of only partial shadow, as during an eclipse
penumbra
point in the path of a celestial body when it is nearest the sun
perihelion
point in the path of a celestial body when it is farthest from the sun
aphelion
dark spot occasionally visible (usually only through a telescope) on the sun's surface, associated with a strong magnetic field
sunspot
eruptive plume of hydrogen gas, causing a sudden brightness, from the sun's surface, ranging in magnitude from A, B, C, M, to X class, the latter being the most powerful in peak flux
solar flare
outflowing of plasma through or from the sun's corona
coronal mass ejection (CME)
orbiting celestial body (composed of ice and dust around a bright nucleus) that develops a long tail and becomes observable when near the sun
comet

orbiting rocky celestial body (esp. between the orbits of Mars and of Jupiter), ranging considerably in size

asteroid, planetoid

stony or metallic solid body in motion in space and smaller than an asteroid

meteoroid

meteoroid that becomes a bright streak in the sky from friction when it encounters the earth's atmosphere

meteor, shooting star, falling star, fireball

meteor, or what remains of it despite vaporizing on contact with the earth's atmosphere, that reaches or impacts the surface of the earth

meteorite

as seen through a thin cloud or haze, a luminous, faintly colored ring appearing around the moon or sun and caused by diffracted light from suspended droplets

corona

radiant streams of light visible at night in the upper atmosphere of earth's magnetic polar region (caused by charged solar particles) occurring sporadically in middle and high latitudes of either hemisphere

aurora

aurora occurring in the Southern Hemisphere

aurora australis, southern lights

aurora occurring in the Northern Hemisphere

aurora borealis, northern lights

measure of reflectiveness of a celestial body

albedo

Clouds

Note: For remembering these Latinate cloud classifications (introduced in 1803 by English chemist Luke Howard), it is helpful to know the meanings of the key affixes: *cumulo-*, heap or pile; *strato-*, cover or layer; *cirro-*, curl or hair; *alto-*, high; and *nimbo-*, rain cloud.

Low-Elevation Clouds

stratus

cloud mass like a formless gray horizontal sheet, from which may come drizzle; the sky looks heavy and leaden; bases and tops of clouds are uniform.

cumulus

separate, distinctively shaped puffs or fleecy domed or towered piles of cloud, brightly white in sunlight with darker base; upper parts often like cauliflower.

stratocumulus

grayish, rounded, roll-like masses forming an extensive layer; often look like altocumulus but are lower.

cumulonimbus

mountainously high and often dark storm cloud (or thunderheads) with swellings or "towers" and frequently a flattened, anvil-like top plume; often with ragged cloudlets underneath.

Middle-Elevation Clouds

altostratus

a gray and smooth, sometimes striated or fibrous (stringlike) uniform veil of grayish or bluish cloud through which the sun may palely shine (as if through frosted glass)

altocumulus

cloud mass of various shapes, disconnected lumps or patches or a jumble of billowing cloudlets white or gray or both; sometimes lining up in parallel bands; sometimes with "towers," resembling cumulus.

nimbostratus

an amorphous gray or dark cloud layer, blotting out the sun and often unseen because rain or snow is falling from it; sometimes with ragged clouds below.

High-Elevation Clouds

cirrus

delicate white wisps or filaments of cloud, sometimes with a silky look; or like fibrous threads with hooks at the end; often seem to converge at a point on the horizon. A long and narrow cirrus cloud with a flowing appearance is a mare's tail.

cirrostratus

a thin, smooth, fibrous whitish cloud with which one often sees a halo effect around (but not obscuring) the sun; contourless and transparent, with no shadows cast on the ground.

cirrocumulus

a thin white layer of cloud, with no shading and with a ripple or other regular pattern; usually too thin to cause shadows below; often known as mackerel clouds, a mackerel sky, or a buttermilk sky.

QUOTATIONS

A sky-herd of cumulus clouds, on their way to bestow moist blessings on the mountains after cruelly deceiving the parched desert, began blotting out the sun and trailing dark shadow-shapes across the blistered land below, offering intermittent but welcome respite from the searing sunlight. When a racing cloud-shadow wiped its way over the ruins, the novice worked rapidly until the shadow was gone, then rested until the next bundle of fleece blotted out the sun.

—Walter M. Miller Jr., *A Canticle for Leibowitz*

The POWs looked up. There, so high that they appeared to be gleaming slits in the sky, were acres and acres of B-29s, one hundred and eleven of them, flying toward an aircraft factory on the rim of the city. Caught in what would later be called the jet stream, the planes were streaking along at speeds approaching 445 miles per hour, almost 100 miles per hour faster than they were built to fly. The Americans had arrived.

—Laura Hillenbrand, *Unbroken: A World War II Story of Survival, Resilience, and Redemption*

Boo Boo found it queerly difficult to keep Lionel in steady focus. The sun, though not especially hot, was nonetheless so brilliant that it made any fairly distant image—a boy, a boat—seem almost as wavering and refractional as a stick in the water. After a couple of minutes, Boo Boo let the image go. She peeled down her cigarette Army style, and then started toward the pier.

—J. D. SALINGER, "Down at the Dinghy," *Nine Stories*

However the street led us to a square,and I saw the towers of a church sitting in the sky;between them the round yellow big moon looked immensely and peacefully conscious . . . no one was stirring in the little streets,all the houses were keeping the moon's secret.

We walked on.

I was too tired to think. I merely felt the town as a unique unreality. What was it? I knew—the moon's picture of a town. These streets with their houses did not exist,they were but a ludicrous projection of the moon's sumptuous personality. This was a city of Pretend,created by the hypnotism of moonlight.

—E. E. CUMMINGS, *The Enormous Room*

This was the manner of its coming. Before it, there was clear sky, and the sun shining upon new-fallen snow, a soft breeze from the west, moist and not cold. Then to the north was a line of high-banked, slate-gray cloud, and the mutter of thunder. Next, suddenly, the clouds darkened sun and sky, the north wind struck frigidly, and the air was thick with furious snow. —GEORGE R. STEWART, *Storm*

Night falls quickly on the Equator; one minute it was sunny, the next it was dark, the Southern Cross low in the sky and the Milky Way thick overhead, the blackness of the river and its unpopulated banks impenetrable. Heat lightning flashed along the horizon, and I played a simple card-slapping game with Kleyton and five kids.

—CARL HOFFMAN, *The Lunatic Express: Discovering the World . . . via Its Most Dangerous Buses, Boats, Trains, and Planes*

Ragged edges of black clouds peeped over the hills, and invisible thunderstorms circled outside, growing like wild beasts. . . . Before sunset the growling clouds carried with a rush the ridge of hills, and came tumbling down the inner slopes. Everything disappeared; black whirling vapours filled the bay, and in the midst of them the schooner swung here and there in the shifting gusts of wind.

—JOSEPH CONRAD, "Karain: A Memory," *Heart of Darkness and Other Tales*

Years before her parents had given a dinner party. They had set up the long table in their parched and dry garden. It was the end of May but the drought had gone on and on and still there was no monsoon. Then, towards the end of the meal, the rains began. Anil woke in her bedroom to the change in the air, ran to her window and looked out. The guests were scurrying under the thickness of the downpour, carrying antique chairs into the house. But her father and the woman he was beside continued to sit at the table, celebrating the break in seasons, as earth turned to mud around them.

—MICHAEL ONDAATJE, *Anil's Ghost*

That afternoon Peter, Kevin and I went fishing in the little outboard. The weather was hot, muggy, clouded over, and we waited in vain for a bite. We'd dropped anchor in a marsh where hollow reeds surrounded us and scratched the metal sides of the boat. I was sweating freely. Sweat stung my right eye. A mosquito spoke in my ear. The smell of gasoline from the engine (tilted up out of the shallow water) refused to lift and float away.

—EDMUND WHITE, *A Boy's Own Story*

The jet stream is not steady; it convulses like a loose firehose, careening off mountains, veering across plains. These irregularities create continent-sized eddies that come ballooning out of the Arctic as deep cold fronts. They are called anticyclones because the cold air in them flows outwards and clockwise, the opposite of a low.

—SEBASTIAN JUNGER, *The Perfect Storm*

It is no easy matter to proceed, though, for the wind pours down the lane as through a funnel, and the road is of slippery bare slate, worn here and there into puddles of greasy clay, and Elsley slips back half of every step, while his wrath, as he tires, oozes out of his heels.

—CHARLES KINGSLEY, *Two Years Ago*

The eastern sun, full and fiery orange, just risen clear of the horizon, began slowly to sink back into the gray ocean of clouds as the plane started down; the sky altered; clouds changed aspects. To the southeast, delicate as frozen breath, an icy herd of mare's tails rode high and sparkling in the upper light of the vanishing sun; they were veiled in crystalline haze as the plane descended through stratocirrus, the sun in iridescent halo at its disappearing upper limb. And below, slowly rising closer, the soft floor of carpeting clouds gradually changed into an ugly boil of endless gray billows, ominous, huge. —H. L. HUMES, *The Underground City*

Above the whole valley, indeed, the sky was heavy with tumbling vapors, interspersed with which were tracts of blue, vividly brightened by the sun; but, in the east, where the tempest was yet trailing its ragged skirts, lay a dusky region of cloud and sullen mist, in which some of the hills appeared of a dark-purple hue.

—NATHANIEL HAWTHORNE, *The Marble Faun*

I looked outside, watching the full moon hover in the sky beyond the tip of the aeroplane wing, childishly imagining it to be catching a free ride. We travelled for a while like that, the moon surfing on the wing, until the pilot warned us, in that proper British accent that we have come to associate with efficiency, to prepare for landing.

—MUKOMA WA NGUGI, *Nairobi Heat*

But of course the texture of that morning is clearer than the present, down to the drenched, wet feel of the air. It had rained in the night, a terrible storm, shops were flooded and a couple of subway stations closed; and the two of us were standing on the squelching carpet outside our apartment building while her favorite doorman, Goldie, who adored her, walked backwards down Fifty-seventh with his arm up, whistling for a taxi. Cars whooshed by in sheets of dirty spray; rain-swollen clouds tumbled high above the skyscrapers, blowing and shifting to patches of clear blue sky, and down below, on the street, beneath the exhaust fumes, the wind felt damp and soft like spring. —DONNA TARTT, *The Goldfinch*

Down river, from Andy's Landing, a burned-off cedar snag held the sun spitted like an apple, hissing and dripping juices against a grill of Indian Summer clouds. All the hillside, all the drying Himalaya vine that lined the big river, and the sugar-maple trees farther up, burned a dark brick and over-lit red. —KEN KESEY, *Sometimes a Great Notion*

I asked why he'd wanted to leave their hometown of Budapest.

"Because Budapest is the City of Egrets," she said.

She means the City of Regrets, I thought, then reminded myself—this was Borka.

City of egrets, city of tall, thin, spooky, watchful people.

We emerged from the metro in a neighborhood where apartment buildings yielded to stand-alone houses. The air was dirtier, the heated smog hovering at the height of the rain gutters in a tobacco-colored band.

—HEIDI JULAVITS, *The Vanishers*

This morning as always Maxine finds the oversize stoop aswarm with pupils, teachers on wrangler duty, parents and sitters, and younger siblings in strollers. The principal, Bruce Winterslow, acknowledging the equinox in a white suit and panama hat, is working the crowd, all of whom he knows by name and thumbnail bio, patting shoulders, genially attentive, schmoozing or threatening as the need arises. —THOMAS PYNCHON, *Bleeding Edge*

To-day is a grey day, and the sun as I write is hidden in thick clouds, high over Kettleness. Everything is grey—except the green grass, which seems like emerald amongst it; grey earthy rock; grey clouds, tinged with the sunburst at the far edge, hang over the grey sea, into which the sand-points stretch like grey fingers. The sea is tumbling in over the shallows and the sandy flats with a roar, muffled in the sea-mists drifting inland. The horizon is lost in a grey mist. All is vastness; the clouds are piled up like giant rocks, and there is a "brool" over the sea that sounds like some presage of doom. —BRAM STOKER, *Dracula*

As the second day of their riding drew on, the heaviness in the air increased. In the afternoon the dark clouds began to overtake them: a somber canopy with great billowing edges flecked with dazzling light. The sun went down, blood-red in a smoking haze.

—J. R. R. TOLKIEN, *The Two Towers*

Cudjoe winces. A column of feathers and stinging grit rises from the cobblestones and sluices past him. Wind is steady moan and groan, a constant weight in his face, but it also bucks and roils and sucks and swirls madly, sudden stop and start, gust and dust devil and dervishes ripping the world apart. Clouds scoot as if they're being chased.

—JOHN EDGAR WIDEMAN, *Philadelphia Fire*

Sometimes, when they came down from the cirrus levels to catch a better wind, they would find themselves among the flocks of cumulus—huge towers of modelled vapour, looking as white as Monday's washing and as solid as meringues. Perhaps one of these piled-up blossoms of the sky, these snow-white droppings of a gigantic Pegasus, would lie before them several miles away.

—T. H. WHITE, *The Once and Future King*

The storm bore down on the mountain with a primordial intensity unlike anything Paljor had ever experienced. The temperature plunged to minus 50, cold enough to freeze exposed flesh straight through in minutes. Gusts approaching eighty miles per hour ripped across the high escarpments, threatening to fling Paljor off the ridge like a bit of straw. —NICK HEIL, *Dark Summit*

Outside, the clouds above the mountain had lowered while Trudi changed her clothes, and a white mist had blanked out the summit, which meant alpine weather on the way but they were dressed for it. They walked through the town past the little shops and the statue of Goethe, then started up one of the trails. About twenty minutes later a few flakes of snow came drifting down—big, soft flakes that spun through the still air. Trudi wiped her face with her mitten. Orlova's cap turned from red to white. A wind stirred, then grew stronger and sighed through the forest, while the branches of the pine trees bowed with the weight of the new snow.

—Alan Furst, *Mission to Paris*

. . . the train is rolling eastward and the changing wind veers for the moment from an easterly quarter, and we face east, like Swedenborg's angels, under a sky clear save where far to the northeast over distant mountains whose purple has faded, lies a mass of almost pure white clouds, suddenly, as by a light in an alabaster lamp, illumined from within by gold lightning, yet you can hear no thunder. . . .

—Malcolm Lowry, *Under the Volcano*

But by early June the southwest monsoon breaks and there are three months of wind and water with short spells of sharp, glittering sunshine. . . . The countryside turns an immodest green. Boundaries blur as tapioca fences take root and bloom. Brick walls turn mossgreen. Pepper vines snake up electric poles. Wild creepers burst through laterite banks and spill across the flooded roads. Boats ply in the bazaars. And small fish appear in the puddles that fill the PWD potholes on the highways.

—Arundhati Roy, *The God of Small Things*

When the sky was furrowed with wispy bands of altostratus cloud the colour ranged from the most delicate pearl-pinks to the deepest fiery red. Sometimes it was so breathtakingly beautiful that Donald and I rushed for our cameras to capture its ephemeral glory.

—John Lister–Kaye, *The White Island*

At this moment the door burst open and Giorgio staggered into the living room, mesmerizing its four occupants. He was drenched, and his luxuriant wavy hair was plastered to his skull, giving him the look of some Cro-Magnon charmer. The topers by the fire became aware that the blizzard had changed to a torrential downpour.

—John Ashbery and James Schuyler, *A Nest of Ninnies*

After an hour of heavy rain in tunnel-darkness, the light reveals a fog cloud hugging the grass. How long has it been right in front of me, invisibly close and an acre wide? A giant *fogbow* appears in the rising light. This one shines blue to orange and arches across the road like a mystical staircase. I've known them to be double the size of common rainbows and sweep 360 degrees to include the whole vista.

—Diane Ackerman, *Dawn Light*

High gauzes and drags of cloud, in where the blue was strongest: he'd learned what that meant. "Cirrostratus . . . moisture . . . It freezes up there. Everything freezes up there." Catching the idea before it pushed in any further and turned nasty. "There'll have been a storm somewhere. Earlier."

—A. L. Kennedy, *Day*

It was quieter than the quietest night. And the clouds drifted across the sky with the same terrible, icy, inhuman slowness. Also there were changes of colour. The scene became tinted with mauve. She watched cumulus gather on the horizon; saw it break into three, and with continuous changes of shape and colour the clouds started their journey across the sky.

—D. M. THOMAS, *The White Hotel*

If you could stand it, you could look straight down, nearly a mile down to the canyon floor. Alexandra would like to go try it when she got home. She was sure it would terrify her, even though looking out the little plastic window in the airplane for some reason didn't. Reading about the skywalk, and looking out her window here at the sullen wet day, with its purplish wisps travelling sideways across a backdrop of dirty-white rolls of nimbus cloud, made her miss the West—its dryness, its bisque color, like a landscape all of pottery.

—JOHN UPDIKE, *The Witches of Eastwick*

After his car had backed out of the driveway, I just lay in my lower bunk, looking up at the slats of Patty's bed above me, listening to the soft, comforting sound of my sister's breathing, and thought of climbing the ladder and getting in beside her. Outside, I heard the howl of a coyote again—the new moon brought them out—and shivered. It felt as if the whole rest of the world was falling apart, and all I wanted was to hold on tight to the one person who wasn't going anywhere.

—JOYCE MAYNARD, *After Her*

The moon, it has been reported, was full, and the light that rained down cast the leaves of the eucalyptuses into spectral coin. —JUNOT DÍAZ, *The Brief Wondrous Life of Oscar Wao*

I recognized the tortuous, tattered band of the Milky Way, with Vega very bright between sun and earth; and Sirius and Orion shone splendid against the unfathomable blackness in the opposite quarter of the heavens. The Pole Star was overhead, and the Great Bear hung over the circle of the earth. And away beneath and beyond the shining corona of the sun were strange groupings of stars I had never seen in my life—notably, a dagger-shaped group that I knew for the Southern Cross.

—H. G. WELLS, *Under the Knife*

The colors that are actually seen depend strongly on the observer's eyesight and the strength of the aurora. Weak aurorae often appear almost colorless, or a pale green. People who have poor low-light red sensitivity may be unable to see the red and purple-violet tints in even major displays, despite seeing the pale green coloration easily. Red aurorae are often mistaken for distant fires.

—STORM DUNLOP, *The Weather Identification Handbook*

What in water did Bloom, waterlover, drawer of water, watercarrier, returning to the range, admire?

Its universality . . . its slow erosions of peninsulas and islands, its persistent formation of homothetic islands, peninsulas and downwardtending promontories: its alluvial deposits: its weight and volume and density: its imperturbability in lagoons and highland tarns: its gradation of colours in the torrid and temperate and frigid zones: its vehicular ramifications in continental lakecontained streams and confluent oceanflowing rivers with their tributaries and transoceanic currents, gulfstream, north and south equatorial courses: its violence in seaquakes, waterspouts, Artesian wells, eruptions, torrents, eddies, freshets, spates, groundswells, watersheds, waterpartings, geysers, cataracts, whirlpools, maelstroms, inundations, deluges, cloudbursts . . . its persevering penetrativeness in runnels, gullies, inadequate dams, leaks on shipboard: its properties for cleansing, quenching thirst and fire, nourishing vegetation: its infallibility as paradigm and paragon: its metamorphoses as vapour, mist, cloud, rain, sleet, snow, hail: its strength in rigid hydrants: its variety of forms in loughs and bays and gulfs and bights and guts and lagoons and atolls and archipelagos and sounds and fjords and minches and tidal estuaries and arms of sea: its solidity in glaciers, icebergs, icefloes . . . the noxiousness of its effluvia in lacustrine marshes, pestilential fens, faded flowerwater, stagnant pools in the waning moon.

—JAMES JOYCE, *Ulysses*

ANIMALS

TYPES OF ORGANISMS

single-celled or acellular animal
  protozoon
organism without a spinal column
  invertebrate
organism with a spinal column
  vertebrate
small, elongated, flexible, soft-bodied invertebrate usually with few or no obvious limbs or appendages
  worm
small, segmented invertebrate with a head, thorax, and abdomen and three pairs of legs
  insect
cold-blooded aquatic (saltwater or freshwater) vertebrate
  fish
warm-blooded feathered vertebrate with wings
  bird
invertebrate usually with a segmented body and jointed limbs (and including insects, arachnids, and crustaceans)
  arthropod
invertebrate whose anterior segment has four pairs of legs and no antenna
  arachnid
usually aquatic arthropod with an exoskeleton or shell
  crustacean

animal that crawls on its belly or on small short legs
reptile
animal adapted to both land and water and zoologically between fish and reptiles
amphibian
animal with hair that nourishes young with milk
mammal, mammalian
animal in family Hominidae (or that of man)
hominid
animal in superfamily of primates (man and apes)
hominoid
hoofed, odd-toed, and usually horned herbivorous animal
ungulate
hoofed, even-toed, cud-chewing herbivorous animal
ruminant
animal with an abdominal pouch for the young
marsupial
animal feeding on refuse or carrion
scavenger
small and large members of the cat family
felines
squirrels and other relatively small gnawing animals
rodents
seals and other carnivorous, flippered aquatic animals
pinnipeds
organism living in an extreme hot or cold environment
extremophile

GENERAL ANIMAL TRAITS

Size

very large, giant
large
greater
standard
medium, intermediate
miniature
lesser
small
very small, toy, teacup, pygmy

General Behavior

feral, wild, undomesticated
tame, domesticated
active
dormant
solitary, reclusive
gregarious, social
sedentary, settled
nomadic, migrating

Development

full-grown, mature
young, immature

Body

long-bodied
short-bodied
heavy-bodied, stocky, stubby, chunky

low-slung
sleek-bodied, slender

Areas of Body

above
below
on the back or top side, dorsal
on or along the side, lateral
on the stomach or underside, ventral
upperpart
underpart
front, anterior
hind, posterior
close together
widely spaced
joined
webbed
separated
near the attachment point, proximal
in the middle, mesial
at the end or extremity, distal, terminal

Parts of Body

well-developed
poorly developed
undeveloped or no longer used as a body part, vestigial
prominent, conspicuous
projecting, bulbous
distinguishing
sharply defined

protective
humped
armored
mantled (fold-like or hood-like)
elongate, elongated
broad
narrow
widening
tapering
flattened
convex
concave, dished (face)
sharp, pointed
blunt, rounded
angular, squarish, flattened
enlarged
reduced
erect
trailing
stiff
loose
legless
limbless
long-legged
short-legged
long-tailed
short-tailed
bushy-tailed
keeled (upright and ridge-like)
odd-toed
even-toed

opposable (thumb)
long-snouted
short-snouted
long-necked
short-necked
lidded
lidless
fixed (upper or lower jaw)
movable
long-eared
short-eared
branched horns
unbranched horns
with claws
without claws
smooth
wrinkled
light-furred
dark-furred
bushy, shaggy, luxuriant
fringed
barbed
glossy
dull
silky
velvety
cottony
leathery
light-plumaged
dark-plumaged

Coloration

plain
colorful
marked
unmarked
regular (markings)
irregular
uniform
variable
alternating
dense
scattered
tinged, tinted, tipped, spotted, blotched, calico
ringed
striped, banded, tabby
streaked, flecked, brindled
buff
tawny
dusky
grizzled
roan
tuxedo

GENERAL DESIGNATING ADJECTIVES

alligator
loricate
ant
formic
anteater
vermilingual

antelope

bovid, alcelaphine, bubaline

ape

australopithecine, anthropoid, pongid

armadillo

tolypeutine

ass or donkey

asinine

baboon

cynocephalous

badger

meline

barracuda

sphyraenoid, percesocine

bat

vespertilian

bear

ursine, arctoid

beaver

casteroid

bee

apian, apiarian

beetle

coleopterous, coleopteral

bird

avian, avine, volucrine, ornithic

bison

bisontine, bisonic

buffalo

buteonine

bull

bovine, taurine

butterfly

lepidopteral, lepidopteran, lepidopterous, papilionaceous, pierid, rhopalocerous

buzzard

buteonine

calf

vituline

camel

cameline

cat

feline, feliform

catfish

silurid, siluroid

centipede

myriapodous, myriapodan

chameleon

vermilingual

chipmunk

spermophiline

cobra

cobriform

cod

gadoid

cow

vaccine

crab

carcinomorphic, arthropodous, arthropodal, porcellanid

cricket
grilled, grilline
crocodile
loricate, crocodilian, emydosaurian
crow
corvine
cuckoo
cuculine
deer
cervine
dinosaur
dinosaurian, dinosauric
diving bird
urinatorial
dog
canine, cynoid
dolphin
delphin
donkey or ass
asinine
dove (also, pigeon and dodo)
columbine
dragonfly
odonatous, libelluloid
duck
anatine
dugong
sirenian
eagle
aquiline

earthworm
lumbricoid

eel
anguilliform

elephant
elephantine, pachydermoid, proboscidian

elk
alcine

falcon
falconine, falconoid

fish
ichthyoid, piscial, piscine

flamingo
phoenicopterous

flea
pulicid, pulicous

fly
muscid

fowl (chicken, turkeys, etc.)
gallinaceous, galline

fox
vulpine, vulpecular, alopecoid

frog
ranine, raniform, batrachian

giraffe
giraffine, camelopardine

goat
hircine, culiciform, capric, caprine

goose
anserine

gopher
spermophiline

gorilla
gorilloid, gorilline, gorillian

grasshopper (also, cricket)
orthopterous

gull
larine, laridine

hamster
cricetine

hare
leporine, lagomorphic

hawk
acciptrine

hedgehog
erinaceous

hen
gallinaceous

hermit crab
pagurian

heron
grallatory

herring
clupeoid

hippopotamus
hippopotamic

hog
suilline

horse
equine, caballine, chevaline

housefly
muscid, musciform

hyena
hyenic, hyaenic

insect
entomologic, insectaean, insectival

jellyfish
acalephan

kangaroo
macropodine, macropoid

king crab
limuloid

lamb
agnine

leech
hirudinoid, bdelloid

lemur
lemurine, lemuroid

leopard
pardine, feline

lion
leonine

lizard
lacertilian, lacertine, lacertian, saurian

lobster
crustacean, macrural, homarine, homaroid

lynx
lyncian

mackerel
scombrid, scombroid

manatee
sirenian, manatine, trichechine

mite, tick
acaridal, acarine

mole
talpine

mongoose
herpestine

monkey
simian, simioid, simious, pithecoid, pithecan

mosquito
culicine, culicid

moth
heterocerous

mouse
murine, murid

octopus
octopean, octopine, cephalopodous

ostrich
struthious, struthionine

otter
lutrine

owl
strigine

oyster
ostreoid, ostriform

panther
pantherine

parrot
psittacine, psittaceous

parrot fish
scaroid
peacock
pavonine
penguin
spheniscine, impennate
pig
porcine, suine
pigeon
peristeronic
poisonous snake
thanatophidian
porcupine
hystricoid, hystricine
porpoise
phocaenine
pouched animal
marsupial, didelphian
pronghorn
antilocaprid
python
pythonic
rabbit
cunicular
raccoon
procyanine
ram
arietine
rat
murine, murid

rattlesnake
crotaline

ray
batoid

reindeer
rangiferine

reptile
reptilian, reptiloid, herpetiform

rhinoceros
rhinocerotic, rhinocerine, rhinoceroid

rodent
glirine, gliriform, rodential

seacow
sirenian

seal
sphragistic, phocine, pinnepedian, otarine

shark
squaloid, squaliform, selachian

sheep
ovine

shrew
soricine, soricoid

shrimp
caridoid

skunk
mephitine

sloth
edentate

slug
limacine

snail

gastropodous

snake

ophidian, sinerous, anguine, anguineous, serpentine, anguiform

songbird

oscine

spider

arachnoid, araneiform

squirrel

sciuroid, sciurine, spermophiline

starfish

asteroidal

stork

ciconine, herodian, herodionine

swan

cygnine

tapeworm

taeniid, taenial

tarantula

theraphosid

tick, mite

acaridal, acarine

tiger

tigerish, tigrine, tigerine, feline

tortoise

testudinal

turtle

chelonian

viper

viperine

vulture
vulturine, vulturial
wading bird
grallatorial
walrus
pinniped
wasp
vespine
water buffalo
bubaline
weasel
musteline
whale
cetacean, cetaceous
wild boar
aprine
wolf
lupine
woodpecker
piciform, picine
worm
vermicular, vermiform, vermian
zebra
zebrine, hippotigrine

ZOOLOGICAL TERMS

warm-blooded
endothermic, homoeothermic
cold-blooded
ectothermic, poikilothermic

active during daylight
diurnal

active at night
nocturnal

active at dawn or twilight
crepuscular

emitting light
bioluminescent

passing the winter in a lethargic and low-metabolic state
hibernating

passing the summer in a lethargic and low-metabolic state
aestivating

two-legged
bicrural

two-footed
biped, bipedal

four-footed
quadruped, quadrupedal, tetrapod, tetrapodal

many-footed
polyped, polypod, polypodous

having no feet
apodal, apodan, apodous

having handlike feet
pedimanous, pedimane

having arms
brachiate

two-handed
bimanous

having nails or claws
unguiculate

having feathered feet
plumiped, plumipede, braccate
web-footed
palmiped
capable of grasping
prehensile
capable of being extended
protractile, protrusile
capable of being drawn back
retractile
extended forward, as a mandible or antenna
porrect
scratching the ground for food
rasorial
having ears
aurated
having a tail
caudate
having no tail
anurous, acaudal
having a tail with colored bands
ring-tailed
having horns
corniculate
having no horns
acerous
having two teeth
bidentate
having no teeth
edentate

having two antennae or tentacles
dicerous

not adapted to flying
flightless

having wings
pennate, alate

having no wings
apterous

having feathers
plumaged, plumose

having a beak
rostrate, rhamphoid

curved downward (as a beak)
decurved

curved backward or inward
recurved

having scales
squamate, squamous, squamose

shedding or peeling off scales
desquamate

having a supportive external covering
exoskeletal

having a bony or horny shell-like case
loricate

shell or shell-like protective case
carapace

having gills
branchiate

having a thick hide
pachydermatous

having a rough skin with sharp points
muricate

having no hair
naked, hairless

having fur (pelage)
furred, furry

having shiny fur
sleek-furred

having soft hair
pilose

having bristles or spines
spiny, hispid, setaceous

covered with bristles or spines
echinate

covered with small bristles or spines
echinulate

divided into defined segments or sections
segmented

of two colors
bicolored

of three colors
tricolored

having stripes
striped, banded

having long markings or somewhat uneven stripes
streaked

having longitudinal stripes
vittate

having transverse or crosswise stripes
cross-banded, cross-barred

having spots of color (or black and white)
spotted, mottled, maculate, liturate
having small spots of color (or black and white)
flecked, freckled, speckled, specked, stippled, irrorate
having large and irregular spots
blotched
having black-and-white blotches
piebald
having patches of white and a color not black
skewbald
having a masklike facial marking or coloration
masked
having a visibly collar-like part or marking
collared, ruffed
having a tuft or ridgelike formation on the head or back
crested
having a fin along the back
fin-backed
having a highly developed sense of smell
macrosmatic
having a weakly developed sense of smell
microsmatic
having virtually no sense of smell
anosmatic
imitative in color or form
apatetic
warning off by colors or changes in the body
aposematic
serving to conceal
cryptic

imitating other things by using something as a covering
allocryptic
giving birth to young rather than producing eggs
viviparous
laying eggs
oviparous
laying eggs but retaining them until hatching time
ovoviviparous
widely distributed around the globe
cosmopolitan
dwelling in a particular region
endemic
dwelling in the same region or overlapping regions without interbreeding
sympatric
dwelling in different regions
allopatric
dwelling in the air
aerial
dwelling on the ground
terrestrial, terricolous
dwelling (insects) at or near the ground's surface
epigeal
dwelling underground
subterranean, hypogeous
dwelling in caverns
cavernicolous
dwelling in burrows
cunicular
dwelling (insects) under a stone
lapidicolous

dwelling in a tube
tubicolous

dwelling in mud
limicolous

dwelling in dung
coprophilous, coprozoic, stercoricolous

dwelling in the desert
deserticolous

dwelling (or burrowing) in sand
arenicolous

dwelling in meadows or fields
practicolous, arvicoline

dwelling in woodlands
silvicolous

dwelling in trees
arboreal

dwelling in hedges
sepicolous

dwelling in mountains
montane

dwelling in rocks
petricolous, saxicolous, rupicolous

dwelling on land and in water
amphibian

dwelling in water
aquatic

dwelling in fresh water
freshwater

dwelling in the sea
oceanic, pelagic, marine, maricolous

dwelling in active or moving waters
lotic
dwelling in still or slow-moving waters
lentic
dwelling along the seacoast
littoral, orarian, limicoline
dwelling in rivers or streams
riverine, riparian, riparial, riparious, riparicolous
dwelling in marshes
palustrine, helobious, paludicolous, paludous
dwelling in estuaries
estuarine
dwelling in the deep sea
autopelagic
dwelling in deep water but coming at times to the surface
spanipelagic
dwelling on the bottom of a body of water or of the sea
benthic, benthonic
migrating from fresh water to the sea to spawn
catadromous
migrating from the sea to streams to spawn
anadromous
nest-building
nidificant
staying in the nest for a period after hatching
nidicolous
leaving the nest soon after hatching
nidifugous
dwelling in or sharing a nest with another animal
nidicolous

dwelling in the nest of another species
inquiline
helpless when hatched and needing parental care for a considerable time
altricial
independently active to a considerable degree after hatching
precocial
eating one type of food
monophagous
eating virtually everything
omnivorous
eating living organisms
biophagous
eating few types of food
stenophagous
eating a moderate variety of foods
polyphagous
eating a wide variety of foods
euryphagous, pantophagous
animal- and vegetable-eating
omnivorous, amphivorous
flesh-eating
carnivorous, amophagous, creophagous
feeding on other animals
predatory, predaceous, raptorial
eating its own kind
cannibalistic
eating human flesh
anthropophagous
eating horse flesh
equivorous

plant-eating
herbivorous, vegetarian
plant-eating (insects and lower animals)
phytophagous, phytivorous
fish-eating
piscivorous, ichthyophagous
fruit-eating
frugivorous, fructivorous
insect-eating
insectivorous
carrion-eating
necrophagous, scavenging
dung-eating
coprophagous
feeding on decomposing matter
saprophagous
grass-eating
graminivorous
grain-eating
granivorous
berry-eating
baccivorous
nut-eating
nucivorous
rice-eating
oryzivorous
leaf-eating
phyllophagous
worm-eating
vermivorous

bone-eating
ossivorous
wood-eating
hylophagous
egg-eating
oophagous
seed-eating
seminivorous
feeding on ants
myrmecophagous
feeding on flowers
anthophilous, anthophagous
capable of movement
motile
"sitting" or not capable of movement
sessile
walking with the body erect
orthograde
walking with the body virtually horizontal
pronograde
walking on the sole of the foot
plantigrade
walking with the back part of the foot raised
digitigrade
walking on hoofs
unguligrade
walking by fins or flippers
pinnigrade
walking backward
retrograde

moving sideways
laterigrade
creeping
reptant, repent
creeping like a worm
vermigrade
climbing
scansorial
wading
grallatorial
burrowing
fossorial
moving by swinging the arms
brachiating
slow-moving
tardigrade

QUOTATIONS

In fact the koala is not a bear at all, but merely suggests one—a bear divested of danger, smaller, cuter, altogether a more predictable fellow. It has the slanted, beady eyes of a fearsome martinet, but they are rendered comical by bushy ears sprouting up like two enormous cowlicks. The koala's mouth is a tight and stubborn slit, but its severity is wholly undone by what appears to be a black rubber nose. The complete effect suggests an attempt at an authoritative demeanor that has turned out rather less than one had hoped—a dour schoolteacher proceeding through the geography lesson, unaware that his toupee is all askew.

—JAMES SHREEVE, *Nature: The Other Earthlings*

The waterfalls of the Sierra are frequented by only one bird,—the Ouzel or Water Thrush (*Cinclus Mexicanus, Sw.*). He is a singularly joyous and lovable little fellow, about the size of a robin, clad in a plain waterproof suit of bluish gray, with a tinge of chocolate on the head and shoulders. In form he is about as smoothly plump and compact as a pebble that has been whirled in a pot-hole, the flowing contour of his body being interrupted only by his strong feet and bill, the crisp wing-tips, and the up-slanted wren-like tail.

—JOHN MUIR, *The Mountains of California*

At no time since hominids first arose on Earth has Australia not been an island. Any human beings who arrived there must have come by sea, in large enough numbers to start a breeding population, after crossing sixty miles or more of open water without having any way of knowing that a convenient landfall awaited them.

—BILL BRYSON, *A Short History of Nearly Everything*

Just as surprised as I, he stood up. He must have construed the sounds of my advance to be those of another sheep or goat. His horns had made a complete curl and then some; they were thick, massive and bunched together like a high Roman helmet, and he himself was muscly and military, with a grave-looking nose. A squared-off, middle-aged, trophy-type ram, full of imposing professionalism, he was at the stage of life when rams sometimes stop herding and live as rogues.

—EDWARD HOAGLAND, *Walking the Dead Diamond River*

In the shed, the slick squirming balls are gone. In their places are new fluffy, downy balls. They almost look like chicks. Their eyes are still sealed shut, still thin black lines that look like closed mouths. But their mouths are open. They are wheezing and huffing and mewling in squeaks that would be barks. They are rolling against each other, tumbling one over the other to land against China's side. She watches me. Skeetah closes the curtain.

—JESMYN WARD, *Salvage the Bones*

It was a biped; its almost globular body was poised on a tripod of two froglike legs and a long thick tail, and its fore limbs, which grotesquely caricatured the human hand, much as a frog's do, carried a long shaft of bone, tipped with copper. The colour of the creature was variegated; its head, hands, and legs were purple; but its skin, which hung loosely upon it, even as clothes might do, was a phosphorescent grey. And it stood there blinded by the light.

—H. G. WELLS, *In the Abyss*

One of the best known *Chelodina* species must be the Australian snake-neck, which, as its name implies, has a neck almost as long as the rest of its body (which may grow to a length of 15–20 cm). It is a rather plainly colored reptile, the head, neck, limbs, and carapace being a uniform olive-brown, while the plastron is dirty yellow. It has very noticeable yellow staring eyes with round pupils.

—JO COBB, *Turtles and Terrapins*

At first, I thought he just had heat exhaustion or something. I mean, it was a crazy-hot July day (102 degrees with 90 percent humidity), and plenty of people were falling over from heat exhaustion, so why not a little dog wearing a fur coat? I tried to give him some water, but he didn't want any of that.

He was lying on his bed with red, watery, snotty eyes. He whimpered in pain. When I touched him, he yelped like crazy.

It was like his nerves were poking out three inches from his skin.

I figured he'd be okay with some rest, but then he started vomiting, and diarrhea blasted out of him, and he had these seizures where his little legs just kicked and kicked and kicked.

And sure, Oscar was only an adopted stray mutt, but he was the only living thing that I could depend on.

—SHERMAN ALEXIE, *The Absolutely True Diary of a Part-Time Indian*

The grizzly is set apart from other bears not only by its light-colored shaggy coat but by its high shoulder hump, formed by a mass of powerful muscles that drive the front legs. Its head is massive, its ears small and its forehead high—all of which combine to give its face a concave, or "dished," profile.

—PETER FARB, *The Land and the Wildlife of North America*

In country like this there were probably animals, all kinds of animals, jungly things. Not lions or elephants, of course, but snakes, certainly, and even monkeys, perhaps—the kind that screamed at night—and small nocturnal creatures that looked like big cats or rats and frolicked through ruins of huts where people had recently lived.

—DEBORAH EISENBERG, "Across the Lake," *The Collected Stories of Deborah Eisenberg*

Lo and behold, here in the creek was a silly-looking coot. It looked like a black and gray duck, but its head was smaller; its clunky white bill sloped straight from the curve of its skull like a cone from its base. I had read somewhere that coots were shy. They were liable to take umbrage at a footfall, skitter terrified along the water, and take to the air. But I wanted a good look. So when the coot tipped tail and dove, I raced towards it across the snow and hid behind a cedar trunk. As it popped up again its neck was as rigid and eyes as blank as a rubber duck's in the bathtub.

—ANNIE DILLARD, *Pilgrim at Tinker Creek*

His captor had been clearing grass for a new maize garden when he disturbed an adult serval. He found a single male kitten in a nest in the tall grass. It had a long, fluffy, soft coat—a pale sandy-brown color—very closely spotted over the dorsal surface. His eyes were open but he could not really see well. The little ears were already erect, very black, and with a dull, dirty-white crossbar.

—VIVIAN J. WILSON, *Orphans of the Wild: An African Naturalist in Pursuit of a Dream*

All but one of the goats were pygmies. These were small, about knee-height, and distinguishable at first mainly by their color. Spanky was black with a white patch on either side. (He looked as if he'd been spanked with hands dipped in white paint.) Pearl was all white, and her sister, Onyx, was all black. Their mother, Suzie, was salt-and-pepper.

—BEN DOLNICK, "Goodnight Moon," *Central Park: An Anthology* (Andrew Blauner, ed.)

The Hawaiian monk seal has wiry whiskers and the deep, round eyes of an apologetic child. The animals will eat a variety of fish and shellfish, or turn over rocks for eel and octopus, then haul out on the beach and lie there most of the day, digesting. On the south side of Kauai one afternoon, I saw one sneeze in its sleep: its convex body shuddered, then spilled again over the sand the way a raw, boneless chicken breast will settle on a cutting board. The seals can grow to seven feet long and weigh 450 pounds.

—Jon Mooallem, "Who Would Kill a Monk Seal?" *New York Times Magazine*, May 8, 2013

The golden hamster hardly ever climbs, and gnaws so little that he can be allowed to run freely about the room where he will do no appreciable damage. Besides this, this animal is externally the neatest little chap, with his fat head, his big eyes, peering so cannily into the world that they give the impression that he is much cleverer than he really is, and the gaily coloured markings of his gold, black and white coat. Then his movements are so comical that he is ever and again the source of friendly laughter when he comes hurrying, as though pushed along, on his little short legs, or when he suddenly stands upright, like a tiny pillar driven into the floor and, with stiffly pricked ears and bulging eyes, appears to be on the look-out for some imaginary danger.

—Konrad Lorenz, *King Solomon's Ring*

Though her ears are high, the rhinoceros makes no move at all, there is no twitch of her loose hide, no swell or raising of the ribs, which are outlined in darker gray on the barrel flanks, as if holding her breath might render her invisible. The tiny eyes are hidden in the bags of skin, and though her head is high, extended toward us, the great hump of the shoulders rises higher still, higher even than the tips of those coarse dusty horns that are worth more than their weight in gold in the Levant. Just once, the big ears give a twitch; otherwise she remains motionless, as the two oxpeckers attending her squall uneasily, and a zebra yaps nervously back in the trees.

—PETER MATTHIESSEN, *Sand Rivers*

Desert bighorns are blocky, long-necked ungulates, grayish brown in color, sometimes more gray than brown, or pale beige, or with a russet cast. Their noses are moist and their rumps are white. They eat dry, abrasive plants, digesting them with four-chambered stomachs and the help of protozoa and bacteria.

The five gaits of bighorn sheep reflect their mental state, from a pompous, show-offy walk to an exuberant trot down a near-vertical rock face or a twenty-five-mile-per-hour escape run.

—ELLEN MELOY, *Eating Stone: Imagination and the Loss of the Wild*

The smallest of the group is the mouse lemur, with a snub nose and large appealing eyes, that scampers through the thinnest twigs. The indri has a closely related nocturnal equivalent, the avahi, very similar in appearance and size except that its fur, instead of being black and white is grey and woolly. Oddest and most specialized of all is the aye-aye. Its body is about the size of that of an otter, it has black shaggy fur, a bushy tail and large membranous ears. One finger on each hand is enormously elongated and seemingly withered, so that it has become a bony articulated probe.

—DAVID ATTENBOROUGH, *Life on Earth*

Averaging perhaps twenty pounds, the wildcat seems to be a miniature cross between a tiger and a leopard, with a bit of mountain lion thrown in. Its rust-brown coat shows spots and flecks above and a suggestion of dark stripes below, blending into a white belly. Heavy lines on its wide-flaring cheek fur break up the outline of its face so it can see without being seen. A little tuft of hair on each ear serves as an antenna which is sensitive to sounds or air currents. Its whiskers, bedded in delicate nerves, may lie back—or reach out to determine if a certain opening will admit its body.

—LES LINE, *The Audubon Wildlife Treasury*

I have named her Maxi, short for Maxitail, as hers is rather long. She is a complex character. She is very grabby, but her grabbiness stems from fright. She shuts her eyes as she grabs and simultaneously covers them by bringing her tail up over her head to form long bangs. Frightened as she may be, however, she has demolished the screen; she cannot—or refuses to—understand that the number of nuts that issue from our house is not infinite. At the moment, she is the most troublesome squirrel we have encountered.

—GRACE MARMOR SPRUCH, *Squirrels at My Window: Life with a Remarkable Gang of Urban Squirrels*

The alligator when full grown is a very large and terrible creature, and of prodigious strength, activity and swiftness in the water. I have seen them twenty feet in length, and some are supposed to be twenty-two or twenty-three feet. Their body is as large as that of a horse; their shape exactly resembles that of a lizard, except their tail, which is flat or cuneiform, being compressed on each side, and gradually diminishing from the abdomen to the extremity, which with the whole body is covered with horny plates or squammae, impenetrable. . . .

—WILLIAM BARTRAM, *Bartram's Travels*

The bulky body of the Muskrat is about a foot long and is covered with two kinds of hair: a short beautiful undercoat of soft and silky brown fur and a long coat of coarser hair. Its stout naked tail—almost as long as its body—is vertically flattened to aid in propulsion and steering when the animal is swimming. Its hind feet are partially webbed as another aid to progress in the water.

—JOHN KIERAN, *A Natural History of New York City*

In his sleep he could hear the horses stepping among the rocks and he could hear them drink from the shallow pools in the dark where the rocks lay smooth and rectilinear as the stones of ancient ruins and the water from their muzzles dripped and rang like water dripping in a well and in his sleep he dreamt of horses and the horses in his dream moved gravely among the tilted stones like horses come upon an antique site where some ordering of the world had failed and if anything had been written on the stones the weathers had taken it away again and the horses were wary and moved with great circumspection carrying in their blood as they did the recollection of this and other places where horses once had been and would be again. —Cormac McCarthy, *All the Pretty Horses*

Finally he was in the top of the tree, a hundred or so feet from the ground. Just above him was the little squirrel, more beautiful, more perfect, up close than it had looked from the ground. The fur of its back and sides was gray but touched, brushed over, with tones of yellowish red and reddish yellow, so that against the light it seemed surrounded with a small glow, and the fur of its underside was immaculately white. Its finest features were its large, dark eyes alight with intelligence and the graceful plume of its tail as long as its body.

—Wendell Berry, "Nothing Living Lives Alone," *The PEN O. Henry Prize Stories 2012*

My first mountain beaver had gone head-first into a trap set at its burrow mouth by my cousin, Mary V., on her parents' ranch above the Oregon coast. It was a grayish, unprepossessing-looking creature about a foot long, weighing two to five pounds. The appearance, to my five-year-old eyes, was grotesque: squinched slits where the eyes should be; crinkly, bare ears; no tail worthy of the name; toes splayed out exactly like those in illustrations of dinosaurs (but otherwise no similarity to the giant reptiles); four curving teeth stained as if from eons of conscientious tobacco chewing.

—Irving Petite, *The Elderberry Tree*

Despite being arboreal the gibbons of the subfamily Hylobatinae are the only monkeys that spontaneously adopt the bipedal stance when on the ground. Their walk is, however, rather odd and clumsy. The gibbons are also noteworthy for their exceptionally long arms and legs, especially the former, and for the absence of a tail.

—Augusto Taglianti, *The World of Mammals*

There is a mysterious quality about the beaver, one that conjures up racial memories of trolls and gnomes and "little people." It isn't just that the animal works magic and can dramatically transform its surroundings during the dark of a single night; its odd and lumpy shape is like that of no other creature. In fact, it looks like some kind of mythical beast put together out of a grab bag of parts belonging to other animals. Its front paws are five-fingered, raccoonlike, and able to manipulate all kinds of material with skill. Its hind feet are totally different from its front ones, big webbed paddles like those of a loon or a duck. Its body is similar to that of a woodchuck who has fattened up in anticipation of a long winter's fast. Its tail might have been taken from a duckbilled platypus; it is flat and paddle-shaped with a surface that is beautifully etched, as if tooled by a skilled leather craftsman.

—Hope Ryden, *Lily Pond: Four Years With a Family of Beavers*

The diet of tree-shrews is largely insectivorous and partly frugivorous, but in fact they are omnivorous and will eat anything that is digestible. — M. F. ASHLEY MONTAGU, *An Introduction to Physical Anthropology*

Where the brown bear is broad-shouldered and dish-faced, the polar bear is narrow shouldered and Roman-nosed. His neck is longer, his head smaller. He stands taller than the brown bear but is less robust in the chest and generally of lighter build. The polar bear's feet are larger and thickly furred between the pads. The toes are partially webbed, the blackish-brown claws sharper and smaller than the brown bear's. It lacks the brown bear's shoulder hump and more expressive face, with its prehensile lips, well suited to stripping bushes of their berries.

—BARRY LOPEZ, *Arctic Dreams*

Then there was the whirring noise of wings as large brown birds burst out of the willows and one bird flew only a little way and lit in the willows and with its crested head on one side looked down, bending the collar of feathers on his neck where the other birds were still thumping. The bird looking down from the red willow brush was beautiful, plump, heavy and looked so stupid with his head turned down and as Nick raised his rifle slowly, his sister whispered, "No, Nickie. Please no. We've got plenty." —ERNEST HEMINGWAY, "The Last Good Country," *The Nick Adams Stories*

The havtagai which, like domestic camels, have long lashes to shade their eyes from the sun's glare, nostrils that can be closed against wind-driven sand, and two toes linked by pads that spread their weight over the shifting sand, differ from them in being uniformly sandy-colored, whereas domestic camels may also be dark brown, black, or even white. They differ also in their longer though fine-boned legs (lacking callosities) and small feet and pads that leave a footprint about half the size of a domestic camel's, in the thinner texture of their coats and the absence of mane and beard, and in their humps, which are small pointed cones and invariably firm, in contrast to those of domestic camels, which vary in size and condition according to their owner's health.

—RICHARD PERRY, *Life in Desert and Plain*

Back on dry land, another marvel of evolution would have made their tread appear to be considerably lighter than that of much smaller animals. The skeletal structure of their feet is angled in a way that has been compared to a platform shoe, so they walk on their toes, the weight spreading evenly toward the heel on a cushioning pad of fatty tissue. The pad is similar to the seismic tissue that whales and dolphins use to detect and receive sound waves in the sea and may enable elephants to detect vibrations in the ground. The footpads as well as the trunks contain Pacinian corpuscles, liquid capsules surrounded by layers of tissue and gel and containing nerve endings so sensitive to pressure as to enable these biggest of land beasts to detect the faintest of stirrings. —MICHAEL DALY, *Topsy: The Startling Story of the Crooked-Tailed Elephant, P. T. Barnum, and the American Wizard, Thomas Edison*

Go to the meatmarket of a Saturday night and see the crowds of live bipeds staring up at the long rows of dead quadrupeds. Does not that sight take a tooth out of the cannibal's jaw? —HERMAN MELVILLE, *Moby-Dick*

In the beginning were the howlers. They always commenced their bellowing in the first hour of dawn, just as the hem of the sky began to whiten. It would start with just one: his forced, rhythmic groaning, like a saw blade. That aroused others near him, nudging them to bawl along with his monstrous tune. Soon the maroon-throated howls would echo back from other trees, farther down the beach, until the whole jungle filled with roaring trees. —BARBARA KINGSOLVER, *The Lacuna*

The snow leopard, or ounce, is slightly smaller than the common leopard, and among the most attractive of all the great cats. In winter coat the fur, particularly on the lower parts, is unusually long, with thick wooly underfur. This, in conjunction with the short muzzle, has the effect of making the head appear disproportionately small. The general ground colour is pale charcoal, faintly tinged with cream: the under parts up to the chin are milk white. The black rosettes are large, irregularly shaped, and randomly distributed. The markings on the head, along the spine, and on the upper part of the tail are well defined, but where the fur is long they are somewhat blurred: the pattern is more distinct in summer coat. The tail is long and densely furred, with large rosettes on the upper surface, white beneath, and black-tipped.

—NOEL SIMON AND PAUL GEROUDET, *Last Survivors: The Natural History of Animals in Danger of Extinction*

The cow has a smooth body and a face that looks much like that of a mouse, with a sharp-pointed nose and whiskers, but the bull is different. His nose has a large hump on it which hangs down over his mouth. His skin is rough and looks like wet earth that has dried in the sun and cracked. He is an ugly animal.

—SCOTT O'DELL, *Island of the Blue Dolphins*

Suddenly the water heaved and a round, shining, black thing like a cannon-ball came into sight. Then he saw eyes and mouth—a puffing mouth bearded with bubbles. More of the thing came up out of the water. It was gleaming black. Finally it splashed and wallowed to the shore and rose, steaming, on its hind legs—six or seven feet high and too thin for its height, like everything in Malacandra. It had a coat of thick black hair, lucid as sealskin, very short legs with webbed feet, a broad beaver-like or fish-like tail, strong forelimbs with webbed claws or fingers, and some complication half-way up the belly which Ransom took to be its genitals. It was something like a penguin, something like an otter, something like a seal; the slenderness and flexibility of the body suggested a giant stoat. The great round head, heavily whiskered, was responsible for the suggestion of seal; but it was higher in the forehead than a seal's and the mouth was smaller. —C. S. Lewis, *Out of the Silent Planet*

For the first time in his life, Paul got a clear view of a gorilla—an adult male with a tuft of silver hair on its back. It rose onto two legs when it saw the hunters and appeared to stand almost six feet tall. The forearms bulged with the promise of strength, its neck a massive pillar of solid muscle. The animal must have weighed nearly four hundred pounds.

—Monte Reel, *Between Man and Beast: An Unlikely Explorer, the Evolution Debates, and the African Adventure That Took the Victorian World by Storm*

I am not a naturalist, nor have we on board a book of zoology, so the most I can do is to describe him. He is almost my height (nearly five feet ten inches) and appears to be sturdily built. Feet and hands are human in appearance except that they have a bulbous, skew, arthritic look common to monkeys. He is muscular and covered with fine reddish-brown hair. One can see the whiteness of his tendons when he stretches an arm or leg. I have mentioned the sharp, dazzling white teeth, set in rows like a trap, canine and pointed. His face is curiously delicate, and covered with orange hair leading to a snow-white crown of fur. My breath nearly failed when I looked into his eyes, for they are a bright, penetrating blue.

—Mark Helprin, "Letters from the Samantha," *Ellis Island and Other Stories*

Thirty-five yards into the grass the big lion lay flattened out along the ground. His ears were back and his only movement was a slight twitching up and down of his long, black-tufted tail. He had turned at bay as soon as he had reached this cover and he was sick with the wound through his full belly, and weakening with the wound through his lungs that brought a thin foamy red to his mouth each time he breathed. His flanks were wet and hot and flies were on the little openings the solid bullets had made in his tawny hide, and his big yellow eyes, narrowed with hate, looked straight ahead, only blinking when the pain came as he breathed, and his claws dug in the soft baked earth. —ERNEST HEMINGWAY, "The Short Happy Life of Francis Macomber," *The Short Stories of Ernest Hemingway*

She gazed down at me, her ears splayed open in the shape of Africa, her eyes kind and concerned. Then, lifting one huge foot, she began to feel me gently all over, barely touching me. Her great ears stood out at right angles to her huge head as she contemplated me lying helpless, merely inches from the tip of two long, sharp tusks.

—DAPHNE SHELDRICK, *Love, Life, and Elephants: An African Love Story*

The eyes of the buffalo were glazing over, his tongue stuck out, and blood was streaming into the dry ground. Round and round the dead beast Clint walked, looking again and again at the great black head with its short shiny dark horns, the shaggy shoulders and breast, the tufts of hair down the forelegs.

—Zane Grey, *Fighting Caravans*

Adela Pingsford said nothing, but led the way to her garden. It was normally a fair-sized garden, but it looked small in comparison with the ox, a huge mottled brute, dull red about the head and shoulders, passing to dirty white on the flanks and hind-quarters, with shaggy ears and large bloodshot eyes.

—Saki, "The Stalled Ox," *The Complete Saki*

An argument of great weight, and applicable in several other cases, is, that the above-specified breeds, though agreeing generally with the wild rock-pigeon in constitution, habits, voice, colouring, and in most parts of their structure, yet are certainly highly abnormal in other parts; we may look in vain through the whole great family of Columbidae for a beak like that of the English carrier, or that of the short-faced tumbler, or barb; for reversed feathers like those of the Jacobin; for a crop like that of the pouter; for tail-feathers like those of the fantail.

—Charles Darwin, *On the Origin of Species*

It began with a helicopter landing right in front of us, a hundred feet from the D-20's open door. A man in a reflective vest hustled out and hitched a fluorescent orange cable connected to the chopper's undercarriage to the pile of black netting on the ground. Then out of the Quonset hut came a small ATV, towing a plywood flatbed. The tranquilized polar bear was on it, flat on its belly, positioned to face backward, so that the ATV didn't blow exhaust in its face. Its fur was yellowing and crimped in places. Its huge muzzle was black with dirt.

—Jon Mooallem, *Wild Ones: A Sometimes Dismaying, Weirdly Reassuring Story about Looking at People Looking at Animals in America*

Fearsome lizards five or six feet long pounded over the ground and leaped lithely for high tree branches, as at home off the earth as on it; they were goannas. And there were many other lizards, smaller but some no less frightening, adorned with horny triceratopean ruffs about their necks, or with swollen, bright-blue tongues.

—Colleen McCullough, *The Thorn Birds*

No coral snake this, with slim, tapering body, ringed like a wasp with brilliant colors; but thick and blunt with lurid scales, blotched with black; also a broad, flat murderous head, with stony, ice-like, whity-blue eyes, cold enough to freeze a victim's blood in its veins and make it sit still, like some wide-eyed creature carved in stone, waiting for the sharp, inevitable stroke—so swift, at last, so long in coming. —W. H. Hudson, *Green Mansions*

The result, however, is a continuous sequence of 20 ft of colour film which seems to show a female Sasquatch, about 7 ft high and weighing an estimated 350 pounds. Her pendulous breasts are clearly visible, and she is covered with short shiny black hair, with the exception of the area just around her eyes. On the back of her head there is a kind of ridge (a bony crest observed on other

Sasquatch, which also occurs, incidentally, on large female gorillas), and she has a very short neck, heavy back and shoulder muscles. The creature walked upright, swinging its arms, in a humanlike manner.

—MYRA SHACKLEY, *Still Living?: Yeti, Sasquatch, and the Neanderthal Enigma*

The straw-coloured fruit-bat, called *abu regai* or *el hafash* by the Baggara Arabs and *ko-jok* by the Nuba, is a very handsome creature for a bat. It is readily recognized by the orange-yellow ruff, brown back and blackish wings but otherwise straw-yellow body. Large specimens have a wingspan of nearly two and a half feet and a body about eight inches long. With tall pointed ears, long foxy face and large, dark, intelligent eyes it is an attractive animal.

—R. C. H. SWEENEY, *Grappling with a Griffon*

The tadpoles in the quiet bay of the brook are now far past the stage of inky black little wrigglers attached by their two little sticky pads to any stick or leaf, merely breathing through their gills, and lashing with their hair-fine cilia. A dark brown skin—really gold spots mottling the black—now proclaims the leopard frogs they will become.

—DONALD CULROSS PEATTIE, *An Almanac for Moderns*

Twelve years later it's the length and weight of a full-grown alligator—six feet long head to tail and twenty-seven pounds—and no longer cute. Definitely not decorative. Its thick muscular body is covered with dark gray scales. A raised jagged dorsal fin runs from its head along its back and down the long tail. It's a beast straight from the age of dinosaurs but to the Kid its appearance is as normal as his mother's. Dewlaps drape in soft fans from its boney jaw and there are thin fringes of flesh on its clawed toes that stiffen and rise as if saluting him when the Kid approaches. It wears its eardrums on the outside of its head behind and below the eyes. On top of its head is a primitive third eye—a gray waferlike lens that keeps a lookout for overhead predators which are large birds mainly.

—RUSSELL BANKS, *Lost Memory of Skin*

Sometimes King Pellinore could be descried galloping over the purlieus after the Beast, or with the Beast after him if they happened to have got muddled up. Cully lost the vertical stripes of his first year's plumage and became greyer, grimmer, madder, and distinguished by smart horizontal bars where the long stripes had been.

—T. H. WHITE, *The Once and Future King*

The cottonmouth (*Agkistrodon piscivorus*) may grow 6 feet long, though the average is about half that size. It is brown with indistinct black bands; its yellow belly may have dark markings as well, and a dark band runs from the eye to the corner of the mouth. It is distinguished from nonpoisonous water snakes by its deep spade-shaped head, light lips and white mouth.

—PHILIP KOPPER, *The Wild Edge: Life and Lore of the Great Atlantic Beaches*

Seeing this great gathering of chiru reminds me of the Mongolian gazelles on the eastern steppes of Mongolia, which I studied during the 1990s, work that is still continued by Kirk Olson. Over one million gazelles persist there, the largest such surviving population of a wild ungulate in Asia. —GEORGE B. SCHALLER, *Tibet Wild: A Naturalist's Journeys on the Roof of the World*

With renewed enthusiasm I dug on and was soon rewarded by the sight of the inhabitant—a gopher tortoise. Reaching into the tunnel, I grasped one stubby foreleg and tried to pull it out but found that it had apparently wedged itself so tightly in the narrow passage that I was forced to dig again. Eventually I dug around the specimen and hauled the struggling creature out. It was an adult, about eight inches across and slate-black in color. Its feet were elephant-like and bore blunt claws instead of toes, an ideal arrangement for digging. Its dome-like carapace was set with diamond-shaped plates in which the yearly growth rings or zones could clearly be discerned.

—ROSS E. HUTCHINS, *Island of Adventure: A Naturalist Explores a Gulf Coast Wilderness*

But this was not a beaver. Although its fur, like a beaver's, was rich brown and glossy, I could see that the animal was smaller. Besides, I knew muskrats on sight, having trapped them when I was a boy. This one weighed about three pounds—they weigh from one and a half to four pounds—and it was about twenty inches long from the tip of its moist black nose to the end of its naked tail.

The nine-inch tail, had I any doubt of what the animal was, identified it for me: a black, slender, thinner-than-high tail; not the wide, flat, boardlike tail of a beaver.

—JOHN K. TERRES, *From Laurel Hill to Siler's Bog: The Walking Adventures of a Naturalist*

The whole family tree of Darwin's finches is marked by this kind of eccentric specialization, and each species has a beak to go with it. Robert Bowman, an evolutionist who studied the finches before the Grants, once drew a chart comparing the birds' beaks to different kinds of pliers. Cactus finches carry a heavy-duty lineman's pliers. Other species carry analogues of the high-leverage diagonal pliers, the long chain-nose pliers, the parrot-head gripping pliers, the curved needle-nose pliers, and the straight needle-nose pliers.

—JONATHAN WEINER, *The Beak of the Finch: A Story of Evolution*

But hold it I did, and looked it over well, for it isn't often I can close my hands on such an exquisite manikin. Its snippet of a buff nose came to a rounded point under high-perched eyes brightly edged in gold. One brown polka-dot marked the space between each two lines of its cross, and narrow bands of brown decorated its frantically springing thighs. The soft skin of its underparts was finely granular, beigey-white with a hint of greenish, and its wrinkled throat was lightly touched with yellow. No webbing at all between its long fingers and only a trace between its toes. Fingers and toes so delicate, so fine, and the climbing discs upon them infinitesimal but distinct. The whole adult peeper so minute it hid itself completely under the end of my thumb.

—Mary Leister, *Wildlings*

There is almost no way to explain a takin. Part this, part that, it looks as if it humbly adopted all the attributes that other goats and antelopes refused. Ponderous and unwieldy, its heavy body sits on fat, stubby legs, and is covered with a dingy, drab coat. Its horns look like a cross between those of the gnu and musk ox, and its face seems to have suffered a terrible accident, while the expression of its droopy lips makes one think it has been sucking a mixture of lemon and garlic.

—Edward W. Cronin Jr., *The Arun: A Natural History of the World's Deepest Valley*

He was a mongoose, rather like a little cat in his fur and his tail, but quite like a weasel in his head and his habits. His eyes and the end of his restless nose were pink; he could scratch himself anywhere he pleased with any leg, front or back, that he chose to use; he could fluff up his tail till it looked like a bottle-brush, and his war-cry as he scuttled through the long grass was: *Rikk-tikk-tikki-tikki-tchk*! —Rudyard Kipling, *The Jungle Book*

Now—the date being October 21, 1945—I hold in the hollow of my hand the body of a little bird killed last night in its migration by flying against a railing atop the roof. I saw it lying in the sunlight on the tarred roof this morning, when I went up there, a creature hardly larger than a mouse, with flaming gold breast streaked with black, and gold elsewhere or russet blending into brown and black. It has a slender, pointed black bill. Its fragile, polished black feet simply hang from it, the toes grasping nothing. You would be surprised, holding it in your hand, at how soft and thick is its coat of feathers. The plumage is most of the bird, for the body is simply a small hard core at the center which you feel with your fingers pinching through the downy mass.

—LOUIS J. HALLE, *Spring in Washington*

Although very light birds, they are fairly large, with a wingspan of about seven feet; when sitting they cross their wings swallowlike over their backs. Although their feet are small, unwebbed, and useless for walking or swimming, frigates can perch with great ease on twigs and branches, either with two toes forward and two back, or three forward and one back. The beak is about four inches long, strongly hooked, and has a sharp tip. It is perfectly adapted for snatching fish from just below the surface, picking up floating organic debris, or lifting twigs from the ground or from another bird, while in full flight.

—IAN THORNTON, *Darwin's Islands: A Natural History of the Galápagos*

For when Charley is groomed and clipped and washed he is as pleased with himself as is a man with a good tailor or a woman newly patinaed by a beauty parlor, all of whom can believe they are like that clear through. Charley's combed columns of legs were noble things, his cap of silver blue fur was rakish, and he carried the pompon of his tail like the baton of a bandmaster. A wealth of combed and clipped mustache gave him the appearance and attitude of a French rake of the nineteenth century, and incidentally concealed his crooked front teeth.

—JOHN STEINBECK, *Travels with Charley*

The living examples of the group (*Chimaera* itself, *Hydrolagus*, *Neoharriotta*, *Rhinochimaera*, *Harriotta*, *Callorhynchus*) bear little resemblance to a typical shark, with their rat-like tails, long probing snouts, a hook-like copulatory organ on the forehead, skin flaps covering the gills, fan-shaped pectoral fins, a large spine in front of the dorsal fin, and crushing toothplates for pulverising the shells of the mollusks on which they feed—the upper jaw being solidly fused to the skull for additional strength.

—RODNEY STEEL, *Sharks of the World*

The shrew is a ferocious and deadly little animal. If it were larger—it is less than the size of a mouse—it would perhaps be one of the most feared animals in the world. It has a narrow, tapering snout; close, dark, sooty-velvet fur; and needle teeth. A poison gland in its mouth sends venom into its victim when it bites, and its prey dies quickly.

—VIRGINIA S. EIFERT, *Journeys in Green Places: The Shores and Woods of Wisconsin's Door Peninsula*

The pronghorns are distinctive in other ways. Both sexes may have horns, but the horns of the female never exceed the length of the ears. The horns are composed of fused hairs which cover a bony core. The horn sheath is shed annually. The rump patch, which resembles a huge powder puff when the hairs are erected, acts as an alarm device. When the white hairs are erected they reflect a large amount of light. —DAVID F. COSTELLO, *The Prairie World: Plants and Animals of the Grassland Sea*

Hedgehogs are curious creatures. Small and covered in one-inch spines, they look like ambulatory toilet brushes without the handles, or like turtles, if turtles were a little bit taller and had prickles glued on their shells. But the pragmatic Hebridean islanders have no romantic notions about their spiny garden friends. The only time they generally notice them is when they see their flattened corpses on the roads. If it came down to a contest, they would tend to choose the birds over the hogs. "Rats with prickles," is how one islander described hedgehogs to me.

—SARAH LYALL, *The Anglo Files: A Field Guide to the British*

About half the bulk and weight of thar, chamois are natives of European and Asian alps. For their handsome appearance, golden brown in summer with dark facial stripe between the sharply pointed ears and muzzle, black legs and short upright horns curved backwards at the tops to form semicircular hooks, they were considered "royal" beasts, being also a challenge to hunt, good to eat, and providing buckskin.

—BETTY BROWNLIE AND RONALD LOCKLEY, *The Secrets of Natural New Zealand*

I have even mentioned White-footed mice. Yes, it is a *kind* of mouse, with—giving a splendid boost to the good sense of name-givers—white feet. It (this mouse) also has a white belly and a bi-colored tail, the under half of which is white all down its length. He eats whatever mice eat (which is not at all cheese, but native seeds, roots, and some small insects), and has white whiskers and a line of demarcation between the expansive white belly and his back which is a soft, fawn-colored brown (generally). He has large ears, two cutting incisors above and two below, and large coal-black eyes, and his name is *Peromyscus*. He is clean, noninfectious, industrious, and thoroughly American. And, as I say, he has white feet.

—RUSSELL PETERSON, *Another View of the City: A Chronicle of a Heritage Besieged*

We can let a population of Evolvabots loose in a simplified world, and that population will evolve under the combined effects of history, randomness, and selection. We know that we can use Evolvabots to test hypotheses about the evolution of early vertebrates.

—JOHN LONG, *Darwin's Devices: What Evolving Robots Can Teach Us About the History of Life and the Future of Technology*

We had just climbed over a high dune, when we saw a strange-looking creature moving along the top of a ridge ahead of us. It appeared to be a rat and had very long back legs, and a long tail ending in a bushy tuft. Its body was upright and its small forelegs were tucked under its chin. It walked along on its hind legs like a kangaroo. Then it caught sight of us with its massive saucer eyes, or sensed our presence with its lengthy moustache hairs. Its great ears twitched and it turned its head to look at us for a brief moment.

—VICTOR HOWELLS, *A Naturalist in Palestine*

The smaller one was flattened against the ground, front legs tensed, ready to spring. Its mate circled slowly to the left, keeping its distance, until it was only possible to hold them both in her field of vision by letting her eyes flicker between them. In this way she saw them as a juddering accumulation of disjointed: the alien black gums, slack black lips rimmed by salt, a thread of saliva breaking, the fissures on a tongue that ran to smoothness along its curling edge, a yellow-red eye and eyeball muck spiking the fur, open sores on a foreleg, and, trapped in the V of an open mouth, deep in the hinge of the jaw, a little foam, to which her gaze kept returning. The dogs had brought with them their own cloud of flies.

—IAN MCEWAN, *Black Dogs*

Like all wildcats, the Arabian/North African wildcat has a "mackerel" striped tabby coat, varying in color from gray to brown—darkest in forest-dwelling animals, palest in those that live on the edges of deserts. It is generally larger and leaner than a typical domestic cat, and both its tail and legs are especially long; indeed, the front legs are so long that when it sits, its posture is characteristically upright, as depicted by the Ancient Egyptians in statues of the cat goddess Bast.

—John Bradshaw, *Cat Sense: How the New Feline Science Can Make You a Better Friend to Your Pet*

On his knees, and with his chin level with the top of the table, Stephen watched the male mantis step cautiously towards the female mantis. She was a fine strapping green specimen, and she stood upright on her four back legs, her front pair dangling devoutly; from time to time a tremor caused her heavy body to oscillate over the thin suspending limbs, and each time the brown male shot back. He advanced lengthways, with his body parallel to the table-top, his long, toothed, predatory front legs stretching out tentatively and his antennae trained forwards: even in this strong light Stephen could see the curious inner glow of his big oval eyes.

—Patrick O'Brian, *Master and Commander*

A magnificent Shire, all of eighteen hands with a noble head that he tossed proudly as he paced towards me. I appraised him with something like awe, taking in the swelling curve of the neck, the deep-chested body, the powerful limbs abundantly feathered above the massive feet.

—James Herriot, *Every Living Thing*

Chipmunks, however, are smaller, less plump and have stripes along the sides of their heads, which the ground squirrel lacks. The stripes down the backs of both the golden-mantled ground squirrel and chipmunks serve to camouflage the animals from their numerous predators, blending with the irregular textures and broken patterns of light characteristic of the forest floor.

—Stephen Whitney, *A Sierra Club Naturalist's Guide to the Sierra Nevada*

The dog climbed out through tall saturated grass, through dying pussy willows and stagnant silt, and onto a large flat red stone that still held the late-afternoon warmth from the sun. Here she lay panting, quivering. Her feet were tender and there was a new rip on her belly from the rocks. Wet, she showed her wolflike physique, the slender sneaky profile of her face, the alert damp fan of her tail. Her coloring was dark, her thick fur stippled, and her tongue mottled, like a chow's, but her slender skeletal underpinnings were those of a wild creature, fox or coyote, something nocturnal and sly.

—Antonya Nelson, *Bound*

Black-chinned nectar hunters hovered now before the crimson of a mallow, now before the blue of a morning-glory. One rufous hummingbird perched on the same twig during periods of rest for three days in a row. According to the angle of the light, its tail appeared rufous or cinnamon-hued. Turning in the sun, a female Anna's hummingbird, larger than a ruby-throat, flashed on and off like the beam of a lighthouse, a dazzling red spot that shone jewellike at its throat. Once Connie pointed out the slightly decurved bill and deeply forked tail of a Lucifer hummingbird.

—Edwin Way Teale, *Wandering through Winter*

A hound it was, an enormous coal-black hound, but not such a hound as mortal eyes have ever seen. Fire burst from its open mouth, its eyes glowed with a smouldering glare, its muzzle and hackles and dewlap were outlined in flickering flame. Never in the delirious dream of a disordered brain could anything more savage, more appalling, more hellish be conceived than that dark form and savage face which broke upon us out of the wall of fog.

—ARTHUR CONAN DOYLE, *The Hound of the Baskervilles*

Next to Mary a small gaunt man was sitting, rigid and erect in his chair. In appearance Mr. Scogan was like one of those extinct bird-lizards of the Tertiary. His nose was beaked, his dark eye had the shining quickness of a robin's. But there was nothing soft or gracious or feathery about him. The skin of his wrinkled brown face had a dry and scaly look; his hands were the hands of a crocodile. His movements were marked by the lizard's disconcertingly abrupt clockwork speed; his speech was thin, fluty, and dry. —ALDOUS HUXLEY, *Crome Yellow*

The heart rates of animals as distantly related as fish and rodents also decrease, sometimes suddenly, when frightened. Loud, startling noises have been demonstrated to induce extremely slow heart rates in fawns and alligators as well as not-yet-born human infants. This heart slowing, called "fear" or "alarm" bradycardia, is a protective reflex that may keep the animal still and silent, making it less detectable to predators.

—Barbara Natterson-Horowitz and Kathryn Bowers, *Zoobiquity: What Animals Can Teach Us about Health and the Science of Healing*

A neck stretches long; legs drape behind. Wings curl forward, the length of a man. Spread like fingers, primaries tip the bird into the wind's plane. The blood-red head bows and the wings sweep together, a cloaked priest giving benediction. Tail cups and belly buckles, surprised by the upsurge of ground. Legs kick out, their backward knees flapping like broken landing gear. Another bird plummets and stumbles forward, fighting for a spot in the packed staging ground along those few miles of water still clear and wide enough to pass as safe.

—Richard Powers, *The Echo Maker*

Two kinds of geckoes live in these highlands. On the tree trunks lives the Leaf-tailed Gecko. In day-time he is a mere mottled green smudge as he lies flattened against a giant tree trunk and is virtually invisible. His fringed sides and broad tail do not even cast a tell-tale shadow and his huge lidless eyes are a maze of green and black squiggles which also match his surroundings. No bird or other predator has sight keen enough to detect him. As long as he does not move he is safe.

—Stanley and Kay Breeden, *Wildlife of Eastern Australia*

Tia and Tallulah watched the arrival of Bad Bull with great interest. He was a massive animal with two jaggedly broken tusks and a large V notch out of the bottom of his right ear. About 45 years old, he stood at least two feet taller than the medium-sized bulls and his head, particularly his forehead and the space between his tusks, was extraordinarily broad. His temporal glands, one on each side of his face, located midway between the eye and ear, were grotesquely swollen and secreting a copious, viscous fluid. —CYNTHIA MOSS, *Elephant Memories: Thirteen Years in the Life of an Elephant Family*

PEOPLE

THE BODY

BODY TYPES, FRAMES, AND STATURES

of average or medium size or height

average, medium, middling, normal

having a smooth body

hairless

having a hairy body

hirsute, shaggy, furry, fuzzy

having a thick or somewhat stout build

stocky, thickset, heavyset, chunky, heavy-built, bulky, compact, beefy, burly

muscular

sinewy, well-built, solid, athletic, brawny, husky, mesomorphic, sturdy, robust, muscle-bound

having good posture

upright, straight, rigid, ramrod

having a flexible body

limber, supple, lithe, lithesome, lissome, pliant, agile, nimble, rubbery

not erect or upright

bent, stooped, bent over, slumped, hunched over

having the shoulders bent forward

round-shouldered, stoop-shouldered

large or big

hulking, gigantic, strapping, oversized, hefty, massive, elephantine, heavy-bodied, lumpish, looming, monstrous, a colossus, a goliath, a giant

having a large bone structure relative to one's flesh

big-boned

small or little

slight, diminutive, tiny, undersized, small-boned, wee, a shrimp, a snip, a pipsqueak

tiny and slim (female)

petite

small or lean and supple

wiry, sinewy

short and pudgy

plump, chubby, rotund, tubby, blubbery, roly-poly, round-bodied, pyknic, endomorphic

fat

obese, stout, corpulent, overweight, portly, adipose, fattish, stoutish, fleshy, beefy, bloated, gross, a blimp, a tub of lard, having embonpoint

fat and short-winded

pursy

having loose or limp flesh

flabby, flaccid, soft, slack, irresilient, quaggy

having hanging flesh

pendulous, baggy, loppy, drooping, droopy, nutant

thin

slim, slender, slight, spare, skinny, ectomorphic, thin as a rail, bony, reedy, underweight, angular

thin and fit or with well-defined musculature
trim, lean, toned, buffed, buff, ripped, cut, having definition

elegantly or sleekly thin
willowy, svelte, lissome

delicately thin
wraith-like, sylph-like, fragile, wispy, undernourished

thin and large framed
rawboned

thin and worn-looking
haggard, gaunt, emaciated, shriveled, underfed, scrawny, scraggy

deathly thin
anorectic, anorexic, spectral, cadaverous, skeletal, consumptive, wasted away, emaciated, skin and bone

tall
tallish, long-limbed

tall and thin
gangling, gangly, rangy, long-limbed, loose-jointed, spindly, slab-sided, a beanpole, lanky

short
undersized, runty, runtish, dwarfish, bantam

short and fat
a butterball

short and heavy
squat, pudgy, fubsy (British), stumpy, like a fireplug

shapelessly short and thick
dumpy

broad-shouldered
square-shouldered, square-built

having a broad upper torso

barrel-chested

having a large belly

pot-bellied, paunchy, abdominous, swag-bellied, ventripotent, gorbellied (obsolete), beer-bellied

having a proportionally short upper body (or high waistline)

short-waisted

having large hips

broad in the beam, hippy

having thin hips

slim-hipped, narrow-hipped

having long arms and legs

long-limbed

having long legs

leggy

having shapely buttocks

callipygous, callipygian

having lardy buttocks

steatopygic, steatopygous

(of a woman) having imposing and stately beauty

statuesque, Junoesque, goddess-like

(of a woman) large and strong

Amazonian

(of a woman) attractively or gracefully thin

svelte, willowy, gracile, slender, slight

(of a woman) large and rounded

full-figured, developed, ample, opulent, full-blown

(of a woman) having large breasts

large-breasted, big-breasted, big-chested, bosomy, big-bosomed, buxom, busty, top-heavy, well-built, built, full-bosomed, well-endowed

(of a woman) having deep cleavage
bathycolpian

(of a woman) having a flat chest
flat-chested, small-breasted

(of a woman) having a full and shapely body
voluptuous, shapely, pneumatic, curvaceous, zaftig, Rubensian, Rubenesque, pleasingly plump

(of a woman) having a small waist
wasp-waisted, having an hourglass figure

HEAD, FACE, COMPLEXION, AND SKIN

extremely round-headed
trochocephalic

extremely short- or broad-headed
brachycephalic

extremely large-headed
macrocephalic

extremely long-headed
dolichocephalic, high-crowned

having a high or dome-like head with short hair
bullet-headed, domey

having well-defined or shapely facial features
fine-featured, chiseled, delicately sculptured, sculpturesque

having delicate, almost translucent-like facial features
porcelain

having thick (or thickened) features
blunt, coarse, heavy, gross

having thick features with wide lips and large eyes
frog-like

having a long face

horse-faced, horsey

having a round face

moon-faced

having a wide forehead and a narrow chin

heart-shaped face

having a small and pretty face

doll-faced

having a thin face with angular features

hatchet-faced, sharp-faced, gaunt, severe, hollow-cheeked, with sunken cheeks

having a flat and round face

pie-faced, flat-faced

having a fat and expressionless face

pudding-faced

having a hook nose and protruding chin

having a nutcracker face

lined face

wrinkled, wizened, furrowed, creased, rugose

having heavy or drooping cheeks

jowly

having a pink or reddish face

pink-faced, rosy-faced, ruddy, florid, flushed, rubicund, rubescent, suffused, roseate

ruddy in a coarse way

blowzy, blowsy

looking crisply clean and fresh

well-scrubbed

having an open and guileless face

fresh-faced, sweet-faced

having an expressionless face
blank, unreadable, deadpan, inscrutable, masklike, vacant look, impassive, empty, poker-faced, stone-faced

face showing pain or a difficult life
pinched, hard-bitten

worn face
weather-beaten, weathered, haggard, withered, shriveled, rough, rugged-looking, craggy (features)

tight or tense face
taut, drawn, hardened, hard (features)

skull-like face
skull-faced, spectral, hollowed

having a fleshy face
puffy, bloated, jowly, heavy-jowled

having a concave face
push-faced, dish-faced

having an elfin face
impish, pixieish, mischievous

baby-faced
cherubic

looking worried or depressed
grim, grim-faced, gloomy, saturnine, with a February face

looking wholesomely neat and regular
clean-cut

smooth-skinned
lustrous, unwrinkled, shining, glowing, glabrous, flawless

having a healthfully rosy complexion
ruddy, rosy-cheeked, apple-cheeked, rubicund, rubescent

cracked, roughened, or reddened from wind or cold
chapped

having large pores
large-pored, grainy

aged skin
withered, shriveled, dried up, wizened, like parchment, puckered, cracked, shrunken

weathered skin
tough, leathery, leathern

having freckles
freckled, lenticular

having small spots or discolorations
mottled, blotchy, splotchy, splodgy (British), having a maple face (obsolete)

having warts
warty, verrucose

having pockmarks
pockmarked, pocked, pitted

pimply
papuliferous, eruptive, acned, broken out

glossy
shiny-faced

oily-skinned
oleaginous, greasy

pale
pallid, wan, chalky, pasty, blanched, doughy, etiolated, peaked, whey-faced

dark

swart, swarthy, dark-complexioned

white

alabaster, pearly, creamy, porcelain, milk white, translucent, light-complexioned

sunburned

sunburnt, tan, bronzed, brown, coppery

brown

cocoa, chocolate, coffee

beige-yellow

olive

black

coal black, ebony

yellowish

sallow, waxen, jaundiced, waxlike, parchment-colored, tallow-hued

reddish

ruddy, raw, blowzy, flushed, florid, suffused

blushing

flushing, mantled

reddish brown

liverish

bluish

cyanotic

black and blue

livid

spotted in coloring

mottled, blotched, liver-spotted

HAIR AND HAIRSTYLES

hair

tress, lock, strand, shock, hank, coil, tendril, curl, ringlet, swirl, tuft

having neatly coiffed or combed hair

kempt

hairy

hirsute, unshaven, shaggy, crinose

having no hair

hairless, bald, bald-headed, glabrous, depilous, a cueball

having little hair

balding, thin, thin on top, sparse, wispy, scant, thinning

attempt to cover a bald spot or receding hairline with strands of hair

comb-over

mid-forehead point formed by the hairline

widow's peak

monk's circular fringe or shaven crown

tonsure

having a full or bushy head of hair

mop-headed, mop top, lion-headed, leonine, thick-haired, luxuriant

having short hair

close-cropped, close-thatched, cropped, short-cropped

having very light or whitish hair (like spinning fiber)

towheaded

having soft and lustrous hair

silken-haired

having fine hair
fine-haired, thin-haired

hair with turns or twists
crinkly

hair in disorder
unkempt, messy, mussed up, unruly, tangled, ratty, tousled, rumpled, snarled, straggly

wild and thickly coiled (snake-like) hair
Medusa-like

long and loose
flowing

loose or streaming in the wind
windblown, flyaway

lacking body
lank, stringy, thin, flat

stiff
bristly, brushlike, en brosse

rough
bristly, bristling, scraggy, scrubby, coarse

with pointed tufts
spiky

in thick strands
ropy

formed into curls or ringlets
curled, crimped

formed into small and tight curls
frizzed, frizzed out, frizzy

given more body by combing toward the scalp
teased, back-combed

combed up toward the top of the head
upswept, swept back, raked back

dried (and usually given a fluffed shaping) with a blow dryer
blow-dried
cut in different lengths for a fuller look
layered
oiled
greased, slicked, slick, pomaded, brilliantined, plastered, pasted
matted patches of hair
elflocks
lock hanging at the front of the head
forelock
groomed curl of hair displayed against the forehead or side of the face
spit curl
curled lock of hair
ringlet
tuft of hair growing awry or that won't lie flat
cowlick
curl or lock of hair worn in front of the ear
earlock, sidelock, sidecurl
dampened curl held with a hairpin or clip
pin curl
twisted or intertwined length of hair
braid, plait
woman's hairstyle with a braid or braids "woven" close to the head and attached with pins
French braid
tight braid usually worn down the back of the head
pigtail, rat's tail, rat tail

cinched lock of hair hanging loosely down the back of the neck or head

ponytail

hair divided into braids and worn flat against the scalp

cornrows

hairstyle cut short in the front and on the sides and left long in the back

mullet

knot of hair worn at the back (or on both sides) of the head

bun

tightly wound bun pulled into a knot low at the back of the head

chignon

short, layered hairstyle associated with character played by Jennifer Aniston on the television sitcom *Friends*

Rachel

knot of folded-under hair at the back of the head

French knot, French twist

knot of hair worn on the top of the head

topknot

wave set in lotioned or wet hair with a finger

finger wave

long and rope-like braids as worn by Rastafarians

dreadlocks, dreads

single long lock worn on a bare scalp

scalp lock

attachable woman's hairpiece for creating a hanging length of hair down the back of the head

fall, extension

any attachable thick strand of hair for a woman's coiffure

switch

front down-hanging hair cut evenly across the forehead
bangs, fringe

woman's conical coil of hair worn at the back of the neck
Psyche knot

roll of hair combed up from the forehead or temples
roach

cylindrical roll of hair
puff

curl that is tubular
sausage curl

curl that is spiral
corkscrew curl

certain strands bleached or colored
highlighted, streaked, frosted, tinted, lightened, darkened

hairstyle in which the hair is chemically curled or waved
permanent wave, permanent, perm, cold wave

permanent wave that is looser and gives more body to the hair
body wave

hairstyle in which the (curly or frizzy) hair is chemically straightened and flattened or slightly waved
conk, process

given aligned soft waves (by means of a heated curling iron)
marceled

perm styling, popularized among African-Americans in the 1970s, that rolls or loosens curls
Jheri curl

hairstyle in which the hair is slicked back from either side to meet, at a part, or overlap behind
ducktail, duck's ass, DA

hairstyle featuring spiky or irregularly chopped hair
punk

haircut created with use of a razor, as for a shaggy look or bob
razor cut

rounded cut (with no attention to sides) with hair shaped and hanging like an inverted bowl
bowl cut

short and brushlike haircut
crewcut, butch, burr-cut, buzz cut, brush-cut, Ivy League

short and brushlike haircut with a flattened top
flattop

short men's hairstyle, brushed forward, with a horizontally straight cut fringe over the forehead
Caesar cut

short haircut that makes one's ears appear large
crop-eared

hairstyle with a brushlike strip down the center of an otherwise shaved head
Mohawk

hairstyle in which the hair is a naturally round and bushy mass
Afro

hairstyle in which the hair shape widens above the head to a flat top but is progressively tapered (or "faded") toward the ears
fade

hairstyle in which the brushed-up hair appears as a full and loose roll around the face
pompadour

woman's choppy, layered coiffure in which the hair is cut in downward overlapping and uneven layers
shag

woman's coiffure in which the hair is cut short and evenly all around the head

bob

woman's coiffure in which the short cut is neither layered nor graduated

blunt cut

woman's coiffure in which the hair is cut irregularly short toward the face and with the ears exposed

pixie, French cut

woman's coiffure in which the hair is teased for a puffed-out look

bouffant

woman's conical coiffure

beehive

woman's coiffure with a rounded or cap-like top that is tapered at the back of the neck

mushroom

coiffure in which the usually shoulder-length hair is combed down and turned under or inward at the ends in a roll and with even bangs over the forehead

pageboy, Prince Valiant

woman's coiffure with bangs and the unlayered hair at chin length

Buster Brown, cap cut

woman's coiffure in which the combed-down hair is curled outward

flip

woman's coiffure that is short in which the hair arcs over the forehead and forms a triangle at the back

wedge, Dorothy Hamill

woman's coiffure in which the short and uneven-length curls are given feather-like ends

feather cut

woman's coiffure that is close-cropped in layers and short in the back

shingle

woman's coiffure in which the hair is combed or swept up toward the top of the head and held by pins or combs

upsweep, updo

woman's coiffure in which the hair is combed back to form a long or vertical roll at the back of the head

French twist, French roll

woman's coiffure (eighteenth century) with the hair worn in cylindrical rolls or puffs

pouf

artificial covering of (another's or synthetic) hair

hairpiece, wig, postiche

weaving in of false or human hair on the scalp to compensate for thin hair

hairweave

man's covering of hair over a bald spot

toupee, piece, rug

seventeenth- and eighteenth-century man's wig often powdered and gathered at the back

periwig, peruke

woman's fringe of hair or curls worn on the forehead

frisette (archaic)

FACIAL HAIR

free of facial hair
clean-shaven

adolescent facial hair
peach fuzz

downy
fuzzy (face or skin)

untrimmed facial hair (short of a mustache or beard)
unshaven, stubbly, stubbled, scraggy, bristly

soft or fine facial hair
downy

needing a shave
with a five-o'clock shadow

having a mustache
mustached, mustachioed (usually a long mustache)

mustache that is slight and thin
pencil mustache

narrow mustache under the middle of the nose
toothbrush mustache

thickly shaggy or droopy mustache
walrus mustache

thick mustache with long and curving ends
handlebar mustache, military mustache

curving and dressed mustache
waxed mustache

having a beard
bearded

beard covering most of the lower face
full beard, beaver

small chin beard or tuft
goatee
beard that is long and rectangular
patrician, square-cut beard
trim and pointed beard extending back to the ears
Vandyke, pickedevant
beard shaped like a pointed or broad spade
spade beard
pointed beard beginning at the lower lip
imperial beard
beard following the line of the chin
galways
whiskers extending below the ears
sideburns, burnsides, side-whiskers, sideboards
untrimmed sidelocks worn by male Orthodox Jews
payess
side-whiskers that become broader at the lower jaw
muttonchops, muttonchop whiskers, dundrearies

HAIR COLOR

white
hoary, silvery, platinum, snow white
blond
blonde, blondish, straw-colored, flaxen-haired
golden blond
goldilocks
dull rather than bright blond
dirty blond
bleached blond
peroxide blond, bottled blond, drugstore blond

pale grayish blond
ash blond

black or brown
brunette, dark-haired, dark

black
jet, jet black, coal black, ebony

black and shiny
raven-haired

a mix of black and white
salt-and-pepper

brown
chestnut, wheaten, nut brown

drab brown
mouse-colored, mousy

light yellowish brown
sandy

reddish brown
auburn

red-haired
redheaded, a carrot top, ginger, gingery, titian

brownish red or brownish orange
coppery

reddish blond
strawberry blond

gray or partly gray
grizzled, graying, hoary, grizzly

dyed reddish or orangish brown
hennaed

dyed slightly bluish (to offset yellowed coloration)
having a blue rinse

having some long strands chemically lightened in color
streaked
having much of the hair chemically lightened for a two-tone effect
frosted

EYES, EYE COLOR, AND EYEBROWS

Eyes
clear-eyed
limpid
large-eyed
saucer-eyed, wide-eyed, fish-eyed
small-eyed
beady-eyed, piglike, porcine, ferret-like, ferrety
eyes wide apart
wide set, far set
eyes close together
close set
sunken eyes
hollow-eyed, deep set
bulging or protruding eyes
pop-eyed, banjo-eyed, prominent, protuberant, starting, exophthalmic, hyperthyroid, bug-eyed, proptosed, bulbous, goggle-eyed, starting
narrow-eyed
slit-eyed
lively eyes
bright-eyed, twinkle-eyed, flashing, luminous, beaming, glinting, glowing

having a hard, unflinching gaze
steely-eyed
expressionless eyes
flat, cold, dull-eyed, lusterless, blank, fish-like, glassy
blinking frequently (as a tic)
blinky-eyed, blinky
narrowed eyes
squinting, crinkled
having inwardly turned eyes
cross-eyed, cockeyed, strabismic
having outwardly turned eyes
walleyed, cockeyed, strabismic
squinting
cockeyed, strabismic
restless or moving eyes
shifting, shifty, darting, swivel-eyed
having soft and dark eyes
sloe-eyed
having large and innocent eyes
doe-eyed
moist or wet eyes
dewy-eyed, watery, aqueous, glistening, teary-eyed, rheumy-eyed, watery-eyed
having slanted eyes
slanty-eyed, sloe-eyed
having horizontally long or somewhat oval eyes
almond-eyed
having tired or half-closed eyes
heavy-lidded, sleepy-eyed, slumberous, slumbrous
motionless eyes
staring, glaring, transfixed, unblinking, glazed

reddened eyes

red-eyed, bloodshot, pink-veined

having weary or strained eyes

bleary-eyed, puffy-eyed

hoodlike upper lids or eyes looking half-closed

hooded eyes

fleshy folds under the eyes

pouchy, pouched, pouch-eyed, baggy, bagged

wearing eyeglasses

bespectacled

Eye color

blue, cornflower blue, steely blue, icy blue, china blue, sapphire blue, baby blue

brown, velvet brown

gray, gooseberry, slate gray, slaty

green, greenish, emerald

light or golden brown, hazel

violet

amber

Eyebrows

thick

bushy, shaggy

jutting out or projecting

beetle-browed, beetling

thinned to a line with tweezers

tweezed, plucked, threaded

accented cosmetically

penciled

NOSE AND EARS

pronounced downward bend from the bridge of the nose
hook-nosed, hawk-nosed, beak-nosed, parrot-nosed, having an arched nose

slight or fine downward bend from the bridge
Roman, aquiline, patrician

long nose
leptorrhine, blade-like

nose curving out or upward
ski-jump nose

having a wide nose
broad-nosed, flat-nosed

short nose with flattened nostrils
snub-nosed, simous, stubby

having a broad and sometimes turned-up nose
pug-nosed

having a large and bulbous nose
cob-nosed

having a somewhat flattened nose
button-nosed

having a protuberant or swollen-looking (and sometimes reddish) nose
bottle-nosed

having an inflamed nose (as from habitual drunkenness)
copper-nosed

nose turned up at the end
upturned, uptilted, retroussé

wrinkled
crinkled

destructive storm rotating around a low-pressure center, esp. one originating in the southwestern Pacific Ocean or the Indian Ocean

cyclone

persistent, planetary-scale cyclonic circulation of cold arctic air centered around either of the earth's poles and sometimes moving southward

polar vortex

tropical cyclone, esp. of equatorial regions of the Atlantic Ocean or Caribbean Sea, bringing severe wind and rain north, northwest, or northeast

hurricane

severe, destructive storm over a wide area

superstorm

sea spray blown by the wind

spindrift

column of water created by a tornado occurring over water

waterspout

storm in which rain freezes on contact with a cold surface

ice storm

usually polar snow condition in which there are no shadows and the horizon cannot be distinguished

whiteout

violent snowstorm with high winds and low visibility

blizzard

spiraling wind system with a high-pressure center that circles clockwise in the Northern Hemisphere and counterclockwise in the Southern Hemisphere

anticyclone

tropical cyclone less intense than a hurricane

tropical storm

fierce windstorm, accompanied by rain, thunder, and almost continuous lightning (up to 50 times per minute)

derecho

rotating, usually destructive column of wind, usually accompanied by a funnel-shaped extension downward of a cumulonimbus cloud, that advances over land in a narrow path

tornado, twister

severe thunderstorm with a rotating updraft, sometimes producing a tornado

supercell

flashes of electric light without thunder near the horizon, usually on hot summer evenings

heat lightning

rare form of lightning, associated with thunderstorms, taking the form of a luminous floating ball and believed to consist of ionized gas

ball lightning

warm ocean current originating in the Gulf of Mexico and passing Florida and the southeast coast of the U.S. before flowing northeast into the Atlantic Ocean

Gulf Stream

irregularly recurring (every few years) upwelling of warm water above the surface of the Pacific Ocean, generated along the western coast of South America, that disrupts usual regional and global weather patterns

El Niño

irregularly recurring (often following El Niño) upwelling of cold water above the surface of the Pacific Ocean, generated along the western coast of South America, that disrupts usual regional and global weather patterns

La Niña

having large and projecting ears
big-eared, jug-eared

having large and floppy ears
spaniel-eared

having an injury-deformed or battered ear
cauliflower-eared

small or delicately shapely ears
seashell ears

having ears upright and somewhat pointed
prick-eared, having satyr-like ears

MOUTH, LIPS, TEETH, JAW, AND NECK

having a loose or slightly open mouth
slack-mouthed

well-shaped lips
shapely, full, sensuous, sensual, ripe, generous

small but prominent or puffy
bee-stung, Botoxed

thick lips
blubber

having cracked or weathered lips from exposure to wind or cold
chapped

having a thin mouth or lips
thin-lipped, slash-mouthed

crooked or twisted mouth
screw mouth

mouth with a protruding upper lip
satchel mouth, shad mouth

classically shapely upper lip
Cupid's bow

having grayish or reddish brown lips
liver-lipped
lips with much or bright lipstick
rouged
having protruding upper teeth
bucktoothed, having an overbite
having a space or spaces between teeth
gap-toothed, gat-toothed
having a jutting or broken tooth
snaggle-toothed
strong- or wide-jawed
square-jawed, lantern-jawed
straight-jawed
orthognathous
crooked-jawed
skew-jawed, agee-jawed
firm-jawed
with a set jaw
having a projecting lower jaw
wopple-jawed, jimber-jawed, prognathous, prognathic
having a projecting upper jaw
jutting, opisthognathous
having the lower jaw hanging down (often stupidly)
slack-jawed
having a double chin
double-chinned, dewlaps
having a thick neck
bull-necked
long and graceful neck
swanlike

having a short neck

no-neck

fleshy or flabby neck

baggy, wattled

having a scrawny neck

turkey-necked

HANDS AND FINGERS

bent and knobby or somewhat deformed

gnarled, horny, knotted, crooked

short fingers

stubby

fat and ugly fingers

sausage fingers

with knuckles, wrist, and other bones prominent

bony

long fingers

tapered

worn hands

coarse, rough, callused, chapped

LEGS, KNEES, AND FEET

having long legs

leggy, long-limbed, dolichocnemic

stick-legged

spindly, spindle-shanked

bowlegged

bandy-legged

having knees touching
knock-kneed
large knees
knobby
short and thick legs
stumpy, stubby, piano legs
crooked legs
gnarled, twisted
withered legs
atrophied
having turned-in feet
pigeon-toed
having turned-out feet
duck-footed, splayfooted

GAIT

walking
stepping, pacing, treading, ambulating, perambulating
walking in an orderly way
marching, processing, filing
walking in a leisurely, easygoing way
sauntering
walking slowly or dragging the feet
shuffling, shambling
walking slowly or heavily
lumbering, loping, schlepping
walking swiftly
rolling, barreling, swooping
walking with quick and hurried steps
scuttling, darting, scurrying, scampering

walking in a jerky or uncertain way
reeling, lurching, staggering, tottering, toddling, wobbling, unsteady, faltering, stumbling

walking in a rigid, unfluid way
stiff-legged

walking quietly or with muffled sound
tiptoeing, padding

walking in a lively way
bouncy, sprightly, skipping, tripping

walking easily or confidently
light-footed, sure-footed, striding briskly, gliding, ambling, strolling

walking effeminately
mincing, flouncing, flitting

walking haltingly
limping, hobbling, claudicant

walking in search of or with effort
trekking, traipsing, tramping

walking or moving about in search of pleasure
gallivanting

walking awkwardly or loudly
clomping, stomping, galumphing

walking arrogantly
strutting, swaggering, promenading, parading, prancing

walking heavily or wearily
plodding, tramping, trudging, slogging, dragging, straggling

walking with purpose or without hesitation
striding, marching, bearing down

walking aimlessly
rambling, wandering, roving, traipsing, gadding
walking with duck-like short steps
waddling
walking furtively
prowling, skulking, slinking
walking warily or timidly
pussyfooting, creeping
walking or moving in a grand or stylish manner
sweeping
walking in a conspicuous or ostentatious way
sashaying
running or hastening
sprinting, dashing

VOICE

clear
audible, firm, resolute, authoritative, carefully articulated, crisp, distinct
high
high-pitched, soprano, shrill, girlish, treble
squeaky
twittery
low
deep, dark, baritone, basso
cold
hard, steely, dry, chilling, dispassionate, insensible, unfeeling, affectless
warm
friendly, intimate

soft

muted, subdued, whispery, low, breathy, modulated

loud

strong, robust, ringing, stentorian, prodigious, booming, commanding, hearty

loud and irritating

sharp, grating, harsh, piercing, brassy, screechy, ear-splitting, shrieking, strident, caterwauling

pleasant or soothing

euphonious, melodious, sweet, dulcet, mellifluous, velvety, rich, lyrical, languid, sweet, silken, soft, honey-voiced, winsome, appealing

bright or buoyant

chirpy, chirrupy, bubbly

slow-speaking and somewhat mannered (or with prolonged vowels)

drawling

hesitant or without assuredness

halting

mournful

sepulchral, funereal, lugubrious, somber

artificial or pretentious

affected, orotund, stilted

alluring

seductive, spell-binding, hypnotic, entrancing, beguiling, bewitching, enchanting, enticing, cajoling, sirenic

falsely or overly sweet or smug

unctuous, cloying, saccharine, ingratiating, oily, oleaginous

having overly inflected or particularly noticeable S sounds

sibilant, hissing

affectedly elegant, lisping
mincing
stammering or overly excited
stuttering, sputtering, spluttering
unpleasantly loud
brassy
like a flute
fluted, fluty
shrill and piping
reedy
low and throaty
husky, gruff, scratchy, raspy, hoarse, gravel-voiced, wheezy, roupy, guttural, smoky
deep
full, resonant, sonorous
deeply mellow and refined
plummy
hollow
tinny
without intonation
monotonous, monotone, flat
nasal
catarrhal, asthmatic
whiny
whimpering, puling, mewling
rising and falling monotonously
singsong, jingly
nervous
uncertain, quavering, timorous, tremulous, quavery, edgy

with audibility deadened or blocked

muffled

with syllables indistinct or running together

slurred

PHYSICAL STATES AND SYMPTOMS

healthy

hearty, hale, robust, vigorous, sound, red-blooded, vital, strong, glowing

unhealthy

sick, sickly, wan, unwell, ailing, not well, weak, run-down, indisposed, under the weather, out of sorts, lacking vigor, unsound

tired or tiring

weary, faint, fatigued, worn, worn out, enervated, drained, debilitated, exhausted, wilting, wilted, languishing, run-down, spent, enfeebled, sapped, raddled

lacking a sense of balance

unsteady, light-headed, dizzy, dazed, stunned, reeling, wobbly, wobbling, buckling, tottering, staggering, tipsy, unstable, losing one's equilibrium

sleepy

somnolent, nodding, drowsy, slumberous, slumbrous, yawning, lethargic, comatose, half asleep, groggy, soporific, oscitant

having skin that is markedly pale

pallid, etiolated, wan, pasty, drained, whey-faced, chalky, cadaverous, ghostly

having sickly or yellowish skin

sallow, jaundiced, icteric

red-faced

blushing, flushed, reddened, rubescent, ruddy, raddled, florid

lacking feeling or sensation

insensible, insensate, anesthetized, deadened, desensitized, numb, impassible, impassive, insentient, unsusceptible, unresponsive, unexcitable

overly sensitive to touch

hypersensitive, raw, tender

disabled

crippled, incapacitated, out of action, hors de combat, handicapped, challenged, enfeebled

being severely cold or having chills

shivering, shaking, aguish, having shivers, having the shakes, having goose bumps, having gooseflesh

having a seizure or fit

convulsing, trembling, quavering, jerking, spasmodic, quivering, atremble, shuddering, tremulous, having tremors, having paroxysms, palsied

having difficulty breathing

short of breath, gasping, panting, wheezing, having labored breathing, stertorous, rhonchal, rhonchial

infected

impure, contaminated, corrupted, septic

sick to one's stomach

dyspeptic, colicky, having indigestion, nauseated, nauseous, under the weather, green around the gills

stiffness

rigidity, rigor

broken bone

fracture

feeling pain or a type of pain

sore, painful, hurting, smarting, sharp, stinging, aching, throbbing, burning, searing, biting, gnawing, chafing, piercing, stabbing, in the throes, having pangs, shooting, angry, fiery, pounding, acute

feeling severe pain

tormenting, excruciating, agonizing, in agony, hellish, torturous, in anguish, atrocious

perspiring

sweating, having beads of sweat, moist, damp, wet

discolored (tissue)

black and blue, livid, bruised, blemished, contused, ecchymotic

inflamed (tissue)

swollen, tumescent

irritated, worn, or rubbed away by friction

abraded

burned

scorched, singed, scalded, blistered, sunburned, wind-burned

speaking unclearly or incoherently

rambling, babbling, raving, gibbering, gabbling, driveling, maundering

having saliva coming out of the mouth

slobbering, dribbling, drooling

unconscious

in a faint, fainted, blacked out, comatose, knocked out, out cold, out, dead to the world, in a swoon

cut (flesh)

lacerated, stabbed, pierced, punctured, pricked, incised, slit, slashed, gashed, sliced, hacked, axed, knifed

in shock
traumatized
in a drugged state
narcotized, strung out, spaced out, stoned, spacey, spacy, zonked, zonked out
vomiting
regurgitating, disgorgement, puking, retching
bleeding
bloody, sanguinary, hemorrhaging, hemorrhagic, exsanguinating, sanguineous
showing putrefaction
putrid, foul
discharging pus
suppurating, pussy, purulent

MEDICAL TERMS FOR SYMPTOMS

small crack in a bone
stress fracture
partial break or bend in a bone (esp. in children)
greenstick fracture, incomplete fracture
fracture with no open wound in the skin
simple fracture, closed fracture
fracture with an open wound in the skin
open fracture, compound fracture
fracture in which the bone is crushed or splintered
comminuted fracture
fracture in which the bone is pressed together on itself
compression fracture
fracture in which the bone has been twisted apart
spiral fracture, torsion fracture

difficulty breathing or shortness of breath
dyspnea

absence of spontaneous respiration
apnea

deep or rapid breathing
hyperpnea, tachypnea

shallow or slow breathing
hypopnea

high blood pressure
hypertension

low blood pressure
hypotension

high heart rate
tachycardia

low heart rate
bradycardia

cessation of the heartbeat
cardiac arrest

fainting or loss of consciousness
syncope, lipothymia

abnormal physical sensitivity
hyperesthesia

severe reaction to a foreign substance, such as insect toxin, a chemical, or a particular food
anaphylaxis

subnormal body temperature
hypothermia

high fever
hyperpyrexia

inflammation
edema

increased blood flow to a body part
hyperemia

vomiting
emesis

purplish discoloration from ruptured blood vessels
ecchymosis

vomiting blood
hematemesis

bluish skin discoloration due to inadequate oxygen reaching tissue
cyanosis

insufficient oxygen reaching body tissues
hypoxia

insufficient oxygen in blood
hypoxemia

excessive response to a stimulus
hyperirritability

increased CO_2 level in blood
hypercapnia

perspiration
hidrosis

excessive perspiring
hyperhidrosis

lacking or showing no perspiration
anhidrosis

pathological changes caused by inadequate oxygen inhaled from air
asphyxia

interrupted breathing (suffocation) resulting in loss of consciousness or death
asphyxiation

rapid and random contractions of the heart
fibrillation
deficient blood supply due to constriction or obstruction of a blood vessel
ischemia
small bruises or pinpoint hemorrhages
petechiae
abnormal crackling or rattling sound heard while inhaling
rale
redness of skin
erythema
forcibly separated or detached
avulsed
chest pain due to deficient oxygenation of the heart muscles
angina pectoris, angina

DRESS AND GENERAL APPEARANCE

appropriate
correct, proper, decent, suitable, apropos, seemly, decorous, felicitous, kempt
proper and wholesome
respectable, clean-cut, conservative, modest, discreet, fitting, comme il faut, conforming to standards, orthodox, tasteful
formal
dressed up, elegant, dressy, all decked out
inappropriately formal
overdressed
meticulous
exquisite, impeccable, fastidious

fashionable or smart

stylish, modish, chic, swell, a la mode, in vogue, voguish, snappy, toney, sophisticated, debonair, polished, cosmopolitan, dashing, spiffy, snazzy, natty, dressed to the nines, becoming, soigné or soignée, spruce, high-toned, aristocratic, with it, hip, cool

sporty

rakish, jaunty, dapper

inappropriate

in poor taste, tasteless, unsuitable, inapropos, unseemly, outlandish, common, vulgar, crude, raffish

not fashionable

old-fashioned, frumpy, frumpish, drab, dowdy, frowsy, frowzy, shabby

heterogeneous or of different colors

motley

informal

casual, come as you are, undressy, homey, off-handed, relaxed, dressed down

inappropriately informal

underdressed

not neat or tidy

unkempt, disheveled, rumpled, slovenly, shabby, grubby, sloppy, untidy, slobby, grungy

flashy

showy, flamboyant, garish, foppish, frilly, extravagant, obvious, out there

cheap

gaudy, vulgar, tacky, common, tawdry, meretricious, cheapjack

immodest

sexy, provocative, revealing, daring, lewd, salacious, lascivious, sluttish, slutty, scantily clad, shameless, scandalous

worn

ragged, frayed, shopworn, threadbare, shabby, tatterdemalion, seedy, ragtag, ratty, tattered

shabby but trying to appear dignified

shabby-genteel

PERCEIVED ATTRACTIVENESS

attractive or beautiful

pretty, handsome, comely, prepossessing, becoming, lovely, appealing, beauteous, exquisite, adorable, gorgeous, cute, pulchritudinous, ravishing, stunning, good-looking, fair, well-favored, pleasing, breathtaking, bonny, fetching

ordinary

nondescript, forgettable, plain, undistinguished, unremarkable, commonplace, prosaic

unattractive

unbecoming, unappealing, ugly, homely, unprepossessing, unsightly, hideous, repugnant, repellent, repulsive, ghastly, unlovely, ill-favored, ill-featured, uncomely, not much to look at

Medical Terms for Bones and Other Anatomical Parts

skull
cranium

roof and upper sides of cranium
parietal bones

posterior floor and walls of cranium
occipital bones

sides and base of cranium
temporal bones

forehead
frontal bone

cheekbones
zygomatic bones

lower jawbone
mandible

upper jaw bones
maxillary bones, maxillae, maxillas

bones in the neck
cervical vertebrae

Adam's apple
thyroid cartilage

shoulder blade
scapula

collarbone
clavicle

backbone
spinal column, vertebral column

upper arm bone
humerus

forearm bones
ulna and (smaller) radius

"*funny bone*"
olecranon process

wrist bones
carpals

finger bones
phalanges (singular: phalanx)

bony enclosing wall of the chest
rib cage

breastbone
sternum

shinbone
tibia

thigh bone
femur

kneecap
patella

behind the knee
popliteal muscles, vessels, and ligaments

lower leg
tibia or shinbone and (smaller) fibula

ankle (projections)
malleoli

heel bone
calcaneus

foot bones
metatarsals

toe bones
phalanges (singular: phalanx)

QUOTATIONS

Perhaps inspired by the sun breaking through the tail end of a cumulus cloud riding a fair, southwesterly breeze, or maybe it comes out of the nicotine from his first cigarette in more than five minutes. Mako stretches for the sky. He's a big man, six foot five, thick in all the right places, his shoulders barely squeezing through hatchways. An athlete in profile, he casts a shadow considered the largest anywhere on the waterfront. He has plenty of jet-black hair and a set of long legs attached to an unpadded thirty-six-inch waist. He elicits playful looks from divorcées years younger than he. They all love what they see: Liam Neeson goes to sea.

—Rory Nugent, *Down at the Docks*

Murphy had often inspected Mr. Endon's eyes, but never with such close and prolonged attention as now.

In shape they were remarkable, being both deep-set and protuberant, one of Nature's jokes involving sockets so widely splayed that Mr. Endon's brows and cheekbones seemed to have subsided. And in colour scarcely less so, having almost none. For the whites, of which a sliver appeared below the upper lid, were very large indeed and the pupils prodigiously dilated, as though by permanent excess of light. The iris was reduced to a thin glaucous rim of spawnlike consistency, so like a ballrace between the black and white that these could have started to rotate in opposite direction, without causing Murphy the least surprise. —SAMUEL BECKETT, *Murphy*

He was a large heavy man. He was bearded. His hair was overgrown and unkempt. His eyes were blue and set in a field of pink that suggested a history of torments and conflicts past ordinary understanding. His weight and size seemed to amplify the act of breathing, which took place through his mouth. His nose looked swollen, a web of fine purple lines ran up his cheeks from the undergrowth, and all the ravage together told of the drinker.

—E. L. DOCTOROW, *Loon Lake*

"Let's try something closer to your level. What is this?" she asked, raising her thumb.

"I believe that is a thumb."

"No," she said. "It is the first digit composed of the metacarpal, the proximal phalange, and the distal phalange."

"That's another way of saying it."

—ANTHONY MARRA, *A Constellation of Vital Phenomena*

Webb is the oldest man of their regular foursome, fifty and then some—a lean thoughtful gentleman in roofing and siding contracting and supply with a calming gravel voice, his long face broken into longitudinal strips by creases and his hazel eyes almost lost under an amber tangle of eyebrows. He is the steadiest golfer, too. The one unsteady thing about him, he is on his third wife; this is Cindy, a plump brown-backed honey still smelling of high school, though they have two little ones, a boy and a girl, ages five and three. Her hair is cut short and lies wet in one direction, as if surfacing from a dive, and when she smiles her teeth look unnaturally even and white in her tan face, with pink spots of peeling on the roundest part of her cheeks; she has an exciting sexually neutral look, though her boobs slosh and shiver in the triangular little hammocks of her bra.

—JOHN UPDIKE, *Rabbit Is Rich*

A couple ducked in late, slid into the pew next to her, and promptly closed their eyes in prayer, leaving Dellarobia free to scrutinize them. The man wore sporty sunglasses pushed on top of his head as if he'd just hopped out of a convertible. But if that was the wife with him, there was no convertible in the story. She'd probably spent two hours getting her hair organized and congealed, the bangs individually shellacked into little spears, all pointing eyeward, which made Dellarobia cringe. She had a thing about eyes. Preston had a habit that killed her, of poking himself along the hairline with his pencil while pondering what to write. Every pointed jab went into her own flesh, her own eyes wincing reflexively.

—BARBARA KINGSOLVER, *Flight Behavior*

And he saw her, with the dumb, pale, startled ghosts of joy and desire hovering in him yet, a thin, vivid, dark-eyed girl, with something Indian in her cheekbones and her carriage and her hair; looking at him with that look in which were blended mockery, affection, desire, impatience, and scorn; dressed in the flamelike colors that, in fact, she had seldom worn, but that he always thought of her as wearing. —JAMES BALDWIN, *Go Tell It on the Mountain*

Joanie, Joanie, my friend with the webbed toes, why do I make Dr. Torbein so uncomfortable, don't you think he'd be used to this by now, he must get it all the time, even if he doesn't get it *all* all the time, you know what I mean? (Joanie smiles and looks at her feet a lot.) I mean, he's got his glasses so far down here, see, that he has to tuck two of his chins back into the recesses of his throat in order to read The Clipboard, which seems to grow out of his gut like some visceral suburbia, and unless we are speaking of the ferrous content of blood, he is utterly ill at ease with irony and gets twitches, like this, see? (Horrid, feeble humor.) —LORRIE MOORE, "Go Like This," *Self-Help*

Students called Zolo "Rolo," because, if only in stature and complexion, he happened to resemble that particularly chewable chocolate caramel candy. He was short, tan and round, wore bright plaid Christmas pants regardless of the time of year, and his thick, yellow-white hair encrusted his shiny freckled forehead as if, ages ago, Hidden Valley Ranch salad dressing had been dribbled all over him. —MARISHA PESSL, *Special Topics in Calamity Physics*

Winnie was barely into her thirties but she had a sane and practiced eye for the half-concealed disasters that constitute a life. A narrow face partly hidden by wispy brown ringlets, eyes bright and excited. She had the beaky and hollow-boned look of a great wading creature. Small prim mouth. A smile that was permanently in conflict with some inner stricture against the seductiveness of humor. —DON DELILLO, *White Noise*

"I have the address. I wrote it down. It was on her knapsack like mine is." Louise said the name of the street, which was east, out St. Claude, almost to the parish line, in the part of town where many houses had been destroyed by the hurricane, two years ago. "They're leaving today," she said. Louise had long straight honey-brown hair and wore tortoiseshell glasses that made her look older than thirteen, made her look businesslike, which in a way she was. She was wearing her blue gingham Trinity skirt and her uniform white blouse and her white kneesocks. She looked perfect.

—RICHARD FORD, "Leaving for Kenosha," *The New Yorker*, March 3, 2008

Otto has a face like a very ripe peach. His hair is fair and thick, growing low on his forehead. He has small sparkling eyes, full of naughtiness, and a wide, disarming grin, which is much too innocent to be true. When he grins, two large dimples appear in his peach-blossom cheeks.

—CHRISTOPHER ISHERWOOD, *Goodbye to Berlin*

After he had finished his long process of washing I went for a walk with my father, along the Embankment, past Cleopatra's Needle and the Sphinxes, black beasts which the pigeons had decked with a white crust. He was a tall man, over six foot in height, with fair hair which left the top of his head but never went grey. His legs were long and very thin, his feet and hands small, his stomach grew in swelling isolation. He had a high forehead; but his nose was thick, his chin grew fat and his lower jaw protruded so that he couldn't be called handsome. His eyes were a clear, light blue; and now that he could no longer see he had abandoned his spectacles.

—JOHN MORTIMER, *Clinging to the Wreckage*

His face was not as square as his son's and, indeed, the chin, though firm enough in outline, retreated a little, and the lips, ambiguous, were curtained by a moustache. But there was no external hint of weakness. The eyes, if capable of kindness and good-fellowship, if ruddy for the moment with tears, were the eyes of one who could not be driven. The forehead, too, was like Charles's. High and straight, brown and polished, merging abruptly into temples and skull, it had the effect of a bastion that protected his head from the world.

—E. M. FORSTER, *Howards End*

You're probably imagining my dad as this maladjusted, socially inept FOB who didn't know what he was saying to me. He was just the opposite. At home, he'd walk around in his underwear and house sandals, but if he had a meeting out came the Jheri curl, gator shoes, and Cartier sunglasses. —EDDIE HUANG, *Fresh Off the Boat*

She was one of those women who are middle-aged too soon, her skin burned into the colors of false health. Thin, nervous, her face was screwed tight, and in those moments when she relaxed, the lines around her forehead and mouth were exaggerated, for the sun had not touched them. Pale haggard eyes looked out from sun-reddened lids. She was wearing an expensive dress but had only succeeded in making it look dowdy. The bones of her chest stood out, and a sort of ruffle fluttered on her freckled skin with a parched rustling movement like a spinster's parlor curtain.

—NORMAN MAILER, *The Deer Park*

"Good evening, Nathaniel," said MARBLE. Slight British accent from the assignment in London, leavened by his time in New York. A whim to use English, to be closer to his case officer, despite Nate's nearly fluent Russian. MARBLE was short and stocky, with deep brown eyes separated by a fleshy nose. He had bushy white eyebrows, which matched his full head of wavy white hair, giving him the appearance of an elegant boulevardier.

—JASON MATTHEWS, *Red Sparrow*

It was the French Lieutenant's Woman. Part of her hair had become loose and half covered her cheek. On the Cobb it had seemed to him a dark brown; now he saw that it had red tints, a rich warmth, and without the then indispensable gloss of feminine hair oil. The skin below seemed very brown, almost ruddy, in that light, as if the girl cared more for health than a fashionably pale and languid-cheeked complexion. A strong nose, heavy eyebrows . . . the mouth he could not see.

—JOHN FOWLES, *The French Lieutenant's Woman*

She was much older than me, at least eleven. Her red-brown hair was worn relatively short, for a girl, and her nose was snub. She was freckled. She wore a red skirt—girls didn't wear jeans much back then, not in those parts. She had a soft Sussex accent and sharp gray-blue eyes.

—NEIL GAIMAN, *The Ocean at the End of the Lane*

The author of the paper, Albert O. Birdless, nineteen, from Marathon, Cascadia, was majoring in vocational education. His build reminded Levin of a young tugboat. He was stocky, with a short neck, heavy shoulders and legs, and stubby feet in square-toed shoes. His longish crewcut appeared to have gone to seed. On his head he usually wore a freshman beanie.

—BERNARD MALAMUD, *A New Life*

Clare is already seated in a booth and she looks relieved when she sees me. She waves at me like she's in a parade.

"Hello," I say. Clare is wearing a wine-colored velvet dress and pearls. She looks like a Botticelli by way of John Graham: huge gray eyes, long nose, tiny delicate mouth like a geisha. She has long red hair that covers her shoulders and falls to the middle of her back. Clare is so pale she looks like a waxwork in the candlelight. I thrust the roses at her. "For you." —AUDREY NIFFENEGGER, *The Time Traveler's Wife*

At thirteen she went every day to the dancing school, and at thirteen Jenny had deliciously slim legs and a figure as lithe as a hazel wand. Her almond eyes were of some fantastic shade of sapphire-blue with deep grey twilights in them and sea-green laughters. They were extraordinary eyes whose underlids always closed first. Her curls never won back the silver they had lost in the country; but her complexion had the bloom and delicate texture of a La France rose, although in summer her straight little nose was freckled like a bird's egg. Her hands were long and white, her lips very crimson and translucent; but the under-lip protruded slightly, and bad temper gave it a vicious look. Her teeth were small, white and glossy as a cat's. —COMPTON MACKENZIE, *Carnival*

Looking in the huge mirror, she considers her hair, a cloud of maddened bees. In lieu of an hour with hot irons and pins, she catches one honey-brown curl and thrusts it back into the hive. —EMMA DONOGHUE, *Frog Music*

For one thing, it provides the extra dash of suspense that comes with every Harrison Ford picture: What will he do with his hair? Throughout *Star Wars*, you stared at Han Solo and wondered how a civilization advanced enough to wage war in space could still allow its heroes to wear their hair over their ears, like midcareer Beatles. Ford turned up in *Presumed Innocent* with an unexpected razor cut, and now, in *The Fugitive*, he has shaggy locks and a beard. They give him an ecclesiastical air; if he slipped on a robe and held up two fingers, he could pose for a Greek icon. —ANTHONY LANE, *Nobody's Perfect: Writings from* The New Yorker

"Don't be nervous. Remember, she wants you here," Obinze whispered, just before his mother appeared. She looked like Onyeka Onwenu, the resemblance was astounding: a full-nosed, full-lipped beauty, her round face framed by a low Afro, her faultless complexion the deep brown of cocoa. Onyeka Onwenu's music had been one of the luminous joys of Ifemel's childhood, and had remained undimmed in the aftermath of childhood.

—CHIMAMANDA NGOZI ADICHIE, *Americanah*

Phineas had soaked and brushed his hair for the occasion. This gave his head a sleek look, which was contradicted by the surprised, honest expression which he wore on his face. His ears, I had never noticed before, were fairly small and set close to his head, and combined with his plastered hair they now gave his bold nose and cheekbones the sharp look of a prow. —JOHN KNOWLES, *A Separate Peace*

"Her axillary temp was fifty degrees," Scarpetta continued. "The low last night was thirty-four; the high during the day was forty-seven. The mark left by the scarf is a superficial circumferential dry brown abrasion. There's no suffusion, no petechia of the face or conjunctiva. The tongue wasn't protruding." —PATRICIA CORNWELL, *The Scarpetta Factor*

Journalist First Class Mac Lean was a small round-bellied man wearing parts of a Seabee uniform with a forty-five holstered on his guard belt. His arms were freckled and thickly tattooed; he had a pink boozer's face adorned with a sinister goatee and wraparound sunglasses.

—ROBERT STONE, *Dog Soldiers*

Mom's gestures were all familiar—the way she tilted her head and thrust out her lower lip when studying items of potential value that she'd hoisted out of the Dumpster, the way her eyes widened with childish glee when she found something she liked. Her long hair was streaked with gray, tangled and matted, and her eyes had sunk deep into their sockets, but still she reminded me of the mom she'd been when I was a kid, swan-diving off cliffs and painting in the desert and reading Shakespeare aloud. Her cheekbones were still high and strong, but the skin was parched and ruddy from all those winters and summers exposed to the elements. To the people walking by, she probably looked like any of the homeless people in New York City. —JEANNETTE WALLS, *The Glass Castle*

The charm of Edna Pontellier's physique stole insensibly upon you. The lines of her body were long, clean and symmetrical; it was a body which occasionally fell into splendid poses; there was no suggestion of the trim, stereotyped fashion-plate about it.

—Kate Chopin, *The Awakening*

Dio, but she was a beauty. Perhaps seventeen or eighteen years old, laced into a rosy silk gown draped over her mare's white flanks in such abundant pleats that I could list at least three broken sumptuary laws. Breasts like white peaches, a pale column of a neck, a little face all rosy with happiness—and hair. Such hair, glinting gold in the sunlight, twined with pearls and tucked with cream-colored roses.

—Kate Quinn, *The Serpent and the Pearl: A Novel of the Borgias*

Directly next to me, on the first cross seat, is a very fine-looking girl. She is a strapping girl but by no means too big, done up head to toe in cellophane, the hood pushed back to show a helmet of glossy black hair. She is magnificent with her split tooth and her Prince Val bangs split on her forehead. Gray eyes and wide black brows, a good arm and a fine swell of calf above her cellophane boot. One of those solitary Amazons one sees on Fifty-seventh Street in New York or in Neiman Marcus in Dallas.

—Walker Percy, *The Moviegoer*

She was beautiful. Fin liked her hair, which was long. He liked her teeth. She thought they were too big, but she was wrong. She was like a horse. Not one of the Pounds' heavy Morgan horses with short sturdy necks and thick clomping legs. She was like a racehorse. Jittery. Majestic. Her long neck and long legs—and her face, too. She had a horsey face, in a beautiful way. And bangs, like a forelock. —CATHLEEN SCHINE, *Fin & Lady*

He just look her up and down. She bout seven or eight months pregnant, bout to bust out her dress. Harpo so black he think she bright, but she ain't that bright. Clear medium brown skin, gleam on it like on good furniture. Hair notty but a lot of it, tied up on her head in a mass of plaits. She not quite as tall as Harpo but much bigger, and strong and ruddy looking, like her mama brought her up on pork. —ALICE WALKER, *The Color Purple*

Henry watched his mother's eyes meet Dr. Luke's: the doctor paused, then nodded. At the door of his parents' room, Henry could smell Buddhist incense burning, along with some kind of cleaning solution. His mother turned on a small lamp in the corner. As Henry's eyes adjusted, he beheld his father, looking small and frail. He lay like a prisoner of his bed—the covers pulled up tight around his chest, which seemed to move in a jerky, uneven rhythm. His skin was pale, and one side of his face looked bloated, like it had been in a fight while the other side watched and did nothing. His arm lay at his side, palm up; a long tube connected at his wrist led to a bottle of clear fluid that hung from the bedpost.

—JAMIE FORD, *Hotel on the Corner of Bitter and Sweet*

He walked over to her as quietly as if she were asleep, feeling strange to be by himself, and stood on tiptoe beside her and looked down into her sunbonnet towards her ear. Her temple was deeply sunken as if a hammer had struck it and frail as a fledgling's belly. Her skin was crosshatched with the razor-fine slashes of innumerable square wrinkles and yet every slash was like smooth stone; her ear was just a fallen intricate flap with a small gold ring in it; her smell was faint yet very powerful, and she smelled like new mushrooms and old spices and sweat, like his fingernail when it was coming off.

—JAMES AGEE, *A Death in the Family*

Most of the time the swelling eventually went down and I could get the leg straight enough to put weight on it. And then I would forget about the incident and try to return as swiftly as possible to the pressing duties of being an energetic boy. Finally, on one occasion that I have blocked from my memory, I had such a massive bleeding that the knee slowly jackknifed. I would not be able to put weight on it again for more than seven years.

With a marvelous combination of sympathy and challenge, my parents helped me fight off the occasional bouts of depression that would seize me when I was confined to my bed.

—BOB MASSIE, *A Song in the Night: A Memoir of Resilience*

Andrew is just as thin as I am fat, and his clothes hang on him in the most comical way. He is very tall and shambling, wears a ragged beard and a broad Stetson hat, and suffers amazingly from hay fever in the autumn.

—CHRISTOPHER MORLEY, *Parnassus on Wheels*

If Miss Baeza could get a man, anyone could. Rogelia Baeza ruled the typing roost at Cabritoville High. She was short, broad-faced, with a good, solid D-cup on her. Her wide hips anchored her spindly bowlegged goat's legs on the ground. Her small, hooflike feet were unbelievably nimble. She moved without sound and would sneak up on you as you were quietly fff fvf vvv fff fvf vvv fff fvf vvv fvfing.

—DENISE CHÁVEZ, *Loving Pedro Infante*

The other was a remarkable fellow. He was in his middle forties, slim, a bit stoop-shouldered. His eyes were black and deep-set. His eyebrows were bushy. He had long arms and wrists, and although he used his hands constantly in making conversation, they were relaxed and delicate in their movements.

—JAMES A. MICHENER, *Tales of the South Pacific*

When Claude walked into my apartment for the first time he looked like he had never had a good day in his life. He wore a jacket and shirt and clean blue jeans and real shoes, not sneakers. That told you something positive right there. He was thin and handsome—my guess was one parent with ancestors in Japan and another with history in Africa, with a few different coasts of Europe thrown in, and later I found out I was right.

—SARA GRAN, *Claire DeWitt and the Bohemian Highway*

Their commander was a middle-aged corporal—red-eyed, scrawny, tough as dried beef, sick of war.

—KURT VONNEGUT, *Slaughterhouse Five*

But the sweet young girl was the daintiest thing these premises, within or without, could offer for contemplation: delicately chiseled features, of Grecian cast; her complexion the pure snow of a japonica that is receiving a faint reflected enrichment from some scarlet neighbor of the garden; great, soft blue eyes fringed with long curving lashes; an expression made up of the trustfulness of a child and the gentleness of a fawn; a beautiful head crowned with its own prodigal gold; a lithe and rounded figure, whose every attitude and movement was instinct with native grace.

—MARK TWAIN, "The Loves of Alonzo Clarence and Rosannah Ethelton," *Best Short Stories by Mark Twain*

Mama uncoiled her braids and let them down and waited for me to unwind them. In truth, she had only to shake her head and the braids unfurled, but she knew I loved to feel the tight plaits go soft and free in my hands. When she wasn't too tired, she let me sit next to her on her bed and practice my seaman's knots on her hair: sheet bend and monkey fist, timber hitch and lineman's loop. Her hair hung in a long pale wave that she sometimes allowed me to brush. I counted the strokes slowly to make them last, her hair popping and crackling as the dark bristles moved through it. —JANICE CLARK, *The Rathbones*

Hurree Babu came out from behind the dovecot, washing his teeth with ostentatious ritual. Full-fleshed, heavy-haunched, bull-necked, and deep-voiced, he did not look like "a fearful man". —RUDYARD KIPLING, *Kim*

Tall, powerful, barefoot, graceful, soundless, Missouri Fever was like a supple black cat as she paraded serenely about the kitchen, the casual flow of her walk beautifully sensuous and haughty. She was slant-eyed, and darker than the charred stove; her crooked hair stood straight on end, as if she'd seen a ghost, and her lips were thick and purple. The length of her neck was something to ponder upon, for she was almost a freak, a human giraffe, and Joel recalled photos, which he'd scissored once from the pages of a *National Geographic,* of curious African ladies with countless silver chokers stretching their necks to improbable heights.

—TRUMAN CAPOTE, *Other Voices, Other Rooms*

Scurvy was common. Foodborne parasites and pathogens made diarrhea almost ubiquitous. Most feared was beriberi, a potentially deadly disease caused by a lack of thiamine. There were two forms of beriberi, and they could occur concurrently. "Wet" beriberi affected the heart and the circulatory system, causing marked edema—swelling—of the extremities; if not treated, it was often fatal. "Dry" beriberi affected the nervous system, causing numbness, confusion, unsteady gait, and paralysis.

—LAURA HILLENBRAND, *Unbroken: A World War II Story of Survival, Resilience, and Redemption*

Mrs. Haydon was a short, stout, hard built, German woman. She always hit the ground very firmly and compactly as she walked. Mrs. Haydon was all a compact and well hardened mass, even to her face, reddish and darkened from its early blonde, with its hearty, shiny cheeks, and double chin well covered over with the up roll from her short, square neck.

—GERTRUDE STEIN, *Three Lives*

In the midst of this brown gloom Mr. Bodiham sat at his desk. He was the man in the Iron Mask. A grey metallic face with iron cheek-bones and a narrow iron brow; iron folds, hard and unchanging, ran perpendicularly down his cheeks; his nose was the iron beak of some thin, delicate bird of rapine. He had brown eyes, set in sockets rimmed with iron; round them the skin was dark, as though it had been charred. Dense wiry hair covered his skull; it had been black, it was turning grey. His ears were very small and fine. His jaws, his chin, his upper lip were dark, iron-dark, where he had shaved. His voice, when he spoke and especially when he raised it in preaching, was harsh, like the grating of iron hinges when a seldom-used door is opened.

—ALDOUS HUXLEY, *Crome Yellow*

Miserable food, ill-timed and greedily eaten, had played havoc with bone and muscle. They were all pale, flabby, sunken-eyed, hollow-chested, with eyes that glinted and shone and lips that were a sickly red by contrast. Their hair was but half attended to, their ears anemic in hue, and their shoes broken in leather and run down at heel and toe. —THEODORE DREISER, *Sister Carrie*

For most people, this restriction is a nuisance. But a few dozen people have moved to Green Bank (population: 147) specifically because of it. They say they suffer from electromagnetic hypersensitivity, or EHS—a disease not recognized by the scientific community in which these frequencies can trigger acute symptoms like dizziness, nausea, rashes, irregular heartbeat, weakness, and chest pains. Diane Schou came here with her husband in 2007 because radio-frequency exposure anywhere else she went gave her constant headaches. "Life isn't perfect here. There's no grocery store, no restaurants, no hospital nearby," she told me when I visited her house last month. "But here, at least, I'm healthy. I can do things. I'm not in bed with a headache all the time."

—JOSEPH STROMBERG, "Refugees of the Modern World," *Future Tense*, Slate, April 12, 2013

Captain Marpole's grizzled head emerged from the scuttle. A sea-dog: clear blue eyes of a translucent truthworthiness: a merry, wrinkled, morocco-coloured face: a rumbling voice. —RICHARD HUGHES, *A High Wind in Jamaica*

This was the first time I had seen Fletcher for nearly a year. He was a tall man who must once have been a handsome figure in the fine clothes he always wore and with his arrogant air and his finely chiseled face set off by his short-cropped black beard and brilliant eyes. Now a heaviness was setting in about his features and a fatty softness was beginning to show in his body. —JACK SCHAEFER, *Shane*

They'd danced each dance together. The band had skiffled faster, her hair had loosened from the French roll she'd copied carefully from the cover of *Bunty*, her feet had ached, but still she'd kept on dancing. Not until Shirley, miffed at having been ignored, arrived aunt-like by her side and said the last bus home was leaving if Laurel cared to make her curfew (she, Shirley, was sure she didn't mind either way) had she finally stopped.

—KATE MORTON, *The Secret Keeper*

She heard the feet cross the diningroom, then the swing door opened and Luster entered, followed by a big man who appeared to have been shaped of some substance whose particles would not or did not cohere to one another or to the frame which supported it. His skin was dead looking and hairless; dropsical too, he moved with a shambling gait like a trained bear. His hair was pale and fine. It had been brushed smoothly down upon his brow like that of children in daguerreotypes. His eyes were clear, of the pale sweet blue of cornflowers, his thick mouth hung open, drooling a little.

—WILLIAM FAULKNER, *The Sound and the Fury*

Seated right next to me, just my luck, was a painfully odd-looking woman with baby bangs and white cat-eye eyeglasses who might well have been there to cure Nosy Nellie disease. She kept leaning over, looking at my handbag, my shoes, sniffing so loudly that I wondered if I should offer her a recommendation for a good ENT doctor.

—Dorothea Benton Frank,
The Last Original Wife

Not much taller than the Bishop in reality, he gave the impression of being an enormous man. His broad high shoulders were like a bull buffalo's, his big head was set defiantly on a thick neck, and the full-cheeked, richly coloured, egg-shaped Spanish face—how vividly the Bishop remembered that face! It was so unusual that he would be glad to see it again; a high, narrow forehead, brilliant yellow eyes set deep in strong arches, and full, florid cheeks,—not blank areas of smooth flesh, as in Anglo-Saxon faces, but full of muscular activity, as quick to change with feeling as any of his features. His mouth was the very assertion of violent, uncurbed passions and tyrannical self-will; the full lips thrust out and taut, like the flesh of animals distended by fear or desire.

—Willa Cather, *Death Comes for the Archbishop*

Their smocks drenched in blood, with the nauseating scent of sepsis and cordite and human excrement fouling the operating theater, they cut and sliced and sawed and cauterized wounds of a sort they never would have known in ordinary practice.

—Wade Davis, *Into the Silence: The Great War, Mallory, and the Conquest of Everest*

He was a big, hefty fellow, good-looking in a rather flashy, sunburnt way. He had the hot, blue eyes usually associated with heavy drinking and loose living. His hair was reddish like his skin. In a few years he would run to fat, his neck bulging over the back of his collar. His mouth gave him away, it was too soft, too pink. I could smell the whisky in his breath from where I stood.

—Daphne du Maurier, *Rebecca*

The eyes—and it was my destiny to know them well—were large and handsome, wide apart as the true artist's are wide, sheltering under a heavy brow and arched over by thick black eyebrows. The eyes themselves were of that baffling protean gray which is never twice the same; which runs through many shades and colorings like intershot silk in sunshine; which is gray, dark and light, and greenish gray, and sometimes of the clear azure of the deep sea. They were eyes that masked the soul with a thousand guises, and that sometimes opened, at rare moments, and allowed it to rush up as though it were about to fare forth nakedly into the world on some wonderful adventure,—eyes that could brood with the hopeless somberness of leaden skies; that could snap and crackle points of fire like those which sparkle from a whirling sword; that could grow chill as an arctic landscape, and yet again, that could warm and soften and be all a-dance with love-lights, intense and masculine, luring and compelling, which at the same time fascinate and dominate women till they surrender in a gladness of joy and of relief and sacrifice.

—Jack London, *The Sea Wolf*

My teeth are only slightly crooked, and most of them are white. I have almost all my hair, which is curly and brown. My chest was concave when I was a child, but if you look closely, this is true of most children, and the weight lifting I did in prison helped with that, and while I don't actually have a barrel chest, I might have half a barrel. My legs aren't nearly as scrawny as they used to be, and have muscles and definition now. My nose would be Roman if my head were smaller. Even though I'm close to legally blind, I don't have to obscure my piercing blue eyes with glasses, because I wear contact lenses.

—Brock Clarke, *An Arsonist's Guide to Writers' Homes in New England*

Mrs. Reed might be at that time some six or seven-and-thirty; she was a woman of robust frame, square-shouldered and strong limbed, not tall, and, though stout, not obese; she had a somewhat large face, the under-jaw being much developed and very solid; her brow was low, her chin large and prominent, mouth and nose sufficiently regular; under her light eyebrows glimmered an eye devoid of ruth; her skin was dark and opaque, her hair nearly flaxen. . . .

—Charlotte Brontë, *Jane Eyre*

He was a muscular, short man with eyes that gleamed and blinked, a harsh voice, and a round, toneless, pock-marked face ornamented by a thin, dishevelled moustache sticking out quaintly under the tip of a rigid nose.

—JOSEPH CONRAD, *Victory*

But shock is not a one-time event. That system-junking you experience at the start goes away, of course. But then a lesser shock keeps showing up, to hurl a big muffling blanket over you. And when you push out of *that*, you feel it almost as a sudden blinking exposure to light. I'm talking about how your mind behaves after the broken circuit *appears* to be back up and running.

—DARIN STRAUSS, *Half a Life: A Memoir*

It was as if I was trying to catch some telltale expression in her eyes. But it wasn't there; she had the same warm, intelligent, confident look. I just looked at her and didn't think about her at all—I just laid there and enjoyed looking at a really fine chick. She had one of those heart-shaped faces with a cupid's-bow mouth, and coal-black hair parted in the middle and pulled tight down over her ears.

—CHESTER HIMES, *If He Hollers Let Him Go*

Her shape was not only exact but extremely delicate, and the nice proportion of her arms promised the truest symmetry in her limbs. Her hair, which was black, was so luxuriant that it reached her middle before she cut it to comply with the modern fashion, and it was now curled so gracefully in her neck that few would believe it to be her own. —HENRY FIELDING, *Tom Jones*

The cousin was so close now, that, when he lifted his hat, Dorothea could see a pair of grey eyes rather near together, a delicate irregular nose with a little ripple in it, and hair falling backward; and there was a mouth and chin of a more prominent, threatening aspect than belonged to the type of the grandmother's miniature.

—GEORGE ELIOT, *Middlemarch*

That November, Mr. Falvo, who taught American history, stopped me on my way out of class. It was my sophomore year. Falvo was a quick-moving, sharp-featured man with flat, razor-scraped cheeks, an Alfalfa cowlick and a shriveled right arm that looked like it belonged on an eight-year-old and felt—I knew because he insisted on shaking hands with it, hunching forward to make up the distance—exactly like a warm, dead fish. He'd gotten it in the war—Okinawa, they said. —MARK SLOUKA, *Brewster*

The girls were sisters. One wore a green frock, the other a tunic of mauve jersey with an orange sash around her bottom. Their cheeks were rouged, their hair shingled, and their nostrils were cavernous.

—BRUCE CHATWIN, *On the Black Hill*

Chile was still in the chair when the new-wave barbers came back and began to comment, telling him they could perm what was left or give him a moderate spike, shave the sides, laser stripes were popular.

—ELMORE LEONARD, *Get Shorty*

There was a deep humility in Hale; his pride was only in his profession: he disliked himself before the glass, the bony legs and the pigeon breast, and he dressed shabbily and carelessly as a sign—a sign that he didn't expect any woman to be interested.

—GRAHAM GREENE, *Brighton Rock*

I had only ever seen her briefly—on the few occasions she'd come by to pick Mina up for outings to Red Lobster, their favorite—and there was no other way to put it than to say: She was gargantuan. The loose-falling *kurta* and the neck scarf may have made her seem not quite so outsized as her more tightly fitting Western clothes did, but if so, the effect was minimal. As for the most distinctive aspect of her heft (at least to me)—her layered neck, its bulbous folds of flesh stacked successively, like scoops of a sundae, and topped with a round, reddish head so much smaller than the rest of her—the Pakistani clothes didn't change that one bit.

—AYAD AKHTAR, *American Dervish*

And Loerke was not a serious figure. In his brown velvet cap that made his head as round as a chestnut, with the brown velvet flaps loose and wild over his ears, and a wisp of elf-like, thin black hair blowing above his full, elf-like dark eyes, the shiny, transparent brown skin crinkling up into odd grimaces on his small-featured face, he looked an odd little boy-man, a bat.

—D. H. Lawrence, *Women in Love*

Tashtego's long, lean, sable hair, his high cheek bones, and black rounding eyes—for an Indian, Oriental in their largeness, but Antarctic in their glittering expression—all this sufficiently proclaimed him an inheritor of the unvitiated blood of those proud warrior hunters, who, in quest of the great New England moose, had scoured, bow in hand, the aboriginal forests of the main.

—Herman Melville, *Moby-Dick*

I did not so much look like a woman who had spent the past three weeks backpacking in the wilderness as I did like a woman who had been the victim of a violent and bizarre crime. Bruises that ranged in color from yellow to black lined my arms and legs, my back and rump, as if I'd been beaten with sticks. My hips and shoulders were covered with blisters and rashes, inflamed welts and dark scabs where my skin had broken open from being chafed by my pack.

—Cheryl Strayed, *Wild: From Lost to Found on the Pacific Crest Trail*

His face was pale as death, and far more ghastly; the broad forehead was contracted in his agony, so that his eyebrows formed one grizzled line; his eyes were red and wild, and the foam hung white upon his quivering lip.

—Nathaniel Hawthorne, "My Kinsman, Major Molineux," *The Snow-Image, and Other Twice-Told Tales*

He was a snub-nosed, flat-browed, common-faced boy enough, and as dirty a juvenile as one would wish to see, but he had about him all the airs and manners of a man. He was short of his age, with rather bow-legs, and little, sharp, ugly eyes. —CHARLES DICKENS, *Oliver Twist*

He was tall, slim, rather swarthy, with large saucy eyes. The rest of us wore rough tweed and brogues. He had on a smooth chocolate-brown suit with loud white stripes, suede shoes, a large bow-tie and he drew off yellow, wash-leather gloves as he came into the room; part Gallic, part Yankee, part, perhaps, Jew; wholly exotic.

—EVELYN WAUGH, *Brideshead Revisited*

Poor Maxwell. Ever since his return last month, from a pharmacological botanical specimen-gathering expedition, he's been noticeably agitated, clumsy and distracted in the manner of one plagued by either fever or crisis. Apparently, something strange had happened in Costa Rica, and now Max was walking into things and breaking them, at a rate of about one electrical fixture, decorative serving dish, potted plant, or item of statuary every three days.

"What's wrong with him, do you think?" Vergil whispered barely audibly in my ear.

Together we watched Max kneel unsteadily down among the lamp shards.

—DONALD ANTRIM, *The Hundred Brothers*

He placed himself at a corner of the doorway for her to pass him into the house, and doated on her cheek, her ear, and the softly dusky nape of her neck, where this way and that the little lighter-coloured irreclaimable curls running truant from the comb and the knot—curls, half-curls, root-curls, vine-ringlets, wedding-rings, fledgeling feathers, tufts of down, blown wisps—waved or fell, waxed over or up or involutedly, or strayed, loose and downward, in the form of small silken paws, hardly any of them much thicker than a crayon shading, cunninger than long round locks of gold to trick the heart.

—George Meredith, *The Egoist*

She stands like this often, with her hands on her hips, pointy elbows pushed back like a fledging set of wings. She is pretty to you, Ruby, though her appearance is jarring, the eyes of a griot in the face of a girl. It's an odd mixture of features: pointy chin, jutting cheekbones, tiny nose, initiation scars, village emblems.

—Taiye Selasi, "The Sex Lives of African Girls," *Granta 115: The F Word*

To the eye, the men were less similar: Littlefield, a hedge-scholar, tall and horse-faced; Chum Frink, a trifle of a man with soft and mouse-like hair, advertising his profession as poet by a silk cord on his eyeglasses; Vergil Gunch, broad, with coarse black hair *en brosse*; Eddie Swanson, a bald and bouncing young man who showed his taste for elegance by an evening waistcoat of figured black silk with glass buttons; Orville Jones, a steady-looking, stubby, not very memorable person, with a hemp-colored toothbrush mustache.

—Sinclair Lewis, *Babbitt*

While he was using the lavatory, he began making his Evelyn Waugh face, then abandoned it in favour of one more savage than any he normally used. Gripping his tongue between his teeth, he made his cheeks expand into little hemispherical balloons; he forced his upper lip downwards into an idiotic pout; he protruded his chin like the blade of a shovel. —KINGSLEY AMIS, *Lucky Jim*

Up close the woman looked maybe a year or two younger than the men. Early forties, possibly, rather than mid. She had jet black hair piled up high on her head and tied in a bun. Or a chignon. Or something. Reacher didn't know the correct hairdressing term. She looked to be medium height and lean. Her shirt was clearly a smaller size than the men's, but it was still loose on her. She was pretty, in a rather severe and no-nonsense kind of a way. Pale face, large eyes, plenty of makeup. She looked tired and a little ill at ease. —LEE CHILD, *A Wanted Man*

Dr. Messinger, though quite young, was bearded, and Tony knew few young men with beards. He was also very small, very sunburned and prematurely bald; the ruddy brown of his face ended abruptly along the line of his forehead, which rose in a pale dome; he wore steel-rimmed spectacles and there was something about his blue serge suit which suggested that the wearer found it uncomfortable. —EVELYN WAUGH, *A Handful of Dust*

Col. Grangerford was very tall and very slim, and had a darkish-paly complexion, not a sign of red in it anywhere; he was clean-shaved every morning, all over his thin face, and he had the thinnest kind of lips, and the thinnest kind of nostrils, and a high nose, and heavy eyebrows, and the blackest kind of eyes, sunk so deep back that they seemed like they was looking out of caverns at you, as you may say. His forehead was high, and his hair was gray and straight, and hung to his shoulders. His hands was long and thin. . . .

—MARK TWAIN, *The Adventures of Huckleberry Finn*

. . . Alfred came leaping from the chair fantastically galvanized, horribly smiling, a travesty of enthusiasm, dancing around with rigid jerking limbs and circling the room at double-speed and then falling hard, face down, wham, like a ladder with its legs together, and lying prone there on the execution-room floor with every muscle in his body galvanically twitching and boiling.

—JONATHAN FRANZEN, *The Corrections*

Good heavens! it was Dorian Gray's own face that he was looking at! The horror, whatever it was, had not yet entirely spoiled that marvelous beauty. There was still some gold in the thinning hair and some scarlet on the sensual mouth. The sodden eyes had kept something of the loveliness of their blue, the noble curves had not yet completely passed away from chiseled nostrils and from plastic throat.

—OSCAR WILDE, *The Picture of Dorian Gray*

Believing that their chances will be slightly less negligible in a group, Spillane slowly makes his way toward the lights. He is buoyed up by his life vest and wetsuit and swimming with his broken arm stretched out in front of him, gripping the blanket bag. It takes a long time and the effort exhausts him, but he can see the lights slowly getting closer. They disappear in the wave troughs, appear on the crests, and then disappear again. Finally, after a couple of hours of swimming, he gets close enough to shout and then to make out their faces. It is Dave Ruvola and Jim Mioli, roped together with parachute cord. Ruvola seems fine, but Mioli is nearly incoherent with hypothermia. —SEBASTIAN JUNGER, *The Perfect Storm*

Had orange blossoms been invented then (those touching emblems of female purity imported by us from France, where people's daughters are universally sold in marriage), Miss Maria, I say, would have assumed the spotless wreath, and stepped into the travelling carriage by the side of gouty, old, bald-headed, bottle-nosed Bullock Senior. . . . —WILLIAM THACKERAY, *Vanity Fair*

A withered face, with the shiny skin all drawn into wrinkles! The stretched skin under the jaw was like the skin of a plucked fowl. The cheek-bones stood up, and below them were deep hollows, almost like egg-cups. A short, scraggy white beard covered the lower part of the face. The hair was scanty, irregular, and quite white; a little white hair grew in the ears. —ARNOLD BENNETT, *The Old Wives' Tale*

And the men of the regiment, with their starting eyes and sweating faces, running madly, or falling, as if thrown headlong, to queer, heaped-up corpses—all were comprehended. —STEPHEN CRANE, *The Red Badge of Courage*

His pallid bloated face expressed benevolent malice and, as he had advanced through his tidings of success, his small fat encircled eyes vanished out of sight and his weak wheezing voice out of hearing.

In reply to a question of Stephen's his eyes and his voice came forth again from their lurking places.

—JAMES JOYCE, *A Portrait of the Artist as a Young Man*

His sister, Catherine, was a slender, worldly girl of about thirty, with a solid, sticky bob of red hair, and a complexion powdered milky white. Her eyebrows had been plucked and then drawn on again at a more rakish angle, but the efforts of nature toward the restoration of the old alignment gave a blurred air to her face.

—F. SCOTT FITZGERALD, *The Great Gatsby*

She padded to the bathroom and washed very carefully, brushed her teeth very meticulously. She felt like in school when you've done all your homework. She looked at herself in the mirror and then thought, *Oh, Jesus*, and turned out the bathroom light. —MARCELLE CLEMENTS, *Midsummer*

In softness of features, body bulk, leanness of legs, apish shape of ear and upper lip, Dr. Pavil Pnin looked very like Timofey, as the latter was to look three or four decades later. In the father, however, a fringe of straw-colored hair relieved a waxlike calvity; he wore a black-rimmed pince-nez on a black ribbon like the late Dr. Chekhov; he spoke in a gentle stutter, very unlike his son's later voice. —VLADIMIR NABOKOV, *Pnin*

She held the light at the same level, and it drew out with the same distinctness her slim young throat and the brown wrist no bigger than a child's. Then, striking upward, it threw a lustrous fleck on her lips, edged her eyes with velvet shade, and laid a milky whiteness above the black curve of her brows. —EDITH WHARTON, *Ethan Frome*

. . . while the Haiti-born daughter of the French sugar planter and the woman whom Sutpen's first father-in-law had told him was a Spaniard (the slight dowdy woman with untidy gray-streaked raven hair coarse as a horse's tail, with parchment-colored skin and implacable pouched black eyes which alone showed no age because they showed no forgetting, whom Shreve and Quentin had likewise invented and which was likewise probably true enough). . . . —WILLIAM FAULKNER, *Absalom, Absalom!*

Parsons, Winston's fellow tenant at Victory Mansions, was in fact threading his way across the room—a tubby, middle-sized man with fair hair and a froglike face. At thirty-five he was already putting on rolls of fat at neck and waistline, but his movements were brisk and boyish. His whole appearance was that of a little boy grown large, so much so that although he was wearing the regulation overalls, it was almost impossible not to think of him as being dressed in the blue shorts, gray shirt, and red neckerchief of the Spies.

—GEORGE ORWELL, *Nineteen Eighty-Four*

His body, which was nearly naked, presented a terrific emblem of death, drawn in intermingled colors of white and black. His closely shaved head, on which no other hair than the well known and chivalrous scalping tuft was preserved, was without ornament of any kind, with the exception of a solitary eagle's plume, that crossed his crown and depended over the left shoulder.

—JAMES FENIMORE COOPER,
The Last of the Mohicans

Edward Page turned slowly upon the bed, seeming to do so by a great effort. He was a big, bony man of perhaps sixty with harshly lined features and tired, luminous eyes. His whole expression was stamped with suffering and a kind of weary patience. And there was something more. The light of the oil lamp, falling across the pillow, revealed one half of his face expressionless and waxen. The left side of his body was equally paralyzed and his left hand, which lay upon the patchwork counterpane, was contracted to a shiny cone.

—A. J. CRONIN,
The Citadel

She was a lawyer and lived in my building. I had been noticing her for months in the elevator. Her light blue eyes were heavily made up and looked almost yellow. Her dark eyebrows, however, preserved for them an intensity that would otherwise have been lost. She had high cheekbones and short auburn hair swept straight back. Her skin—at least when I saw her in the elevator—seemed to glow. But it was her eyes, on these occasions, that offered, with stunning insistence, the promise of sexual fulfillment.

—MARK STRAND, "More Life," *Mr. and Mrs. Baby and Other Stories*

He was dressed all in decent black, with a white cravat round his neck. His face was as sharp as a hatchet, and the skin of it was as yellow and dry and withered as an autumn leaf. His eyes, of a steely light grey, had a very disconcerting trick, when they encountered your eyes, of looking as if they expected something more from you than you were aware of yourself. His walk was soft; his voice was melancholy; his long lanky fingers were hooked like claws.

—WILKIE COLLINS, *The Moonstone*

A girl was standing there looking in. She had full, rouged lips and wide-spaced eyes, heavily made up. Her finger-nails were red. Her hair hung in little rolled clusters, like sausages. She wore a cotton house dress and red mules, on the insteps of which were little bouquets of red ostrich feathers.

—JOHN STEINBECK, *Of Mice and Men*

His voice was generally too loud for its setting, for the porch on this homely, leaf-drowned block of wood-frame houses on this somnolent, hot afternoon, for example, but the oversize voice was well matched with his face, long and lean and not the least softened up at its edges by his five-dollar barbershop buzz cut, its narrow span busily occupied by a large, slightly hooked Roman nose and large, hooded green eyes and a wide, mobile mouth and large out-sticking ears, all of which he tirelessly manipulated as a clown would, launching his eyebrows or stretching his grin from one lobe to the other.

—Susan Choi, *My Education*

Elmer Cowley was extraordinarily tall and his arms were long and powerful. His hair, his eyebrows, and the downy beard that had begun to grow upon his chin were pale almost to whiteness. His teeth protruded from between his lips and his eyes were blue with the colorless blueness of the marbles called "aggies" that the boys of Winesburg carried in their pockets.

—Sherwood Anderson, "Queer," *Winesburg, Ohio*

We were, superficially at any rate, a very unlikely pair to become friendly. She was fair-haired and pretty, gaily dressed in corduroy trousers and a bright jersey, while I, mousy and rather plain anyway, drew attention to these qualities with my shapeless overall and old fawn skirt. Let me hasten to add that I am not at all like Jane Eyre, who must have given hope to so many plain women who tell their stories in the first person, nor have I ever thought of myself as being like her.

—Barbara Pym, *Excellent Women*

Those fiery letters, meanwhile, had disappeared; there were ten seconds of complete darkness; then suddenly, dazzling and incomparably more solid-looking than they would have seemed in actual flesh and blood, far more real than reality, there stood the stereoscopic images, locked in one another's arms, of a gigantic negro and a golden-haired young brachycephalic Beta-Plus female.

—Aldous Huxley, *Brave New World*

Outside of Goethe and Byron, my sister was the object of most of my brother's thoughts. She was a beautiful girl who played the piano nearly as well as my brother read and wrote, and it was widely considered a shame that they were related. For my part, I had a bit of a hatchet face. The Germans thought I looked French.

As for my brother and sister, if there was anything improper I never knew it, though when she spoke to him her words were made of cotton, or a sweet that dissolves on your tongue, whereas I was addressed as a cur dog.

—Philipp Meyer, *The Son*

He was a tight brisk little man, with the air of an arrant old bachelor. His nose was shaped like the bill of a parrot; his face slightly pitted with the smallpox, with a dry perpetual bloom on it, like a frost-bitten leaf in autumn. He had an eye of great quickness and vivacity, with a drollery and lurking waggery of expression that were irresistible. —WASHINGTON IRVING, *The Sketch Book*

After fleeing to a nearby brasserie, Fiona and Pauline carefully examined the man in the photograph. His hair was gray-blond, windblown, and boyishly full. It fell onto his forehead and framed an angular face dominated by a small, rather cruel-looking mouth. The clothing was vaguely maritime: white trousers, a blue-striped oxford cloth shirt, a large diver's wristwatch, canvas loafers with soles that would leave no marks on the deck of a ship. That was the kind of man he was, they decided. A man who left no marks. —DANIEL SILVA, *The English Girl*

Aunt Julia was an inch or so taller. Her hair, drawn low over the tops of her ears, was grey; and grey also, with darker shadows, was her large flaccid face. Though she was stout in build and stood erect her slow eyes and parted lips gave her the appearance of a woman who did not know where she was or where she was going. Aunt Kate was more vivacious. Her face, healthier than her sister's, was all puckers and creases, like a shriveled red apple, and her hair, braided in the same old-fashioned way, had not lost its ripe nut colour.

—JAMES JOYCE, "The Dead," *Dubliners*

Her face swelled here. The musket ball moved there. The face bulged there. The musket ball moved here, neither capitulating, each doing a kind of death dance, with her soul as the anxious partner in waiting, until the musket ball quit the game, pushing its way out to the surface, where it bulged just above her left eye, a grotesque grape-sized lump. One night, lying on her back, she reached up to her left temple and felt it, just beneath the skin, and dug her fingers into the gouging mound of pus and blood until the awful gurgling mass of flesh popped open and the ball landed on the floor with a sharp ping as she passed out.

—JAMES MCBRIDE, *Song Yet Sung*

Once, calling at the Primrose Hill branch to take Melissa to lunch, he waited for her on a stool at the back of the shop and took it all in—Lenochka, the assistant with spiky cropped hair dyed black, lisping Russian-inflected Cockney through pierced-tongue jewelry, the piped Tchaikovsky, the scent of sandalwood, a general air of unmockable devotion to children and adults at play.

—IAN MCEWAN, *Solar*

The baroness gave him a flashing, brilliant smile. She was a woman of more than forty, but in a hard and glittering manner extremely beautiful. She was a high coloured blonde with golden hair of a metallic lustre, lovely no doubt but not attractive, and Ashenden had from the first reflected that it was not the sort of hair you would like to find in your soup. She had fine features, blue eyes, a straight nose, and a pink and white skin, but her skin was stretched over her bones a trifle tightly; she was generously *décolletée* and her white and ample bosom had the quality of marble.

—W. Somerset Maugham, "Miss King," *The Complete Short Stories of W. Somerset Maugham*, vol. 1, *East and West*

The circumstances of Greg Fleniken's death, as reported, were unremarkable. On the table before him was a 55-year-old Caucasian male who appeared to be in decent shape. After methodical inspection, the only marks Brown found on the body were a one-inch abrasion on his left cheek, where his face had hit the rug, and, curiously, a half-inch laceration of his scrotum. This was interesting. The sack itself was swollen and discolored, and around the wound was a small amount of edema fluid. The bruising had spread up through the groin area and across the right hip. Something had hit him hard.

—Mark Bowden, "The Body in Room 348," *Vanity Fair*, May 2013

He was wearing mirrored sunglasses, a soft cap with a buttoned visor, white rubber boots, and yellow rubber overalls slashed at the crotch. Of middle height, blond and fine-featured, he had sandy hair around his ears and a large curl in back, like a breaking wave.

—John McPhee, *The Control of Nature*

She willed herself to be strong, and when at last she met her real father, Cuyler Goodwill—he arrived at the Simcoe Street door with sweat on his brow, wearing an ill-fitting suit, looking disappointingly short and dark-complexioned—she braced herself for his kiss. It didn't come, not on that first meeting. He never so much as took her hand. His face had a poor, pinchy look to it, but the mouth was kind.

—Carol Shields, *The Stone Diaries*

Back at the guest house Mrs. Starling introduced me to George Windus, who had sidewhiskers and baggy pants and a florid face. I suspected that Mrs. Starling hoped that Mr. Windus would ask the questions she was too timid to risk.

"What brings you to Teignmouth then?" Mr. Windus said. His nose was swollen, the color of the Burgundy he was drinking.

I was in publishing, I said. I had a week off. I was traveling along the coast.

—Paul Theroux, *The Kingdom by the Sea: A Journey around the Coast of Great Britain*

He had a heavily muscled and sculpted physique, a neck wider than his head—including his ears. Sixteen years of pushups and sit ups and whatever exercise he could manage in his cell had given him a chest that easily extended beyond his chin, and biceps-triceps vises that looked like they could crush walnuts to powder. In the mug shots, his hair had always had a stylized fade. Now his head was clean-shaven and he had used his dome as a canvas for the Lord.

—Michael Connelly, *The Black Box*

She hobbled around, leaning on a gnarled stick, muttering to herself in a language I could not quite understand. Her small withered face was covered with a net of wrinkles, and her skin was reddish brown like that of an overbaked apple. Her withered body constantly trembled as though shaken by some inner wind, and the fingers of her bony hands with joints twisted by disease never stopped quivering as her head on its long scraggy neck nodded in every direction.

Her sight was poor. She peered at the light through tiny slits embedded under thick eyebrows. Her lids were like furrows in deeply plowed soil. Tears were always spilling from the corners of her eyes, coursing down her face in well-worn channels to join glutinous threads hanging from her nose and the bubbly saliva dripping from her lips. She looked like an old green-gray puffball, rotten through and waiting for a last gust of wind to blow out the black dry dust from inside.

—JERZY KOSINSKI, *The Painted Bird*

Dr. Rau turns his plump face to Landsman. The irises of his eyes are like cast iron. "Based on my examination, I would guess that you are going through alcoholic withdrawal, Detective Landsman. In addition to exposure, you're also suffering from dehydration, tremors, palpitations, and your pupils are enlarged. Your blood sugar is low, which tells me you probably haven't been eating. Loss of appetite is another symptom of withdrawal. Your blood pressure is elevated, and your recent behavior appears to have been, from what I gather, quite erratic. Even violent."

Landsman tugs on the wrinkled lapels of the collar of his chambray work shirt, trying to smooth them out. Like cheap window blinds, they keep rolling themselves up.

—MICHAEL CHABON, *The Yiddish Policemen's Union*

Then, amid their laughter, the door opened, and several of the others came in—Eliza's mother, a plain worn Scotchwoman, and Jim, a ruddy porcine young fellow, his father's beardless twin, and Thaddeus, mild, ruddy, brown of hair and eye, bovine, and finally Greeley, the youngest, a boy with lapping idiot grins, full of strange squealing noises at which they laughed.

—THOMAS WOLFE, *Look Homeward, Angel*

So we listened to our Mooshum instead. While he talked, we sat on kitchen chairs and twisted our hair. Our mother had given him a red coffee can for spitting snoose. He wore soft, worn, green Sears work clothes, a pair of battered brown lace-up boots, and a twill cap, even in the house. His eyes shone from the slits cut deep into his face. The upper half of his left ear was missing, giving him a lopsided look. He was hunched and dried out, with random wisps of white hair down his ears and neck. From time to time, as he spoke, we glimpsed the murky scraggle of his teeth.

—LOUISE ERDRICH, *The Plague of Doves*

He was a comely, handsome fellow, perfectly well made, with straight strong limbs, not too large, tall and well-shaped, and, as I reckon, about twenty-six years of age.

He had a very good countenance, not a fierce and surly aspect, but seemed to have something very manly in his face, and yet he had all the sweetness and softness of an European in his countenance, too, especially when he smiled. His hair was long and black, not curled like wool; his forehead very high and large; and a great vivacity and sparkling sharpness in his eyes.

—Daniel Defoe, *Robinson Crusoe*

Ceiling fans stirred the thick humidity; little groups of Indian businessmen huddled together drinking glasses of fluorescent orange passionfruit juice. When the waiter came over I ordered a Tusker beer. "White Cap!" a man sang out at the table next to me. "White Cap is the only good beer in Kenya. It's like a German beer!"

Joaquin Fechner was chubby and pale and wearing a khaki fishing vest over a pink shirt. He was sweating profusely, a Swiss native who'd been living in Africa for twenty-five years, and in Mombasa the past six. "Come join me," he said.

—Carl Hoffman, *The Lunatic Express: Discovering the World . . . via Its Most Dangerous Buses, Boats, Trains, and Planes*

The forehead was high, and very pale, and singularly placid; and the once jetty hair fell partially over it, and overshadowed the hollow temples with innumerable ringlets now of a vivid yellow, and jarring discordantly, in their fantastic character, with the reigning melancholy of the countenance. The eyes were lifeless, and lustreless, and seemingly pupil-less, and I shrank involuntarily from their glassy stare to the contemplation of the thin and shrunken lips. —EDGAR ALLAN POE, *Berenice*

A foot scraped the staircase, a lazy S framed by a mahogany banister missing several spindles leading to an open second-floor hallway. I looked up at five and a half feet of clear brown skin in white shorts and a pink halter top that fell short of her navel and a longer way short of her collarbone, with piles of shimmering blue-black hair and toenails too pink for her natural coloring, in cork sandals. Her makeup was all wrong, too, her lips a candy-corn shade of orange. She'd use a spray gun to put on a perfume that probably came in a drum. She was all of fourteen years old. —LOREN D. ESTLEMAN, *Burning Midnight*

Carey Carr wore spectacles and he had a cleft chin. At forty-two he still looked very young, with round plump cheeks and a prissy mouth, yet to people who knew him this air of cherubic vacancy and bloodlessness, at first so apparent, quickly faded: one knew that his face could reflect decision and an abiding passion.

—WILLIAM STYRON, *Lie Down in Darkness*

Mr. Squeer's appearance was not prepossessing. He had but one eye, and the popular prejudice runs in favour of two. The eye he had was unquestionably useful, but decidedly not ornamental, being of a greenish grey, and in shape resembling the fanlight of a street door. The blank side of his face was much wrinkled and puckered up, which gave him a very sinister appearance, especially when he smiled, at which times his expression bordered closely on the villainous. His hair was very flat and shiny, save at the ends, where it was brushed stiffly up from a low protruding forehead, which assorted well with his harsh voice and coarse manner. He was about two or three and fifty, and a trifle below the middle size; he wore a white neckerchief with long ends, and a suit of scholastic black, but his coat sleeves being a great deal too long, and his trousers a great deal too short, he appeared ill at ease in his clothes, and as if he were in a perpetual state of astonishment at finding himself so respectable.

—CHARLES DICKENS, *Nicholas Nickleby*

After a long moment, Larry sat up. He was on the small side, with a puckish or faun-like quality to his face, which, depending on the light or how much he'd been partying, could look either as high-cheekboned as Rudolf Nureyev or as hollow-cheeked as the figure in Munch's *The Scream*. Right now, it was somewhere in between.

—JEFFREY EUGENIDES, *The Marriage Plot*

Ransie was a narrow six feet of sallow brown skin and yellow hair. The imperturbability of the mountains hung upon him like a suit of armor. The woman was calicoed, angled, snuff-brushed, and weary with unknown desires. Through it all gleamed a faint protest of cheated youth unconscious of its loss.

—O. HENRY, "The Whirligig of Life," *Best Stories of O. Henry*

He was a man of somewhat less than average height, inclined to corpulence, with his hair, worn long, arranged over the scalp so as to conceal his baldness. He was clean-shaven. His features were regular, and it was possible to imagine that in his youth he had been good-looking.

—W. Somerset Maugham,
Of Human Bondage

He had the soft pink cheeks of an adolescent who almost never needed to shave; disheveled hair with the remnant of a part in the middle; wrinkled flannel trousers with a suggestion of a crease; frayed trouser cuffs pinched by metal bicycle clips; a belted double-breasted leather motorcycle jacket with an oversized collar turned up; a beige silk scarf knotted around his throat; motorcycle goggles down around his neck; a worn leather motorcycle bonnet, the kind someone might have worn when motorcycles were first invented, hanging from a wrist.

—Robert Littell, *Young Philby*

Her black hair cascaded over one clavicle, and the gesture she made of shaking it back and the dimple on her pale cheek were revelations with an element of immediate recognition about them. Her pallor shone. Her blackness blazed. The pleated skirts she liked were becomingly short. Even her bare limbs were so free from suntan that one's gaze, stroking her white shins and forearms, could follow upon them the regular slants of fine dark hairs, the silks of her girlhood. The iridal dark-brown of her serious eyes had the enigmatic opacity of an Oriental hypnotist's look (in a magazine's back-page advertisement) and seemed to be placed higher than usual so that between its lower rim and the moist lower lid a cradle crescent of white remained when she stared straight at you. Her long eyelashes seemed blackened, and in fact were. Her features were saved from elfin prettiness by the thickish shape of her parched lips. Her plain Irish nose was Van's in miniature. Her teeth were fairly white, but not very even. —VLADIMIR NABOKOV, *Ada*

Gerard's face, describable as "rugged," had been better characterised by his brother-in-law the art dealer as "cubist." There were a number of strong dominant surfaces, a commanding bone structure, a square even brow, a nose that appeared to end in a blunt plane rather than a point.

—IRIS MURDOCH, *The Book and the Brotherhood*

In front of his stall sat the sickly-looking punk with the almost shaved head and bumpy headbones, smacking flies on his leg with a rolled-up comic. The boy was too young to be in anybody's pay. He must belong to Nebraska. He had his father's curving soapcake of a nose. His fingernail worked some red spot near his mouth corner.

—JAIMY GORDON, *Lord of Misrule*

(The door opens. Bella Cohen, a massive whoremistress, enters. She is dressed in a threequarter ivory gown, fringed round the hem with tasselled selvedge, and cools herself flirting a black horn fan like Minnie Hauck in Carmen. On her left hand are wedding and keeper rings. Her eyes are deeply carboned. She has a sprouting moustache. Her olive face is heavy, slightly sweated and full-nosed with orangetainted nostrils. She has large pendant beryl eardrops.)

BELLA: My word! I'm all of a mucksweat.

(She glances round her at the couples. Then her eyes rest on Bloom with hard insistence. Her large fan winnows wind towards her heated faceneck and embonpoint. Her falcon eyes glitter.) —JAMES JOYCE, *Ulysses*

There were all too many reasons George could need help at any given moment. One poorly propped pillow and his air passage could be cut off. A little vomit or even postnasal drip could asphyxiate him or slide down and infect his already damaged lungs. —ALEX SHAKAR, *Luminarium*

Wolkowicz smiled, his old sardonic grin that narrowed his slanted eyes and lit up his shrewd muzhik face.

—CHARLES MCCARRY, *The Last Supper*

I've been in the Remake Center for more than three hours and I still haven't met my stylist. Apparently he has no interest in seeing me until Venia and the other members of my prep team have addressed some obvious problems. This has included scrubbing down my body with a gritty foam that has removed not only dirt but at least three layers of skin, turning my nails into uniform shapes, and primarily, ridding my body of hair. My legs, arms, torso, underarms, and parts of my eyebrows have been stripped of the stuff, leaving me like a plucked bird, ready for roasting. I don't like it. My skin feels sore and tingling and intensely vulnerable. But I have kept my side of the bargain with Haymitch, and no objection has crossed my lips.

—Suzanne Collins, *The Hunger Games*

Everything about her person is honey-gold and warm in tone; the fair, crisply-trimmed hair which she wears rather long at the back, knotting it simply at the downy nape of her neck. This focuses the candid face of a minor muse with its smiling grey-green eyes. The calmly disposed hands have a deftness and shapeliness which one only notices when one sees them at work, holding a paint-brush perhaps or setting the broken leg of a sparrow in splints made from match-ends.

—Lawrence Durrell, *Justine*

She tells me I look great, and I tell her she looks great, which she does, in her proudly unkempt way: her early white hair hangs past her shoulders, thick and flyaway; and she's unapologetically frumpy in a mid-calf calico skirt and running shoes. She gave up vanity the way other people give up sugar, and her arms and hips and stomach are as soft and plump as bread dough.

—Ann Packer, "Things Said or Done,"
The PEN O. Henry Prize Stories 2012

Avoid trouble. This was the operating principle of Abdul Hakim Husain, an idea so fiercely held that it seemed imprinted on his physical form. He had deep-set eyes and sunken cheeks, a body work-hunched and wiry—the type that claimed less than its fair share of space when threading through people-choked slumlanes. Almost everything about him was recessed save the pop-out ears and the hair that curled upward, girlish, whenever he wiped his forehead of sweat.

—Katherine Boo, *Behind the Beautiful Forevers: Life, Death, and Hope in a Mumbai Undercity*

His fatless, taut, weather-yellowed features, his deep eye sockets and long creased cheeks and dry gray hair were those of a man ending rather than beginning his forties. Jason was forty-two, like Carol. In his arms she looked young, and her broad hips suggested a relaxed and rounded fertility rather than middle-aged spread. Though Jason's eyelids were lowered in their deep sockets, and seemed to shudder in the firelight, Carol's blue eyes were alertly round and her face as pristine and blank as a china statuette's each time the slow music turned her around so Ed could see her. —John Updike, *Couples*

April Watts, who takes the other section, is like a teacher out of a Victorian novel: she has hair like brown cotton candy, whipped into a gauzy attenuated confection around her head, and bottle-bottom glasses through which she peers, vaguely, her blue eyes enlarged and distorted by the lenses like fishes in a tank. Although only in her early fifties, she wears support hose for her varicose veins and she has, poor ghastly thing, absolutely no sense of humor whatsoever. —Claire Messud, *The Woman Upstairs*

But in no regard was he more peculiar than in his personal appearance. He was singularly tall and thin. He stooped much. His limbs were exceedingly long and emaciated. His forehead was broad and low. His complexion was absolutely bloodless. His mouth was large and flexible, and his teeth were more wildly uneven, although sound, than I had ever before seen teeth in a human head. The expression of his smile, however, was by no means unpleasing, as might be supposed; but it had no variation whatever. It was one of profound melancholy—of a phaseless and unceasing gloom. His eyes were abnormally large, and round like those of a cat. The pupils, too, upon any accession or diminution of light, underwent contraction or dilation, just such as is observed in the feline tribe. In moments of excitement the orbs grew bright to a degree almost inconceivable; seeming to emit luminous rays, not of a reflected but of an intrinsic lustre, as does a candle or the sun; yet their ordinary condition was so totally vapid, filmy, and dull, as to convey the idea of the eyes of a long-interred corpse.

—EDGAR ALLAN POE, "A Tale of the Ragged Mountains," *Complete Tales and Poems*

The wrappings fell open. The face was translucent, pale, sunken, yet almost perfectly preserved. They had left his spectacles on the crooked nose: He felt amused derision. Dumbledore's hands were folded upon his chest, and there it lay, clutched beneath them, buried with him.

—J. K. ROWLING, *Harry Potter and the Deathly Hallows*

Godfrey beetled his brows at him, and such was their tangled growth that there was a distinct illusion of salt wind and screaming seagulls.

—JOHN ASHBERY AND JAMES SCHUYLER, *A Nest of Ninnies*

You are the teacher, the incarnation of decrepit, laughingly out of touch with cool, yours the clothes that even Larry, Curly, and Moe said "yuck" to. You all but wear your hair in a comb-over, you've gone spongy in the belly, and you gobble goddamn Lipitor and Primvil because your body—some temple it is, Bunky—has turned on you in outright revolt.

—LEE K. ABBOTT, "One of Star Wars, One of Doom," *All Things, All at Once*

His mother's great chest was heaving painfully. Jimmie paused and looked down at her. Her face was inflamed and swollen from drinking. Her yellow brows shaded eyelids that had grown blue. Her tangled hair tossed in waves over her forehead. Her mouth was set in the same lines of vindictive hatred that it had, perhaps, borne during the fight. Her bare, red arms were thrown out above her head in an attitude of exhaustion, something, mayhap, like that of a sated villain.

—STEPHEN CRANE, "Maggie: A Girl of the Streets," *Maggie: A Girl of the Streets and Other Short Fiction*

She thought how nice-looking he was, and how he seemed to be so unaware of it. He wore a brush cut, in the style of the time—particularly if you were anything like an engineer—and his light-colored skin was never flushed like hers, never blotchy from the sun, but evenly tanned whatever the season.

—ALICE MUNRO, "To Reach Japan," *Dear Life*

The only end in sight was Yossarian's own, and he might have remained in the hospital until doomsday had it not been for that patriotic Texan with his infundibuliform jowls and his lumpy, rumpleheaded, indestructible smile cracked forever across the front of his face like the brim of a black ten-gallon hat. —JOSEPH HELLER, *Catch-22*

Madame Merle was a tall, fair, plump woman; everything in her person was round and replete, though without those accumulations which minister to indolence. Her features were thick, but there was a graceful harmony among them, and her complexion had a healthy clearness. She had a small grey eye, with a great deal of light in it—an eye incapable of dullness, and, according to some people, incapable of tears; and a wide, firm mouth, which, when she smiled, drew itself upward to the left side, in a manner that most people thought very odd, some very affected, and a few very graceful. Isabel inclined to range herself in the last category. Madame Merle had thick, fair hair, which was arranged with picturesque simplicity, and a large white hand, of a perfect shape—a shape so perfect that its owner, preferring to leave it unadorned, wore no rings.

—HENRY JAMES, *The Portrait of a Lady*

It appeared, indeed, from the countenance of this proprietor, that he was of a frank, but hasty and choleric, temper. He was not above the middle stature, but broad-shouldered, long-armed, and powerfully made, like one accustomed to endure the fatigue of war or of the chase; his face was broad, with large blue eyes, open and frank features, fine teeth, and a well-formed head, although expressive of that sort of good humour which often lodges with a sudden and hasty temper. Pride and jealousy there was in his eye, for his life had been spent in asserting rights which were constantly liable to invasion; and the prompt, fiery, and resolute disposition of the man had been kept constantly upon the alert by the circumstances of his situation. His long yellow hair was equally divided on the top of his head and upon his brow, and combed down on each side to the length of his shoulders: it had but little tendency to grey, although Cedric was approaching to his sixtieth year.

—Sir Walter Scott, *Ivanhoe*

Her History of the United States, of Republic of America had proven sufficiently profitable to make her financially independent. She was a statuesque woman of "classic features"—a Roman nose gave her a particularly strong profile—and in her role as a schoolmistress, she dressed invariably in the finest black silk or satin, her head crowned with a white turban.

—David McCullough, *The Greater Journey: Americans in Paris*

At nineteen, I was a hatless type, with a flat, black, not particularly clean, Continental-type pompadour over a badly broken-out inch of forehead.

—J. D. Salinger, "De Daumier-Smith's Blue Period," *Nine Stories*

Therefore Ikey's corniform, be-spectacled nose and narrow, knowledge-bowed figure was well known in the vicinity of the Blue Light, and his advice and notice were much desired.

—O. Henry, "The Love-Philtre of Ikey Schoenstein," *The Best of O. Henry*

The sound of her voice was driving me mad. Its raspiness was so exotic, so utterly feminine. Not under any circumstances would I have taken it for a man's voice laboring to sound womanly. It was a raspy voice, but not a throaty or harsh-sounding one. It was more like the sound of bare feet softly walking on gravel.

—Carlos Castaneda, *The Art of Dreaming*

Two young men, taller than most, loped across the grassy quad in front of the library, in a hurry. One of them, a six-foot-three freshman named Roger Morris, had a loose, gangly build; a tousle of dark hair with a forelock that perpetually threatened to fall over his long face; and heavy black eyebrows that lent him, at first glance, a bit of a glowering look. The other young man, Joe Rantz, also a freshman, was nearly as tall, at six foot two and a half, but more tautly built, with broad shoulders and solid, powerful legs. He wore his blond hair in a crew cut. He had a strong jawline, fine, regular features, gray eyes verging into blue, and he drew covert glances from many of the young women sitting on the grass.

—DANIEL JAMES BROWN, *The Boys in the Boat: Nine Americans and Their Epic Quest for Gold at the 1936 Berlin Olympics*

Her position before was sheltered from the light: now, I had a distinct view of her whole figure and countenance. She was slender, and apparently scarcely past girlhood: an admirable form, and the most exquisite little face that I have ever had the pleasure of beholding: small features, very fair; flaxen ringlets, or rather golden, hanging loose on her delicate neck; and eyes—had they been agreeable in expression, they would have been irresistible—fortunately for my susceptible heart, the only sentiment they evinced hovered between scorn and a kind of desperation, singularly unnatural to be detected there.

—EMILY BRONTË, *Wuthering Heights*

Nora Johnson thought that men might regard travel as fast. Men preferred to marry safer, calmer women. Women who didn't go gallivanting too much. It was only sensible to have advance information about men, Nora Johnson told her daughters. This way you could go armed into the struggle. —MAEVE BINCHY, *Tara Road*

The lieutenant walked in front of his men with an air of bitter distaste. He might have been chained to them unwillingly—perhaps the scar on his jaw was the relic of an escape. His gaiters were polished, and his pistol-holster: his buttons were all sewn on. He had a sharp crooked nose jutting out of a lean dancer's face; his neatness gave an effect of inordinate ambition in the shabby city.

—GRAHAM GREENE, *The Power and the Glory*

I meet few American academics, and was pleasantly surprised that this one was bored by Bloomsbury, and happy to leave the modern movement to his younger and more ambitious colleagues. But then Ed Winterton liked to present himself as a failure. He was in his early forties, balding, with a pinky glabrous complexion and square rimless spectacles: the banker type of academic, circumspect and moral. He bought English clothes without looking at all English. He remained the sort of American who always wears a mackintosh in London because he knows that in this city rain falls out of a clear sky.

—JULIAN BARNES, *Flaubert's Parrot*

He looked fixedly at the young woman, who squirmed and cast her eyes nervously to the fields. A smattering of freckles across her nose and forehead interrupted what was otherwise pale skin. Her eyes were brown and widely set, and there was a large gap between her front teeth. There was something ungainly about her, Blöndal decided. He noted the thick crescents of dirt under her fingernails.

—HANNAH KENT, *Burial Rites*

Billie, however, is obviously a native of these parts, a short pudgy person in, I judge, her middle to late thirties. She really is of a remarkable shape, and might have been assembled from a collection of cardboard boxes of varying sizes that were first left out in the rain and then piled soggily any old way one on top of another. The general effect was not improved by the extremely tight jeans she was wearing, and the black polo-necked jumper that made her large head look like a rubber ball set squarely atop all those precariously stacked cartons.

—JOHN BANVILLE, *Ancient Light*

You must picture Mr. Thomas Marvel as a person of copious, flexible visage, a nose of cylindrical protrusion, a liquorish, ample, fluctuating mouth, and a beard of bristling eccentricity. His figure inclined to embonpoint; his short limbs accentuated this inclination.

—H. G. WELLS, *The Invisible Man*

Drenka was a dark, Italian-looking Croat from the Dalmatian coast, on the short side like Sabbath, a full, firmly made woman at the provocative edge of being just overweight, her shape, at her heaviest, reminiscent of those clay figurines molded circa 2000 B.C., fat little dolls with big breasts and big thighs unearthed all the way from Europe down to Asia Minor and worshiped under a dozen different names as the great mother of the gods. She was pretty in a rather efficient, businesslike way, except for her nose, a surprisingly bridgeless prizefighter's nose that created a sort of blur at the heart of her face, a nose slightly out of plumb with the full mouth and the large dark eyes, and the telltale sign, as Sabbath came to view it, of everything malleable and indeterminate in her seemingly well-deployed nature.

—PHILIP ROTH, *Sabbath's Theater*

One was rather short and very stoutly built, with a big bullet-shaped head, a bristly grey moustache, and small pale-blue eyes, a trifle bloodshot. The other was a slender young fellow, of middle height, dark in complexion, and bearing himself with grace and distinction.

—ANTHONY HOPE, *The Prisoner of Zenda*

Victor Van Allen was thirty-six years old, inclined to a general firm rotundity rather than fat, and he had thick, crisp brown eyebrows that stood out over innocent blue eyes. His brown hair was straight, closely cut, and like his eyebrows, thick and tenacious. His mouth was middle-sized, firm, and usually drawn down at the right corner with a lop-sided determination or with humor, depending on how one cared to take it.

—PATRICIA HIGHSMITH, *Deep Water*

He was pale as salt. Although along his jaw there was, beneath the pale skin, the outline of a black beard. His hair was cut short, but it was clear that left to its own devices it would curve, and then curl. He was not tall, but the fingers that held his hand against his overcoat were exceptionally long and thin. She saw how they moved one at a time against the dark brown felt, pressing themselves against the fabric almost imperceptibly, like a pulse under the skin. The way a child's fingers might move in sleep. —ALICE MCDERMOTT, *After This*

Sometimes, when a fierce wind blows out of the north, the faces of the scurrying citizens, drawn tight by the bluster of it, all seem to acquire a Lappish look, their eyes rather slanted, their cheekbones heightened, their skulls apparently narrowed, until they too, tending as they often do anyway toward an ideal androgyny, seem like a species devised especially for the setting by fablers or geneticists. —JAN MORRIS, *Journeys*

Moore wore a splendid black silk robe with a gold lamé collar and belt. He sports a full mustache above an imperial, and his hair, sleeked down under pomade when he opens operations, invariably rises during the contest, as it gets water sloshed on it between rounds and the lacquer washes off, until it is standing up like the top of a shaving brush. —A. J. LIEBLING, "Ahab and Nemesis," *The Sweet Science and Other Writings*

I can still see Hassan up on that tree, sunlight flickering through the leaves on his almost perfectly round face, a face like a Chinese doll chiseled from hardwood: his flat, broad nose and slanting, narrow eyes like bamboo leaves, eyes that looked, depending on the light, gold, green, even sapphire. I can still see his tiny low-set ears and that pointed stub of a chin, a meaty appendage that looked like it was added as a mere afterthought. And the cleft lip, just left of midline, where the Chinese doll maker's instrument may have slipped, or perhaps he had simply grown tired and careless.

—KHALED HOSSEINI, *The Kite Runner*

When they announced the arrival of flight #894 from Toledo I followed my mother to the gate. I knew it was them right away. I knew it by the way they walked down the airplane stairs, clutching each other. And when they got closer I knew it by my grandmother's shoes—black with laces and fat heels—old lady shoes. My grandfather had white hair around the edges and none on top. He was shorter and fatter than my grandmother.

They looked around a bit before my mother called out, "Here we are—over here."

They walked toward us, growing more excited as they recognized my mother. She gave each of them a short hug. I just stood there feeling dumb until my grandmother said, "And this must be Margaret Ann."

—JUDY BLUME, *Are You There God? It's Me, Margaret.*

In response, the woman reached up and slowly lifted the veil from her face. She was strikingly beautiful, and yet older than Langdon had imagined—in her sixties perhaps, stately and strong, like a timeless statue. She had a sternly set jaw, deep soulful eyes, and long, silver-gray hair that cascaded over her shoulders in ringlets. An amulet of lapis lazuli hung around her neck—a single snake coiled around a staff. —DAN BROWN, *Inferno*

He was taller than Gustav, a thin man with rough-cut dark-grey hair and beard and an aquiline nose. He turned by chance and faced us and I had a full view of his gaunt face. What surprised me was its fierceness. A severity that was almost savagery. I had never seen a face that expressed such violent determination never to compromise, never to deviate. Never to smile. And what eyes!

They were slightly ex-ophthalmic, of the most startling cold blue. Beyond any doubt, insane eyes.

—John Fowles, *The Magus*

Her skin had the transparent shine of glycerine soap, and her eyes bulged ever so slightly, possibly from the effort of trying to emote when every associated muscle had been pumped full of botulinum or lasered into submission. Her thinning orange hair was gelled into a hard pompadour, like the crust on *crème brûlée*.

—Lauren Beukes, *Zoo City*

When he appeared at my door four years ago, I knew nothing about him and he didn't offer much. He wore gray wool trousers and a seersucker jacket that was lightly stained on the breast pocket. His clothes were pressed and his salt hair was combed and brilloed into place. He'd shaved too, but on a face so weathered it didn't do much in the way of brightening or smoothing. He had hazel eyes that squinted from the anticipation of glare. He was no more than five foot eight.

—Amy Grace Loyd, *The Affairs of Others*

Dominating the scene by his height and force was Nathan: broad-shouldered, powerful-looking, crowned with a shock of hair swarthy as a Sioux's, he resembled a more attenuated and frenetic John Garfield, with Garfield's handsome, crookedly agreeable face—theoretically agreeable, I should say, for now the face was murky with passion and rage, was quite emphatically anything but agreeable, suffused as it was with such an obvious eagerness for violence. He wore a light sweater and slacks and appeared to be in his late twenties. He held Sophie's arm tight in his grasp, and she flinched before his onslaught like a rosebud quivering in a windstorm. Sophie I could barely see in the dismal light. I was able to discern only her disheveled mane of straw-colored hair and, behind Nathan's shoulder, about a third of her face. This included a frightened eyebrow, a small mole, a hazel eye, and a broad lovely swerve of Slavic cheekbone across which a single tear rolled like a drop of quicksilver.

—WILLIAM STYRON, *Sophie's Choice*

"Fortune be with you," I told Marco, though I knew well enough that he'd lose, and snapped my cards together. Old worn cards by now, frayed about the edges and greasy with thumb marks and wine stains, but I'd made good money from them over the years. I might look like a seedy fellow down on his luck—my leather doublet was battered, my shirt had patches on the threadbare elbows, and the hose stretching over my crooked legs fit very ill—but it didn't do for a dwarf to look prosperous. We're easy enough marks as it is without wearing embroidered sleeves or fine cloaks. —KATE QUINN, *The Serpent and the Pearl: A Novel of the Borgias*

He runs his finger down her nose, a long straight nose, rather flat, like their father's. Sadie looks—or looked—like him, much more than Luke does, the long oval face, angular jaw, the deep-set flashing eyes, and perfect, perfect teeth behind full lips, though Sadie's lips rarely stopped quivering, working something over and over, always working something.

—Michelle Latiolais, *A Proper Knowledge*

The reddleman turned his head, and replied in sad and occupied tones. He was young, and his face, if not exactly handsome, approached so near to handsome that nobody would have contradicted an assertion that it really was so in its natural colour. His eye, which glared so strangely through his stain, was in itself attractive—keen as that of a bird of prey, and blue as autumn mist. He had neither whisker nor moustache, which allowed the soft curves of the lower part of his face to be apparent. His lips were thin, and though, as it seemed, compressed by thought, there was a pleasant twitch at their corners now and then.

—Thomas Hardy, *The Return of the Native*

His fingers, crept up to his chin, squeezed it tenderly, like a piece of fruit. A clear delineation existed between his neck and face, but still his chin was not the strong, crisp, masculine escarpment it should be. The problem was that there was a smidge too much softness *underneath* his chin, a yielding swag of flesh he had possessed since childhood that tended to swallow the lower edge of his jawline, especially if he wasn't careful and pulled his head back into his neck. Weak chins were for weak men, symptomatic of cowardice, corruption, deviant appetites, and poor breeding, and he was forced to conclude that, both on a cosmetic level and as a sign of his essence, his mandibular failings made his less attractive than he might have been with a perfect, Gregory Peck kind of chin.

—MAGGIE SHIPSTEAD, *Seating Arrangements*

But that sour face of her elderly fury keeps disappearing just as she disappeared. Even this latest face, the one propped on the hospital pillow, the hieratic visage that seems polished and will soon be an object, even this one is hard to keep in focus. I'm sitting here, holding her hand, but it's the ardent face from 1936 that keeps appearing, the face in the photograph placed on the shelf above the piano all the years of my girlhood and beyond. Heart-shaped with high cheekbones and eyes set wonderfully wide, it is the face of a romantic lead.

—PATRICIA HAMPL, *The Florist's Daughter*

She looked about twenty-six and as if she hadn't slept very well. She had a tired, pretty little face under fluffed-out brown hair, a rather narrow forehead with more height than is considered elegant, a small inquisitive nose, an upper lip a shade too long and a mouth more than a shade too wide. Her eyes could be very blue if they tried. She looked quiet, but not mousy-quiet. She looked smart, but not Hollywood-smart.

—RAYMOND CHANDLER, "Mandarin's Jade," *Killer in the Rain*

"I heard you, David. And I've already heard that Mr. Lincoln's here." Mrs. Surratt was a handsome auburn-haired woman with a body that David, who read romantic stories in yellow covers, knew was Junoesque. In some ways, he found Mrs. Surratt more to his taste than her daughter; and this curious preference convinced him that he was probably the monster of depravity that his seven sisters liked to claim he was. —GORE VIDAL, *Lincoln*

She was not more than twenty at the time of independence. She had the flattish, vaguely Asian face that some Sena people had, the high cheekbones, the slanted hooded eyes. Her shaven head revealed its sculptural symmetries, her neck was slender and fragile-seeming. She was very thin, with tight muscles in her arms and legs that gave her a loose springy walk, her small high buttocks beating against her swinging skirt or her wraparound, the red *chitenje* she sometimes wore. —PAUL THEROUX, *The Lower River*

Tom was of that bull-terrier type so common in England; sturdy, and yet not coarse; middle-sized, deep-chested, broad-shouldered; with small, well-knit hands and feet, large jaw, bright gray eyes, crisp brown hair, a heavy projecting brow; his face full of shrewdness and good-nature, and of humor withal, which might be at whiles a little saucy and sarcastic, to judge from the glances which he sent forth from the corners of his wicked eyes at his companion on the other side of the window.

—CHARLES KINGSLEY, *Two Years Ago*

Flat padded faces, flattish noses, and "double" upper eyelids—the epicanthic folds—appear to be adapted to protect the exposed and vulnerable face and eyes from cold.

—M. F. ASHLEY MONTAGU, *Introduction to Physical Anthropology*

. . . I record that Doctor Aziz was a tall man. Pressed flat against a wall of his family home, he measured twenty-five bricks (a brick for each year of his life) or just over six foot two. A strong man also. His beard was thick and red—and annoyed his mother, who said only Hajis, men who had made the pilgrimage to Mecca, should grow red beards. His hair, however, was rather darker. His sky-eyes you know about. Ingrid had said, "They went mad with the colors when they made your face." But the central feature of my grandfather's anatomy was neither color nor height, neither strength of arm nor straightness of back. There it was, reflected in the water, undulating like a mad plantain in the centre of his face . . . Aadam Aziz, waiting for Tai, watches his rippling nose.

—SALMAN RUSHDIE, *Midnight's Children*

Physical features, as best I remember them. He was fair, a good average height and strongly built though not stout. Brown hair and moustache—very small this. Extremely well-kept hands. A good smile though when not smiling his face wore a somewhat quizzical almost impertinent air. His eyes were hazel and the best feature of him—they looked into other eyes, into other ideas, with a real candour, rather a terrifying sort of lucidity. He was somewhat untidy in dress but always spotlessly clean of person and abhorred dirty nails and collars. Yes, but his clothes were sometimes stained with spots of the red ink in which he wrote. There!

—LAWRENCE DURRELL, *Balthazar*

SENSORY IMPRESSIONS, TEMPERAMENT, AND BEHAVIOR

SENSORY IMPRESSIONS (HEARING, SMELL, AND TASTE)

Hearing

sound

noise, pitch, acoustics, timbre, tone, register, sonority

hearable

audible, distinct, clear, plain, distinctive

silent or almost silent

soundless, inaudible, noiseless, quiet, speechless, unspoken, unuttered, unexpressed, unsaid, stifled, muffled, muzzled, muted, mute, tacit, deadened, still, gagged, dull, dampened, hushed, quiescent, whispered, murmured, subdued, soft, unheard, faint, subaudible, indistinct, low, smothered

pleasant-sounding or pleasant-voiced

mellow, rich, harmonious, euphonious, euphonic, agreeable, resonant, honeyed, mellifluous, sonorous, musical, dulcet, lyrical, sweet, melic, canorous, golden-tongued, silver-tongued, mellisonant, lilting, songlike, ariose, velvety

loud or jarring

discordant, grating, raucous, cacophonous, harsh, piercing, strident, shrieking, screeching, shrill, banging, blaring, setting one's teeth on edge, resounding, thunderous, deafening, clamorous, clangorous, booming, ear-splitting, fortissimo, making a din, at a crescendo

repeating as a sound

reverberating, reverberant, echoing, echoic, staccato, drumming, thrumming, resounding, resonating, resonant

ringing

pealing, jingling, tolling, chiming, tinkling, ding-dong, bell-like, tintinnabulating, sounding a knell, clinking, clanking

howling

ululating, yowling, baying, bawling, lowing, mugient, bellowing, braying

whimpering

puling, mewling

hissing

sibilant

Smell

odor

aroma, scent, fragrance, redolence, whiff, breath, emanation, exhalation, essence, olfaction

having a pleasant smell

fragrant, sweet, dulcet, flowery, balmy, aromatic, perfumy, ambrosial, like incense

having a strong smell

odorous, odoriferous, pungent, ripe, reeking, suffocating, asphyxiating, penetrating, sharp, biting, smelly, heady, effluvious, olent

having a bad smell

noxious, rank, noisome, stinking, fetid, miasmic, foul, malodorous, putrid, rotten, offensive, nasty, vile, olid, poisonous, rancid, repellent, sulfurous, graveolent, smelling to high heaven, nidorous, toxic

not smelling fresh

stale, musty, moldy, dusty, stuffy, frowsty, frousty, fusty

having an animal or slightly spoiled smell

gamy, musky, funky

odorless

unscented, deodorized, antiseptic, medicinal, inodorous, scentless, fragrance-free, neutral-smelling

Taste

taste

appetite, gustation, hunger, thirst, flavor, tang, palate, goût

worthy of eating

edible, palatable

worthy of drinking

drinkable, potable

looking tasty

appetizing, tempting, tantalizing, making one's mouth water, fit for a king

tasting sweet

dulcet, saccharine, sugary, syrupy, honeyed

strong or seasoned in taste

salty, spicy, peppery, hot, pungent, sharp, tangy, stinging, biting, having an edge

unappealing to taste

repellent, unappetizing, uninviting, yucky, gross, unsavory, unpalatable

not sweet

tart, sour, bitter, astringent, acerbic, acerb

tasting good

tasty, sapid, saporous, savory, soporific, palatable, flavorful, toothsome, delectable, rich, piquant, tangy, whetting the appetite

smooth tasting

velvety

very tasty

delicious, scrumptious, yummy, juicy, succulent, luscious

overly sweet

cloying, sugary, sickening sweet

tasting bad

distasteful, repellent, foul, nasty, spoiled, overripe, rancid, nauseating, rotten, inedible, uneatable, undrinkable

TEMPERAMENT AND BEHAVIOR

mature

grown-up, adult, mellowed, full-grown, seasoned, full-blown, experienced, veteran, full-fledged

immature

puerile, callow, green, sophomoric, juvenile, half-baked, inexperienced, adolescent, untutored, wet behind the ears, unversed, unseasoned, jejune

innocent

simple, guileless, ingenuous, artless, angelic, naïve, sincere, unsophisticated, unworldly, childlike

humble

self-effacing, modest, unassuming, subdued, down-to-earth, folksy, earthy

lively

alive, animated, vibrant, vivacious, energetic, spirited, feisty, spry, perky, effervescent, bubbly, pert, boisterous, exuberant, rowdy, zesty, ebullient, bright-eyed

brave or venturesome

courageous, undaunted, plucky, spunky, intrepid, bold, doughty, hardy, valiant, mettlesome, fearless, intrepid

intensely curious, interested, or eager

excited, agog, giddy

contented

pleased, placid, at peace, serene, untroubled, unworried

sensible

practical, pragmatic, rational, commonsense, level-headed, sound-thinking

happy

cheerful, delighted, gay, merry, blithe, jolly, glad, joyous, radiant, lighthearted, sunny-faced, in good spirits, in high spirits, cheery, laughing

very happy
exuberant, euphoric, blissful, elated, on cloud nine, beaming, rapturous, beatific, ecstatic

receptive
amenable, willing, well-disposed, responsive, welcoming

eager to please
accommodating, well-disposed, amiable, willing, ingratiating, wheedling, complaisant, obliging, good-natured

enthusiastic
eager, earnest, zealous, avid, with alacrity, welcoming, keen

passionate
impassioned, ardent, fervent, fervid, fevered, feverish, unrestrained, emotional

courteous
considerate, polite, courtly, well-mannered, gracious, obliging, decorous

considerate
gracious, solicitous, thoughtful, empathetic

expectant
hopeful, anticipating, excited

longing
wistful, yearning, dreamy

casual or jaunty
airy, devil-may-care, informal, happy-go-lucky, insouciant, pococurante, breezy, easygoing, leisurely, nonchalant, offhand, carefree, buoyant

mischievous

playful, frolicsome, impish, elfin, whimsical, puckish, roguish, naughty

changeable or unpredictable

capricious, inconstant, flighty, mercurial, fickle, protean

confident

self-confident, assured, self-assured, self-possessed, poised, self-reliant, undaunted, sanguine, optimistic, positive

friendly

personal, sociable, social, warm, gregarious, amiable, amicable, approachable, affable, companionable, chummy, congenial, genial, convivial, neighborly, collegial, agreeable, cordial, likeable, personable, outgoing, simpatico

sympathetic

empathetic, having an affinity with, appreciative, inclined toward, compassionate, understanding, sensitive to, well-disposed toward, pitying

confiding

confidential, reassuring, winking, intimate, meaningful

charming

winning, winsome, engaging, endearing, gallant, debonair, entrancing, appealing, charismatic, disarming

inviting or seductive

beckoning, come-hither, ravishing, alluring, bewitching, entrancing, flirtatious, enticing, beguiling, coquettish, having bedroom eyes

sober

grave, thoughtful, deliberative, meditative, serious, ruminative, reflective, pensive, conscientious, in a brown study

unthinking

thoughtless, heedless, careless, disregardful, mindless, unconscious, uncaring, oblivious, rash, sloppy, reckless, blithe, irresponsible

odd

queer, strange, eccentric, enigmatic, fishy, weird, bizarre, oddball, peculiar, curious, quirky

slow

lethargic, phlegmatic, sluggish, snail-like, stolid, ponderous, laggard, poky, lumbering

alert or watchful

comprehending, sharp, attentive, vigilant, appraising, keen-eyed, focused, transfixed

forward

pushy, offensive, obnoxious, outrageous, brazen, brash

challenging

pointed, fixed, glaring, staring, penetrating, hard-eyed, piercing, gimlet-eyed, unwavering

firm or resolute

tough, stout, stout-hearted, unflinching, strong, solid, sound, unbowed

bold or assertive

audacious, unflinching, shameless, impudent, flinty, steely, unabashed, confrontational, emboldened

overly talkative

chattering, talky, prolix, garrulous, nattering, babbling, loquacious, gabby, long-winded, gassy, prating, blathering, jabbering, running on

shy

timid, sheepish, mousy, diffident, uncertain, reticent, reluctant, timorous, bashful, skittish

awkward

ungainly, uncoordinated, clumsy, graceless, gawky, maladroit, bumbling, cloddish, gauche

quiet

reserved, subdued, retiring, unobtrusive, reclusive, withdrawn, conservative, self-contained, restrained, low-key

sad or given to dark moods

dejected, melancholic, melancholy, downcast, grim-faced, chapfallen, hangdog, bowed, low, blue, crestfallen, dispirited, heavyhearted, depressed, despondent, glum, mopish, mopy, gloomy, disconsolate, inconsolable, down, saturnine, brooding, long-faced, mournful, doleful, grave, woeful, moody, sullen

weeping

crying, sobbing, bawling, blubbering, wailing, whimpering, sniveling, shedding tears, being teary-eyed, lachrymating

unhappy or complaining

joyless, cheerless, ungratified, grim, fretful, whining, griping, querulous, sour

injured or resentful

sulky, pouting, sullen, brooding, mopish, mopey, reproachful, indignant, aggrieved, offended, bruised, begrudging, peeved, peevish, petulant

disappointed

disheartened, unsatisfied, displeased, crestfallen, dejected, crushed

despairing

despondent, low, hopeless, dispirited, downcast, depressed, pessimistic

defeated

discouraged, dispirited, careworn, pessimistic, fatalistic, down, negative, bleak

imposing

impressive, forbidding, intimidating, magisterial, majestic, grand, august, awesome, overbearing, dominating

regal

imperious, kingly, queenly, princely, autocratic, aristocratic, lordly

impulsive

impetuous, rash, hasty, spontaneous, impatient, erratic, flighty. irrepressible

cocky or fresh

bumptious, nervy, cheeky, brash, brazen, impudent, assertive, offensive, impertinent, saucy, pert, smart-alecky, sassy, pushy, obnoxious, cheeky, provocative, peremptory

arrogant

superior, haughty, snobbish, overbearing, patronizing, condescending, stuck-up, supercilious, conceited, sniffy, overweening, haughty

self-important

pompous, self-aggrandizing, pretentious, snooty, egotistic, egocentric, egomaniacal, self-satisfied, smug

self-dramatizing

stagy, dramatic, histrionic, overemotional, theatrical, overplayed, operatic, emoting

vain

preening, gloating, self-congratulatory, conceited, egotistic, narcissistic

dictatorial

demanding, peremptory, autocratic, bossy, imperious

discourteous

impolite, uncourtly, ungracious, rude, boorish, churlish, vulgar

contemptuous

disrespectful, sneering, lordly, spiteful, scornful, sardonic, insolent, abusive, condescending, derisive

straightforward

candid, forthcoming, forthright, frank, open, outspoken, aboveboard, straight, sincere, genuine, up-front, plain, plain-speaking, unreserved, blunt, to the point, unflinching, direct, honest

not candid or forthright

evasive, mealy-mouthed, devious, deceptive, equivocating

scheming

manipulative, guileful, conniving, designing, wily, calculating, untrustworthy, Machiavellian

artificial or false

studied, stagy, mannered, affected, phony, pretentious, practiced, putting on airs

overly earnest or flattering
ingratiating, smarmy, wheedling, cajoling

pious or moralistic
sanctimonious, hypocritical, pharisaical, holier-than-thou, goody-goody, po-faced (British)

sneaky
furtive, false, covert, clandestine, sly, stealthy, surreptitious, secretive, crafty, shifty, duplicitous, close-lipped, incommunicative

disapproving
withering, hard, baleful, stern, glaring, frowning, dismissive, glowering, critical, deprecatory, disdainful, grimacing

displeased
discontented, dissatisfied, unsatisfied, ungratified, malcontent, disgruntled, out of sorts, dyspeptic, querulous

inept
hapless, ineffective, fatuous, ineffectual, feckless

frustrated or annoyed
exasperated, vexed, piqued, irked, aggravated

dismayed
aghast, appalled, horrified, horror-stricken, horror-struck

pained
haunted, wounded, aggrieved, stricken, aching, cut to the quick, agonized, tormented

excitable or overly sensitive
overemotional, volatile, perturbable, prickly, thin-skinned, touchy

irritable or on edge

restless, jumpy, fidgety, testy, tetchy, difficult, fractious, ill-natured, ill-tempered, quarrelsome, querulous, bilious, tense, taut, grumpy

aggressive

scrappy, challenging, provocative, rambunctious, defiant, pugnacious, belligerent, bellicose, truculent, abrasive, contrarian, combative, pushy, forward, competitive, bullying, bumptious

angry or easily angered

short-tempered, snippy, glowering, scowling, incensed, indignant, furious, wrathful, enraged, boiling, outraged, choleric, cross, seething, simmering, hot-tempered, explosive, irate, glaring, dark, black, fulminating

threatening

menacing, intimidating, fierce, ferocious, minatory, frightening, fearsome, scary, warning

guilty

chastened, at fault, peccant, regretful, sinful

shamefaced

embarrassed, mortified, rueful, self-reproaching, sheepish, abashed

sorry or apologetic

regretful, repentant, penitent, contrite, remorseful, rueful, repining

conciliatory

placatory, placating, mollifying, reconciliatory, propitiative, propitiatory, appeasing

subservient

fawning, sycophantic, toadying, servile, obsequious, craven, slavish, cringing, yielding, tractable, submissive, groveling, sequacious

abrupt

brusque, unmannerly, rude, curt, bluff, unceremonious, peremptory, giving short shrift, gruff, crusty

stubborn or unyielding

unrelenting, uncompromising, implacable, unbending, unreachable, obstinate, dogged, balky, contrary, mulish, recalcitrant, pervivacious, inflexible, obdurate, stern, flinty, resistant, dour

disagreeable

morose, dour, sullen, sulky, crabbed, surly, sour, ill-mannered, ill-natured, spiky

unsociable

unfriendly, unapproachable, aloof, standoffish, inamicable, cool, chilly, asocial, antisocial, inimical

careful

cautious, mindful, heedful, deliberate, tentative

defensive

protective, self-protective, guarded, chary, wary, warding off

hostile

antagonistic, malevolent, ill-disposed, antipathetic, contentious, surly, quarrelsome

wicked

sinister, iniquitous, villainous, ungodly, diabolic, diabolical, depraved, satanic, demonic, base, vile, fiendish, infamous, heinous, nefarious, immoral, turpitudinous, despicable, malicious, malignant, malefic, malign

tired or lacking energy

worn, worn out, weary, fatigued, depleted, drained, spent, enervated, lifeless, feckless, listless, leaden, sluggish, debilitated

dissipated

dissolute, debauched, overindulgent, crapulous, self-indulgent, immoderate

without liveliness or flair

stolid, lumpish, plodding, apathetic, unspirited, spiritless, languid

meek

docile, gentle, mild-mannered, lamblike, unassuming

timid

fearful, irresolute, hesitant, diffident, timorous, mousy, pliant

wary or suspicious

hesitant, guarded, regardful, chary, distrustful, questioning, leery, measured

doubting or disbelieving

dubious, incredulous, skeptical

surprised

astonished, astounded, startled, amazed, flabbergasted, bug-eyed

stunned

dazed, dumbfounded, numb, benumbed, agape, stupefied, staggered, startled, unnerved

anxious, upset, or afraid

fearful, scared, apprehensive, worried, concerned, troubled, unnerved, disturbed, agitated, distraught, disquieted, discomposed, discomforted, discomfited, bothered, distressed, fraught

uneasy or worried
restless, fidgety, fluttery, restive, nervous, unnerved, on edge, jittery, ill at ease, apprehensive, tense, skittish, keyed up, anxious, antsy

alarmed
made fearful, apprehensive, panicked, in a tizzy

imperturbable
unflappable, unfazed, airy, unexcitable, serene, unflustered, unruffled, cool, cool as a cucumber, centered

inexpressive
silent, guarded, withdrawn, unforthcoming, untalkative, uncommunicative, unresponsive, mute

expressionless
blank, vacant, vacuous, deadpan, detached, impassive, unfeeling, affectless

inscrutable
mysterious, sphinxlike, unreadable, impenetrable, unknowable

impassive or cold
unfeeling, impervious, icy, affectless, impersonal, stony, stonelike, stiff, apathetic, indifferent, uninterested, dispassionate, unresponsive, unsympathetic, uncaring

unaware
unconscious, oblivious, unmindful, mindless, heedless, out of it

seeming distant or lost
absent, remote, dreamy, faraway, withdrawn

preoccupied
distracted, abstracted, absent-minded, distrait, absorbed, bemused

puzzled or confused

uncomprehending, bewildered, confounded, at sea, befuddled, perplexed, addled, betwixt and between, at sixes and sevens, thrown off, going around in circles, muddled, nonplussed, baffled, mystified, in a quandary, abashed, disconcerted, perturbed, discomposed, agitated, upset, clueless, disquieted, flustered, unsettled, at a loss, lost, overwhelmed, disoriented

speechless

tongue-tied, mortified, paralyzed, dazed, stunned, insensible, overcome, overwhelmed, petrified, struck dumb, mute, dumbstruck, at a loss for words

businesslike

formal, serious, all business, officious, punctilious, methodical, efficient, no-nonsense

stiff

rigid, circumspect, unspontaneous, severe, strict, stringent, harsh, starchy, prim, stilted, reserved, inflexible, unforthcoming, uptight, repressed, inflexible, puritanical, hidebound, straitlaced

Facial Expressions and Head Movements

raise one's eyebrows
knit one's brows
give a look
be wild-eyed
roll one's eyes
stare

look daggers at
look askance (or askant) at
flutter one's eyelashes
blink
blink back tears
glance
be unblinking
glare
leer
squint (or squinch one's eyes)
wink
fix one's gaze on
avert one's eyes
look wide-eyed
have glazed eyes or a glazed look
give a sidelong glance
wrinkle or crinkle one's nose
snort
have flared nostrils
sniffle
sniff
trembling or quivering lips
unsmiling
smirk
purse one's lips
grin
pucker one's lips
pout
be open-mouthed or agape
make a moue
grin

grin from ear to ear
laugh
bite one's lip
stick one's tongue out
grit one's teeth
lick one's lips
smile
have a crooked smile
have a forced smile
smirk
frown
cock an ear
glower
scowl
grimace
contort one's face
have a pained expression
be slack-jawed
be deadpan or straight-faced
be expressionless
nod
shake one's head
throw one's head back (laughing)
scratch one's head

QUOTATIONS

In fact, it isn't bad. The meat is lean and white, without a hint of gaminess. There's no aftertaste. Gradually, my squeamishness fades, and I try to decide what the meat reminds me of, but nothing comes to mind. It simply tastes like rat. —PETER HESSLER, *Strange Stones: Dispatches from East and West*

Elizabeth, or Beth, as everyone called her, was a rosy, smooth-haired, bright-eyed girl of thirteen, with a shy manner, a timid voice, and a peaceful expression which was seldom disturbed. Her father called her "Little Miss Tranquility", and the name suited her excellently, for she seemed to live in a happy world of her own, only venturing out to meet the few whom she trusted and loved.

—LOUISA MAY ALCOTT, *Little Women*

Pulque is low in alcohol—only 4–6 percent alcohol by volume (ABV)—and has a slightly sour flavor, like pears or bananas past their prime. It is something of an acquired taste. Spanish historian Francisco López de Gómara, writing in the sixteenth century, said: "There are no dead dogs, nor a bomb, that can clear a path as well as the smell of [pulque]."

—AMY STEWART, *The Drunken Botanist: The Plants That Create the World's Great Drinks*

At thirteen or fourteen he was a mere bag of bones, with upper arms about as thick as the wrists of other boys of his age; his little chest was pigeon-breasted; he appeared to have no strength or stamina whatever, and finding he always went to the wall in physical encounters, whether undertaken in jest or earnest, even with boys shorter than himself, the timidity natural to childhood increased upon him to an extent that I am afraid amounted to cowardice. This rendered him even less capable than he might otherwise have been, for as confidence increases power, so want of confidence increases impotence.

—SAMUEL BUTLER, *The Way of All Flesh*

I sit down in Studio B and slide on a pair of headphones. The recording is awash with white noise, hisses, a banging like a radiator clanging. There is the soft hum of an elevator motor. The mechanical clunk of an elevator door sliding open. They must be near the elevator. They are in a basement. Every sound is exaggerated and faintly doubled by the echo. I can clearly make out a man's voice, urging, insistent. Is the girl sobbing? It's an awful scene and I am able to project myself there all too easily. I can visualize the location. The girl is pushed against the wall. The man is facing her, his voice more clear and cutting because the sound waves are bouncing off the concrete into her phone's mouthpiece. —KARL TARO GREENFIELD, *Triburbia*

Willie patronized Oscar, who patronized Willie. Oscar was big, languid, and dreamy. Willie was a tolerable pianist; Oscar had no musical talent. But his wit made itself felt: thanks to his mischievous eye, nearly all the boys in the school bore nicknames conferred by him, though good-humoredly enough. His own nickname, which annoyed him, was "Grey Crow," perhaps premonitory of Dorian's surname. —RICHARD ELLMANN, *Oscar Wilde*

The maiden's lips, glossed with a *red*-red lipstick—a color called "Man Hunt"—her full lips curl into a smile. Here, the air hangs so calm that one can detect the scent of her perfume, like flowers left in a tomb, pressed flat and dried for a thousand years. She leans close to the open window and says, "You're too late. It's already tomorrow. . . ." She pauses for a long, lustful wink blanketed in turquoise eye shadow, and asks, "What time is it?"

And it's obvious the man is drinking champagne, because in that quiet moment even the bubbles of his champagne sound loud. And the ticking of the man's wristwatch sounds loud. And his voice within the car says, "It's time for all bad girls to go to bed."

—CHUCK PALAHNIUK, *Doomed*

"Easy, Amy. Only a twitch." He winks at me, then drops what he is doing and strides out of the room. "Have a listen to this," he calls over his shoulder and soon the place is awash with cascades of sound—brittle arpeggios, tumbling fragments of melody. It is very loud.

—PAUL BROKS, *Into the Silent Land: Travels in Neuropsychology*

Lydia Tkach did not expect her grandchildren to run to her arms. Lydia knew that her voice was high and shrill and her manner that of a Gulag prison camp commander. Still, they were well behaved and suffered themselves to be hugged. The hug was long and the children were patient.

—STUART M. KAMINSKY, *A Whisper to the Living*

This time Oscar didn't cry when they drove him back to the canefields. Zafra would be here soon, and the cane had grown well and thick and in places you could hear the stalks clackclack-clacking against each other like triffids and you could hear krïyol voices lost in the night. The smell of the ripening cane was unforgettable, and there was a moon, a beautiful full moon, and Clives begged the men to spare Oscar, but they laughed. You should be worrying, Grod said, about yourself. Oscar laughed a little too through his broken mouth.

—JUNOT DÍAZ, *The Brief Wondrous Life of Oscar Wao*

I've never listened to water quite this way before, with such close attention to its music. "You can change the pitch of a stream by removing a stone." I lift a cobble out of the water. The chord loses some of its brightness, picks up a drone I didn't hear before. "A stream tunes itself over time," Gordon says, "tumbling the rocks into place." A channel gouging through the mud that remains after a hillside has been logged is "only noise. But an old mossy stream? That's a fugue." Once, he tells me, he heard wind move up the Hoh valley, knocking dry leaves off the bigleaf maple trees. "It sounded," he says, "like a wave of applause."

—KATHLEEN DEAN MOORE, "Silence Like Scouring Sand," *Orion*, November/December 2008

The chair smells fetid and deeply damp, unclean; it smells of irreversible rot. If it were hauled out into the street (*when* it is hauled out into the street), no one would pick it up. Richard will not hear of its being replaced.

—MICHAEL CUNNINGHAM, *The Hours*

Hitler's open and unambiguous death threat against the Jewish people had not yet been uttered on the night when the Grynszpans were arrested in Hanover. Herschel Grynszpan, however, an attentive newspaper reader and a participant in anxious and deeply saturnine conversations around the tables at the Aurore and the Tout Va Bien, did not need to wait for any such public proclamation. He had already concluded that the Nazi intentions were both brutal and overtly murderous.

—JONATHAN KIRSCH, *The Short, Strange Life of Herschel Grynszpan: A Boy Avenger, a Nazi Diplomat, and a Murder in Paris*

The night was cool and dark, the air sweet with the scent of flowers growing in front yards and the peppery smell of automobile exhaust.

—TONY ARDIZZONE, *The Whale Chaser*

As with Maria, the serving girl from Aberdeen, as time passed, each personality began to grow and develop on its own timeline. Whatever she learned or experienced in her secondary state stayed with her, and when she returned to it, she would pick up where she had left off, with all her memories from that state preserved. Her new personality was markedly different from the first, far more witty, talkative, and imaginative. She wrote poetry and cultivated a whole new set of friends, having decided that she didn't much like the ones from her original state.

—ANDREW MCCONNELL STOTT, "Split Personalities," *Lapham's Quarterly*, December 28, 2013

When we think of our sense organs, we usually think of these five: tasting, smelling, touching, hearing and seeing. There are more than that, though, since touch includes temperature, pressure, texture, and pain, the heart and the gut respond to emotions, and the hair on the back of the neck might react to an unknown fear.

— RUSSELL TARG, "A Decade of Remote Viewing Research," *Radiant Minds: Scientists Explore the Dimensions of Consciousness* (Jean Millay, ed.)

I recently asked my mother to describe my personality until I hit puberty, and if my behavior changed or was strange in any way during this time. For adjectives, she said that throughout this period I was "adorable, lovable, straightforward, mischievous, inquisitive, capable, cheerful, insightful, likable, friendly, a prankster," and added, "a pain in the ass, take your pick."

—James Fallon, *The Psychopath Inside: A Neuroscientist's Personal Journey into the Dark Side of the Brain*

Once when the Store was full of lunchtime customers, he dipped the strainer, which we also used to sift weevils from meal and flour, into the barrel and fished for two fat pickles. He caught them and hooked the strainer onto the side of the barrel where they dripped until he was ready for them. When the last school bell rang, he picked the nearly dry pickles out of the strainer, jammed them into his pockets and threw the strainer behind the oranges. We ran out of the Store. It was summer and his pants were short, so the pickle juice made clean streams down his ashy legs, and he jumped with his pockets full of loot and his eyes laughing a "How about that?" He smelled like a vinegar barrel or a sour angel.

—Maya Angelou, *I Know Why the Caged Bird Sings*

Cecilia wasn't the kind who was likely to flinch. "You mean the waiting room," she said.

"Down the hall," he said, looking more and more like he was going to chew her up—and spit her out. He took one of his cards out and turned it over and wrote a telephone number on the back. He handed it to her and turned his ambiguous grin into a happy grin, which he hoped she would perceive as ironic and become even more unsettled or at least more confused.

—TOM WOLFE, *Back to Blood*

Zinman has a nimble verbal manner, a cheerful seen-it-all-but-show-me-some-more bluntness, infused with a nasal Yonkers inflection, and a look that would have engaged Daumier—elfin, slightly paunchy, bemused. His red hair has mostly gone white and there's not much left on top, and he has a pink complexion, a neatly trimmed beard, hazel eyes, and a consistent air of benign, sage alertness.

—MARK SINGER, "The Book Eater," *Character Studies: Encounters with the Curiously Obsessed*

Stefano stood up with an irritated shrug and pulled his T-shirt over his head. Bruno did likewise and they began to gather together their belongings. I noticed Bruno slip a couple of DVDs into his bag as he packed, but said nothing. Maddalena couldn't find her top. I brought her an old T-shirt of mine and she made a moue but accepted the shirt. The three of them headed off down the hill.

—NAOMI ALDERMAN, *The Lessons*

Tasting—in the sense of "wine-tasting" and of what Sue Langstaff does when she evaluates a product—is mostly smelling. The exact verb would be *flavoring*, if that could be a verb in the same way *tasting* and *smelling* are. Flavor is a combination of taste (sensory input from the surface of the tongue) and smell, but mostly it's the latter. Humans perceive five tastes—sweet, bitter, salty, sour, and umami (brothy)—and an almost infinite number of smells. Eighty to ninety percent of the sensory experience of eating is olfaction. Langstaff could throw away her tongue and still do a reasonable facsimile of her job.

—MARY ROACH, *Gulp: Adventures on the Alimentary Canal*

And that is *exactly* what a bow tie says. Not that you're powerless, but that you're impotent. People offer to take you home not because you're sexy but because you're sex*less*, a neutered cat in need of a good stiff cuddle. This doesn't mean that the bow tie is necessarily *wrong* for me, just that it's a bit premature. When I explained this to my father, he rolled his eyes. Then he said that I had no personality. "You're a lump."

—DAVID SEDARIS, *When You Are Engulfed in Flames*

Rockwell had to be persistent. He had to climb the steep stairways of brownstones in Greenwich Village, wander hallways, knock politely, hope someone would agree to see him for a minute or two and look at his portfolio of sample illustrations. Although Rockwell was not dashing, he dressed neatly and had a nice personal manner. He said hello in a resonant baritone and shook hands firmly, with the deliberateness of a shy man who was looking for something to hold onto.

—DEBORAH SOLOMON, *American Mirror: The Life and Art of Norman Rockwell*

Mr. Darcy danced only once with Mrs. Hurst and once with Miss Bingley, declined being introduced to any other lady, and spent the rest of the evening in walking about the room, speaking occasionally to one of his own party. His character was decided. He was the proudest, most disagreeable man in the world, and everybody hoped that he would never come there again. Among the most violent against him was Mrs. Bennet, whose dislike of his general behaviour was sharpened into particular resentment by his having slighted one of her daughters.

—JANE AUSTEN, *Pride and Prejudice*

It was thrilling to hear them speak in their deep, baritone voices and to see, up close, the dark razor stubble that shadowed their chins. At the same time, an exotic aroma entered the room, one that made me feel light-headed and flushed, like I'd been on a pogo stick. Only as an adult would I be able to name this intoxicating scent: English Leather.

—AUGUSTEN BURROUGHS, *Magical Thinking: True Stories*

He remembered Harry very well. He was then in his early twenties, thin but wiry build, average height, a sallow complexion, and small eyes. His subservient, eager-to-please manner as he had answered the questions had been off-putting but he had certainly given the impression of being so very, very shocked about Tracey's disappearance.

—MARY HIGGINS CLARK, *Daddy's Gone A Hunting*

The minister didn't speak in a normal tone of voice; he bellowed, like he thought we all suffered from hearing loss (after several Sundays of that, I think we would have—probably an evangelical strategy for quick, resistance-free supplication: deaf lambs don't bleat back, a way to shut the mutton up). It seemed he kept looking directly at me, and I was sure the blank look he found on my face was spurring him on, his voice rising to an increasingly frothy pitch, the way people will gradually begin to yell when talking to recent refugees or immigrants from . . . Tunisia, or Finland, outer Mongolia, say, in the hope that if they bray the words, their listeners will somehow suddenly understand this language that's only recently been stuffed in their mouths and ears.

—KELLIE WELLS, *Skin*

She and her two sisters washed loads of laundry and hung them out to dry on lines stretched across the length of the swampy backyard.

This set my mother apart from her siblings: she was one of them, and not. The role she assumed made her lonely and isolated her, and her natural shyness complicated this. She resented the strength she had to cultivate, the endurance demanded of women in the rural South. She recognized its injustice, even as a child. This made her quiet and withdrawn. By the time she was a teenager and her siblings old enough to not need her constant supervision, my mother was able to act her age, and she dated, frequented the hole-in-the-wall club her godfather owned, and threw a few house parties that her peers still talk about today.

—JESMYN WARD, *Men We Reaped: A Memoir*

My senses awakened with a vengeance. Smell, especially: juniper incense, tobacco and ganja, cow shit, jasmine, frying honey, kerosene and eucalyptus. I spent my afternoons at the Yin Yang Coffee House, filling my journal with a wild energy fueled by hashish, ginger tea, and french fries. As I rode home on my rented Hero bike, the thunderstorms turned the streets and alleys into a slush of cow manure. Primitive electrical lines spat and shorted, with blue and red explosions, above my head. I'd watch the sunset from the roof of the Kathmandu Guest House, waiting for the fruit bats to drop from the trees and soar over the grounds of the Royal Palace. I could follow their path across the valley—which was still, in July 1979, a patchwork of emerald paddies, uncluttered temples, and white palaces.

—JEFF GREENWALD, *Snake Lake*

At Smith College the pervasive obsession with food was expressed at candlelight dinners and at Friday-afternoon faculty teas; in Danbury it was via microwave cooking and stolen food. In many ways I was more prepared to live in close quarters with a bunch of women than some of my fellow prisoners, who were driven crazy by communal female living. There was less bulimia and more fights than I had known as an undergrad, but the same feminine ethos was present—empathetic camaraderie and bawdy humor on good days, and histrionic dramas coupled with meddling, malicious gossip on bad days.

—PIPER KERMAN, *Orange Is the New Black: My Year in a Women's Prison*

If Greer wasn't rigorous or self-critical, she was impassioned and empathetic, with great reservoirs of feeling about the issues she cared about. Her personality, like her writing, was lilting and engaging. And what Nate had once taken to be a certain artificiality on her part, he came to see as theatricality, which was different and was part of what made being with her so vivid. He soon found himself charmed by her quirky interests—her unpredictable enthusiasms for, say, piñatas this week, or tiny little postcards that fit only one sentence the next.

—ADELLE WALDMAN, *The Love Affairs of Nathaniel P.*

Alexander Boris de Pfeffel Johnson, who is forty-eight, has a yellow thatch, a hulking physique, and a voluptuous, sonorous facility befitting a onetime president of the Oxford Union.

—REBECCA MEAD, "Wordplay," *The New Yorker*, June 25, 2012

The mild Mr Chillip could not possibly bear malice at such a time, if at any time. He sidled into the parlor as soon as he was at liberty, and said to my aunt in his meekest manner:

"Well, ma'am, I am happy to congratulate you."

"What upon?" said my aunt, sharply.

Mr Chillip was fluttered again, by the extreme severity of my aunt's manner; so he made her a little bow and gave her a little smile to mollify her.

—CHARLES DICKENS, *David Copperfield*

He was wearing the hotel's bathrobe of white towelling and he had been wearing it ever since his incarceration, except when vainly trying to sleep or, once only, slinking upstairs at an unsociable hour to eat alone in a rooftop brasserie washed with the fumes of chlorine from a third-floor swimming pool across the road. Like much else in the room, the bathrobe, too short for his long legs, reeked of stale cigarette smoke and lavender air freshener.

—JOHN LE CARRÉ, *A Delicate Truth*

Already many of the memories of the previous two weeks had faded: the smell of that small hotel in St. Andrews; that mixture of bacon cooking for breakfast and the lavender-scented soap in the bathroom; the air from the sea drifting across the golf course; the aroma of coffee in the coffee bar in South Street. She should have said something about all that and the light and the hills with sheep on them like small white stones.

—ALEXANDER MCCALL SMITH, *Trains and Lovers*

A hundredweight of ringed and brooched blubber, smelling to high heaven of female smells, rank as long-hung hair or blown beef, her bedroom strewn with soiled bloomers, crumby combinations, malodorous bust-bodices. She had swollen finger-joints, puffy palms, wrists girdled with fat, slug-white upper arms that, when naked, showed indecent as thighs. She was corned, bunioned, callused, varicose-veined.

—ANTHONY BURGESS, *Inside Mr. Enderby*

Even in his twenties, when his published work amounted to no more than a doctoral thesis (profoundly original but little understood) and a few secret papers in the Los Alamos archives, his legend was growing. He was a master calculator: in a group of scientists he could create a dramatic impression by slashing his way through a difficult problem. Thus scientists—believing themselves to be unforgiving meritocrats—found quick opportunities to compare themselves unfavorably to Feynman. His mystique might have belonged to a gladiator or a champion arm wrestler. His personality, unencumbered by dignity or decorum, seemed to announce: Here is an unconventional mind. —JAMES GLEICK, *Genius: The Life and Science of Richard Feynman*

She backed away, buying time, and waited at the end of the anteroom to see if Cross-eyes would retrieve the box. One of the tenants had burned chiles so bad the scent tattooed the air around her for hours.

—HELENA MARIA VIRAMONTES, *Their Dogs Came with Them*

Half the boys went into the girls' classroom, and half the girls came into the boys' classroom, and when they did, the room smelled like a meadow, like a thousand meadows, like a thousand meadows covered in a fine, soothing mist of Aqua Net hair spray, and I inhaled deeply as they walked by, the heels of their shiny black shoes making delicate music, clickety-clackety-click, on the hard tile floors.

—SHALOM AUSLANDER, *Foreskin's Lament*

Undoubtedly, dear reader, you have heard the expression "a body that wouldn't quit." Well Tiffany's body would not only not quit, it wouldn't take five minutes off for a coffee break. Skin like satin, or should I say like the finest of Zabar's novy, a leonine mane of chestnut hair, long willowy legs, and a shape so curvaceous that to run one's hands over any portion of it was like a ride on the Cyclone. This is not to say the one I roomed with, the scintillating and even profound Olive Chomsky, was a slouch physiognomywise. Not at all. In fact she was a handsome woman with all the attendant perquisites of a charming and witty culture vulture and, crudely put, a mechanic in the sack. —Woody Allen, "The Lunatic's Tale," *The Insanity Defense: The Complete Prose*

They weren't really mingling. They were doing something that was more like a stiff list, a drift and sway. The acoustics made it impossible to speak normally and so they found themselves shouting inanities then just falling mute. The noise of the place was deafening as a sea, and the booming heartiness of others seemed to destroy all possibility of happiness for themselves.

—Lorrie Moore, "Foes," *The Guardian*, October 31, 2008

The *lechuga*—lettuce—of Castile, celebrated for its succulence, was worth twice that found in the rest of Spain. Even the water of Guzmán was different from the water of Roa just down the road. "We need to preserve tastes of this magical place for our children," he'd once told me.

—MICHAEL PATERNITI, *The Telling Room: A Tale of Love, Betrayal, Revenge, and the World's Greatest Piece of Cheese*

"Father!"—The girl's voice rang clear through the half light of the wainscoted library. Gwendoline Oxhead had thrown herself about the earl's neck. The girl was radiant with happiness. Gwendoline was a beautiful girl of thirty-three, typically English in the freshness of her girlish innocence. She wore one of those charming walking suits of brown holland so fashionable among the aristocracy of England, while a rough leather belt encircled her waist in a single sweep. She bore herself with that sweet simplicity which was her greatest charm. She was probably more simple than any girl of her age for miles around. Gwendoline was the pride of her father's heart, for he saw reflected in her the qualities of his race.

—STEPHEN LEACOCK, *Literary Lapses*

"Tea?" she asks, and I say, "I would love to, but I have to get home and make dinner." Perhaps that's why we haven't become closer: We are on different schedules. So much of friendship is about being in the right place at the right time. That's how Kiernan's mother, Deborah, and I found each other, both young mothers of young children, both a little overwhelmed, a little lost. Alice is the friend who knew me when I was young and uncertain, Nancy the friend I acquired when I needed someone sure and straightforward and sane to a fault. I'm not sure I have room now for any more friends, even one as nice as Olivia. I'm vaguely sorry about that every time I see her.

—ANNA QUINDLEN, *Every Last One*

Ghosts of a golden time ambled around the sound stages as if they were living people. Judy Garland. Gene Kelly making *Brigadoon*. Donald O'Connor knockoffs. The guileless Bob Fosse fit somewhere in there, though exactly where, no one knew for sure. He didn't have Kelly's hardy build or expansive spirit. He didn't score high on the O'Connor scale of personality. Never mind that he was one of the best dancers on the lot. Close-ups didn't care about that. Bob Fosse was mild of voice, limited of expression, and small onscreen. What did they need him for?

Fosse endured many screen tests, innumerable changes of clothes, hairstyles, poses, and expressions, until the studio finally decided who he was. —SAM WASSON, *Fosse*

She's a small girl and moving close to her I feel, for once, that I have some size. The waxy collar of her jacket prickles the hair on my forearms. Her neck is damp and slippery, and her mouth, as I kiss it, tastes like cigarettes and chocolate. I picture her smoking rapidly, furtively, in the little bathroom on the plane. Her hair smells a little rancid. The perfume she put on this morning has moldered with sweat and travel and now gives off an odor of decayed pear. —PAMELA ERENS, *The Virgins*

She was a small, plump, fair woman, with a bright, clear eye, and an extraordinary air of neatness and briskness. But these qualities were evidently combined with unaffected humility, and the Doctor gave her his esteem as soon as he had looked at her. A brave little person, with lively perceptions, and yet a disbelief in her own talent for social, as distinguished from practical, affairs—this was his rapid mental résumé of Mrs. Montgomery, who, as he saw, was flattered by what she regarded as the honour of his visit. —HENRY JAMES, *Washington Square*

According to the E.U. regulations, extra-virgin oil must have appreciable levels of pepperiness, bitterness, and fruitiness, and must be free of sixteen official taste flaws, which include "musty," "fusty," "cucumber," and "grubby." "If there's one defect, it's not extra-virgin olive oil—*basta*, end of story," Flavio Zaramella, the president of the Corporazione Mastri Oleari, in Milan, one of the most respected private olive-oil associations, told me.

—TOM MUELLER, "Slippery Business:
The Trade in Adulterated Olive Oil,"
The New Yorker, August 13, 2007

"This is a good time. As good as any, I suppose." What excuse was there for keeping him, all of them, away while their father dozed through whatever time remained to him, even though the old man himself did not ask her to send for them? Teddy could have blamed her for letting things get worse without calling him. It was pride, or it was shame that had made her hope Jack would recover himself enough to let the others see that things had been good between them. Though there was their father, too. But she saw nothing of anger or accusation in Teddy's manner. A calm, affable man who went about his doctoring with scrupulous detachment and a heavy heart, he saw enough misery in the ordinary course of his life to avoid adding to it, except when compelled to on medical grounds. —MARILYNNE ROBINSON, *Home*

His father had chosen his name, thinking that it referred to artesian wells. It wasn't until Artemis was a grown man that he discovered he had been named for the chaste goddess of the hunt. He didn't seem to mind and, anyhow, everybody called him Art. He wore work clothes and in the winter a seaman's knitted cap. His manner with strangers was rustic and shy and something of an affectation, since he read a good deal and had an alert and inquisitive intelligence. His father had learned his trade as an apprentice and had not graduated from high school. He regretted not having an education and was very anxious that his son should go to college. Artemis went to a small college called Laketon in the north of the state and got an engineering degree.

—JOHN CHEEVER, "Artemis, the Honest Well Digger," *The Stories of John Cheever*

By nature, Cohn is diffident and modest—not necessarily useful traits in his chosen profession. To compensate, he has developed an orally aggressive manner—a confident staccato, as unstoppable as a bunch of marbles rolling down a hill—that could easily be mistaken for unrestrained egotism. His conversational style is as crisp and breezy as a morning d.j.'s. He laughs a lot—a popping laugh that sounds like a can of beer being opened, followed by a wheeze.

—MARK SINGER, "Professional Doppelgänger," *Mr. Personality: Profiles and Talk Pieces from* The New Yorker

What is not debatable is that a perfect bowl of Hanoi *pho* is a balanced meeting of savory, sweet, sour, spicy, salty, and even umami—a gentle commingling of textures as well: soft and giving, wet and slippery, slightly chewy, momentarily resistant but ultimately near-diaphanous, light and heavy, leafy and limp, crunchy and tender.

—ANTHONY BOURDAIN, *Medium Raw*

He'd spent thirty of his fifty-six years working in the Memphis Public School system. When you first met him, you thought that whatever happened next it wasn't likely to be pleasant. His social manner was, like his salt-and-pepper hair, clipped short. He had the habit of frowning when another would have smiled, and of taking a joke seriously. But after about twenty minutes you realized that though the hard surface was both thin and brittle, beneath was a pudding of sentiment and emotion. He teared up easily, and was quick to empathize.

—MICHAEL LEWIS, *The Blind Side*

The smell of a rich, sweet Germanic tobacco sat in a cloud just above head level, staining the leaves of the highest books yellow, and there was an elaborate smoking set on a side table—spare mouthpieces, pipes ranging from the standard U-bend to ever more curious shapes, snuff boxes, a selection of gauzes—all laid out in a velvet-lined leather case like a doctor's instruments. Scattered about the walls and lining the fireplace were photos of the Chelfen clan, including comely portraits of Joyce in her pert-breasted hippie youth, a retroussé nose sneaking out between two great sheaths of hair.

—ZADIE SMITH, *White Teeth*

The line rang with three more piercing notes—Mercy! they could burst an eardrum, hello? I said Mister Bast is abroad somewhere just a minute, Julia? The card that came yesterday with a picture of a mountain, where, hello . . . ?

—Who in heaven's name . . .

—Well I never! The oddest voice, it sounded like someone talking under a pillow. I thought he said he was a business friend of James, the most awful shrill sounds on the telephone line and then it sounded like a loud bell ringing and he simply hung up.

—WILLIAM GADDIS, *J R*

INDEX OF QUOTED AUTHORS

ABOUT THE AUTHORS

DAVID GRAMBS began his career in publishing as a definer for the original *American Heritage Dictionary*. He has also worked as a juvenile fiction mystery editor and writer, encyclopedia editor, translator, lexicographer, magazine copy editor, and travel reporter.

ELLEN S. LEVINE is a web producer and writer. She's worked in publishing and public relations and holds a master's degree in creative writing.

Both reside in Brooklyn, New York. To contact them, please send email to describersdictionary@gmail.com.